The Modern Venus

The Modern Venus

Dress, Underwear and Accessories in the Late 18th-Century Atlantic World

Elisabeth Gernerd

BLOOMSBURY VISUAL ARTS
LONDON • NEW YORK • OXFORD • NEW DELHI • SYDNEY

BLOOMSBURY VISUAL ARTS
Bloomsbury Publishing Plc
50 Bedford Square, London, WC1B 3DP, UK
1385 Broadway, New York, NY 10018, USA
29 Earlsfort Terrace, Dublin 2, Ireland

BLOOMSBURY, BLOOMSBURY VISUAL ARTS and the Diana logo are trademarks of Bloomsbury Publishing Plc

First published in Great Britain 2024

Copyright © Elisabeth Gernerd, 2024

Elisabeth Gernerd has asserted her right under the Copyright, Designs and Patents Act, 1988, to be identified as Author of this work.

For legal purposes the Acknowledgements on pp. xiv–xv constitute an extension of this copyright page.

Cover design by Tjaša Krivec
Cover image: *A New Conveyance to the Regions of Folly, or the Ladies Balloon Dress for the year 1786*, 17 April, 1786, publ. by W. Wellings. Courtesy of the Library of Congress, Washington D.C.

All rights reserved. No part of this publication may be reproduced or transmitted in any form or by any means, electronic or mechanical, including photocopying, recording, or any information storage or retrieval system, without prior permission in writing from the publishers.

Bloomsbury Publishing Plc does not have any control over, or responsibility for, any third-party websites referred to or in this book. All internet addresses given in this book were correct at the time of going to press. The author and publisher regret any inconvenience caused if addresses have changed or sites have ceased to exist, but can accept no responsibility for any such changes.

A catalogue record for this book is available from the British Library.

A catalog record for this book is available from the Library of Congress.

ISBN: HB: 978-1-3502-9338-0
PB: 978-1-3502-9337-3
ePDF: 978-1-3502-9339-7
eBook: 978-1-3502-9340-3

Typeset by Integra Software Services Pvt. Ltd.
Printed and bound in India

To find out more about our authors and books visit www.bloomsbury.com and sign up for our newsletters.

Contents

List of illustrations vi
Acknowledgements xiv
List of abbreviations xvi

Introduction: Fashioning the modern Venus 1

1 Head first: Brimmed hats and calashes on the tides of fashion 29

2 'Let us examine their tails': The material and satirical lifecycles of cork rumps and bums 73

3 By hand: Silk and fur muffs 109

4 Tight lacing: The motifs and materiality of stays 151

Conclusion: 'The fickle Goddess' 189

Notes 197
Bibliography 239
Index 253

Illustrations

0.1   Mary Hoare, *A Modern Venus – or – a Lady of the Present Fashion in the State of Nature*, 1785, pencil and ink on paper, New York Public Library, New York 2

0.2   Anne Liddell, Countess of Upper Ossory, *A Modern Venus Clothed,* 1785/6, pencil and ink on paper, New York Public Library, New York 4

0.3   *A Modern Venus, or a Lady in the Present Fashion in the State of Nature 1786*, 1786, engraving, New York Public Library, New York 5

0.4   William Hogarth, *The Analysis of Beauty. Plate 1*, 5 March 1753, publ. by William Hogarth, etching and engraving, Lewis Walpole Library, Farmington 7

0.5   Robe à la Française, 1740s, hand-painted silk, Acc. No. 1995.235.a,b, Metropolitan Museum of Art, New York 8

0.6   William Redmore Bigg, *A Lady and Children Relieving a Cottager*, 1781, oil on canvas, Philadelphia Museum of Art, Philadelphia 9

0.7   Shift, *c.* 1780, linen and cotton, Acc. No. 2005.369, Metropolitan Museum of Art, New York 10

0.8   Stays and hoop petticoat, *c.* 1750–1780, linen, cane, baleen, twill, Acc. Nos. M.2007.211.353 and M.2007.211.981, Los Angeles County Museum of Art, Los Angeles 12

0.9   Stays and hoop petticoat, *c.* 1750–1780, linen, cane, baleen, twill, Acc. Nos. M.2007.211.353 and M.2007.211.981, Los Angeles County Museum of Art, Los Angeles 13

0.10 *A Pig in a Poke*, 6 February 1786, publ. by J. Phillips, hand-coloured etching, British Museum, London 14

0.11 *Eve and Her Granddaughter in a Modern Eden*, 1 April 1786, publ. by W. Holland, engraving, Library of Congress, Washington, D.C. 15

0.12 *The Female Combatants, or, Who Shall*, 26 January 1776, hand-coloured etching and engraving, Lewis Walpole Library, Farmington 16

0.13 *Cock and Hen Pouters*, 24 February 1787, publ. by S. W. Fores, hand-coloured etching and engraving, Lewis Walpole Library, Farmington 18

0.14 Handkerchief, 1775–1800, muslin, Acc. No. 1980.444.1, Metropolitan Museum of Art, New York 19

0.15 Francis Alleyne, *Margot Wheatley*, 1786, oil on canvas, Yale Centre for British Art, New Haven 20

0.16 *A New Conveyance to the Regions of Folly, or the Ladies Balloon Dress for the Year 1786*, 17 April 1786, publ. by W. Wellings, hand-coloured etching, Library of Congress, Washington, D.C. 21

0.17 *Miss Macaroni and Her Gallant at a Print-Shop*, 2 April 1773, publ. by John Bowles, mezzotint, Lewis Walpole Library, Farmington 25

1.1 *Oh Heigh Oh, or, A View of the Back Settlements*, 9 July 1776, publ. by Mathew and Mary Darly, hand-coloured etching and engraving, Lewis Walpole Library, Farmington 30

1.2 *Twelve Fashionable Head Dresses of 1778*, 1778, engraving, Museum of Applied Arts and Sciences, Ultimo 32

1.3 Eight of Twelve Interchangeable Coiffeurs, *c.* 1780s, watercolour on paper and pasteboard case, Winterthur Museum, Garden and Library, Winterthur 33

1.4 Bergère, *c.* 1770, straw and silk, Acc. No. 2017.16, Metropolitan Museum of Art, New York 34

1.5 John Singleton Copley, *Frances Tucker Montresor*, *c.* 1778, oil on canvas, The Diplomatic Reception Rooms, U.S. Department of State, Washington, D.C. 35

1.6 George Romney, *Mrs. Bryan Cooke*, *c.* 1787–91, oil on canvas, Metropolitan Museum of Art, New York 37

1.7 Wooden doll with wardrobe, *c.* 1780s, Acc. No. 2005-102,1, DeWitt Wallace Museum of Decorative Arts, Williamsburg 38

1.8 Straw and silk doll's hat, *c.* 1780s, Acc. No. 2005-102, 8, DeWitt Wallace Museum of Decorative Arts, Williamsburg 38

1.9 Black silk brimmed doll's hat, *c.* 1780s, Acc. No. 2005-102, 8, DeWitt Wallace Museum of Decorative Arts, Williamsburg 39

1.10 Green and pink silk calash, *c.* 1775–80, Acc. No. 1960–723, DeWitt Wallace Museum of Art, Colonial Williamsburg Foundation, Williamsburg 40

1.11 Green and pink silk calash, *c.* 1775–80, Acc. No. 1960–723, DeWitt Wallace Museum of Art, Colonial Williamsburg Foundation, Williamsburg 41

1.12 Brown and pink silk calash, 1780–1790, Acc. No. 1.12.771, Fashion Museum, Bath 42

1.13 Brown and pink silk calash, 1780–1790, Acc. No. 1.12.771, Fashion Museum, Bath 43

1.14 'Fashionable Dresses in the Rooms at Weymouth 1774,' *The Lady's Magazine or Entertaining Companion for the Fair Sex*, 1774, engraving, Wellcome Collection, London 45

1.15 *Dress of the year 1778*, 1778, Collection of the Author 49

1.16 *Miss Calash: Drawn by Miss Calash 1778*, 14 October 1778, publ. by William Richardson, etching, British Museum, London 51

1.17 *Miss Calash in Contemplation*, 15 May 1780, publ. by Carington Bowles, hand-coloured mezzotint, Lewis Walpole Library, Farmington 52

1.18 *A Lady in Waiting*, 14 October 1780, publ. by R. Sayer & J. Bennett, mezzotint, British Museum, London 54

1.19 *A Lady in Waiting*, 14 October 1787, publ. by Robert Sayer, hand-coloured mezzotint, British Museum, London 55

1.20 *A Morning Excursion*, publ. by Bowles and Carver, Collection of the Author 57

1.21 *Capt. Calipash & Mrs. Calipee*, 28 October 1777, publ. by Mathew and Mary Darly, crayon manner, Lewis Walpole Library, Farmington 58

1.22 *The Ton at Greenwich, a Lá Festoon dans le Park a Greenwich*, 11 August 1777, publ. by Matthew and Mary Darly, etching, British Museum, London 60

1.23 *The Old Maids Morning Visit, or, The Calash Lady's*, 1777, publ. by Mathew and Mary Darly, etching, Lewis Walpole Library, Farmington 63

1.24 John Collet, *A Morning Visit, or, the Fashionable Dresses for the Year 1777*, 1 January 1778, publ. by Carington Bowles, mezzotint, Wellcome Collection, London 66

1.25 John Collet, *The Spruce Sportsman, or, Beauty the Best Shot*, 24 June 1780, publ. by Carington Bowles, hand-coloured mezzotint, Lewis Walpole Library, Farmington 67

1.26 Detail of John Collet, *The Spruce Sportsman, or, Beauty the Best Shot*, 24 June 1780, publ. by Carington Bowles, hand-coloured mezzotint, Lewis Walpole Library, Farmington 68

2.1 *The Preposterous Head Dress, or, The Feathered Lady*, 20 March 1776, publ. by Matthew and Mary Darly, etching, Lewis Walpole Library, Farmington 74

2.2 *The Utility of Cork Rumps 1777*, 9 June 1777, publ. by John Lockington, etching and engraving, Lewis Walpole Library, Farmington 75

2.3 Silk, Italian gowns, *c.* 1780–85, Acc. Nos. 1976.146a, b and 1970.87a, b, Metropolitan Museum of Art, New York 76

2.4 White linen and horsehair bum, *c.* 1780–1800, Acc. No. 1954.1010, Manchester Art Gallery, Manchester 78

2.5 Detail of white linen and horsehair bum, *c.* 1780–1800, Acc. No. 1954.1010, Manchester Art Gallery, Manchester 78

2.6 Blue silk bum, *c.* 1785–1795, Acc. No. TMM9002, The Museum Centre of Turku, Turku 80

2.7 *The Cork Rump, or, Chloe's Cushion*, 19 November 1776, publ. by J. Walker, etching & aquatint, Lewis Walpole Library, Farmington 81

2.8 *Chloe's Cushion, or, The Cork Rump*, 1 January 1777, publ. by Matthew and Mary Darly, hand-coloured engraving, Lewis Walpole Library, Farmington 82

2.9 False cosmetic supplements including cheek plumpers, eyebrows, patches, and breast pads, 1701–1800, Acc. No. A158810, Science Museum, London 86

2.10 *The Siege of Cork*, 11 April 1777, publ. by Matthew and Mary Darly, etching and engraving, Lewis Walpole Library, Farmington 88

2.11 *Long Corks or the Bottle Companions*, 11 April 1777, publ. by Matthew and Mary Darly, hand-coloured etching and engraving, Lewis Walpole Library, Farmington 89

2.12 John Wilkinson, 'Seamens Preservation', 1766, *Tutamen Nauticum: or, The Seaman's Preservation from Shipwreck, Diseases, and other Calamities incident to Mariners*, New York Public Library, New York 90

2.13 John Wilkinson, 'Seamens Preservation', 1766, *Tutamen Nauticum: or, The Seaman's Preservation from Shipwreck, Diseases, and other Calamities incident to Mariners*, New York Public Library, New York 90

2.14 *The Cork-Rump the Support of Life*, c. 1776, etching, British Museum, London 92

2.15 R. S. [Richard Sheridan], *Miss Shuttle-cock*, 6 December 1776, publ. by Matthew and Mary Darly, etching, Lewis Walpole Library, Farmington 94

2.16 R. S. [Richard Sheridan], *The Back-side of a Front Row*, 1 January 1777, publ. by Matthew and Mary Darly, etching and drypoint, Lewis Walpole Library, Farmington 96

2.17 R. S. [Richard Sheridan], *The New Rigatta*, 20 February 1777, publ. by Matthew and Mary Darly, etching, Lewis Walpole Library, Farmington 97

2.18 R. S. [Richard Sheridan], *Dolefull Dicky Sneer in the Dumps, or, The Lady's Revenge*, 1 April 1777, publ. by Matthew and Mary Darly, etching and drypoint, Lewis Walpole Library, Farmington 98

2.19 *The Bum Shop*, 11 July 1785, publ. by S. W. Fores, hand-coloured etching, British Museum, London 101

2.20 *A Milliner's Shop*, 24 March 1787, publ. by S. W. Fores, hand-coloured etching, Yale Center for British Art, New Haven 103

2.21 Detail of *A Man Millener: The Muff*, 16 February 1787, publ. by S. W. Fores, hand-coloured etching with stipple, Lewis Walpole Library, Farmington 104

2.22 *The Bumless Beauties*, January 1788, publ. by S. W. Fores, etching with stipple, Lewis Walpole Library, Farmington 106

3.1 'The Modern Venus', *Walker's Hibernian Magazine, or, Compendium of Entertaining Knowledge*, March 1786, National Library of Ireland, Dublin 110

3.2 'The Modern Hercules, *Walker's Hibernian Magazine, or, Compendium of Entertaining Knowledge*, December 1785, National Library of Ireland, Dublin 111

3.3 *A Stage Box Scene: Mrs Bruin, Miss Chienne, Miss Renard*, 1 January 1787, publ. by J. Wicksteed, hand-coloured aquatint, Lewis Walpole Library, Farmington 114

3.4 *A Man Millener: The Muff*, 16 February 1787, publ. by S. W. Fores, etching with stipple, Lewis Walpole Library, Farmington 115

x   *Illustrations*

3.5   *The Virgin Unmasked, c.* 1768, publ. by S. W. Fores, etching and engraving, Lewis Walpole Library, Farmington 116

3.6   *The Virgin Unmasked,* 16 June 1786, publ. by S. W. Fores, hand-coloured etching, Library of Congress, Washington, D.C. 117

3.7   J. Elwood, 1790, drawing on paper, British Museum, London 118

3.8   'Inside view of Messrs. Harding, Howell & Co. 89 Pall Mall' in Rudolph Ackermann's *The Repository of Arts, Literature, Commerce, Manufactures, Fashions, and Politics,* 1809, British Library, London 120

3.9   'Elegant Pattern for a Fashionable Muff or Work Bag,' *Walker's Hibernian Magazine, or Compendium of Entertaining Knowledge,* July 1786, New York Public Library, New York 125

3.10   'A Pattern for a Lady's Muff,' *The Lady's Magazine, or Entertaining Companion for the Fair Sex,* December 1779, Bayerische Staatsbibliothek Munich 126

3.11   Silk plain weave muff with silk embroidery, 1770s, Acc. No. M.2007.211.136, Los Angeles County Museum of Art, Los Angeles 127

3.12   Detail of silk plain weave muff with silk embroidery, 1770s, Acc. No. M.2007.211.136, Los Angeles County Museum of Art, Los Angeles 128

3.13   Silk plain weave muff with silk plain weave ribbon embroidery, 1780s, Acc. No. M.2007.211.137, Los Angeles County Museum of Art, Los Angeles 129

3.14   Detail of silk plain weave muff with silk plain weave ribbon embroidery, 1780s, Acc. No. M.2007.211.137, Los Angeles County Museum of Art, Los Angeles 129

3.15   Circle of Sir Joshua Reynolds, *Mrs. Huddesford, c.* 1778, oil on canvas, Private Collection 131

3.16   Detail of 'The Modern Venus', *Walker's Hibernian Magazine, or, Compendium of Entertaining Knowledge,* March 1786, National Library of Ireland, Dublin 133

3.17   Silk satin muff with silk mezzotint, 1782–1800, Acc. No. 43.1820, Museum of Fine Arts, Boston 134

3.18   Silk satin muff with silk mezzotint, 1781–1800, Acc. No. 43.1823, Museum of Fine Arts, Boston 134

3.19   Silk satin muff with silk mezzotint, 1781–1800, Acc. No. 43.1820, Museum of Fine Arts, Boston 135

3.20   Detail of silk satin muff with silk mezzotint, 1782–1800, Acc. No. 43.1820, Museum of Fine Arts, Boston 136

3.21   Detail of silk satin muff with silk mezzotint, 1781–1800, Acc. No. 43.1823, Museum of Fine Arts, Boston 137

3.22   Detail of silk satin muff with silk mezzotint, 1781–1800, Acc. No. 43.1820, Museum of Fine Arts, Boston 138

3.23 Angelica Kauffman, *Felicity*, 1 October 1781, publ. by W. Palmer, stipple engraving, National Galleries of Scotland, Edinburgh 139

3.24 Angelica Kauffman, *Sincerity*, 1 October 1781, publ. by W. Palmer, stipple engraving, Yale Centre for British Art, New Haven 140

3.25 Angelica Kauffman, *Innocence*, 1 February 1782, publ. by J. Walker, stipple engraving, British Museum, London 141

3.26 Silk satin print embroidered screen, 1780s, Acc. No. NN8146, Museum of London, London 143

3.27 Silk satin print embroidered screen, 1780s, Acc. No. NN8145, Museum of London, London 143

3.28 *Winter*, 12 May 1785, publ. by R. Sayer and J. Bennett, mezzotint, British Museum, London 144

3.29 *Winter*, 12 May 1794, publ. by Laurie & Whittle, hand-coloured mezzotint, Lewis Walpole Library, Farmington 145

3.30 Ann Frankland Lewis, *The Dress of the Year 1784*, 1784, watercolour on paper, AC1999.154.1-.32, Los Angeles County Museum of Art, Los Angeles 147

3.31 Detail of Ann Frankland Lewis, *The Dress of the Year 1784*, 1784, watercolour on paper, AC1999.154.1-.32, Los Angeles County Museum of Art, Los Angeles 148

4.1 *Titus Shapes Figure Frames*, 19 January 1778, publ. by W. Humphrey, etching, Wellcome Collection, London 152

4.2 Interior detail of twilled canvas stays, mid-eighteenth century, Acc. No. CAG.1940.598, Manchester Art Gallery, Manchester 153

4.3 William Hogarth, *The Rake's Progress: 3, The Rake at Rose-Tavern, The Orgy*, 1732, oil on canvas, Sir John Soane's Museum, London 154

4.4 Detail of William Hogarth, *The Rake's Progress: 3, The Rake at Rose-Tavern, The Orgy*, 1732, oil on canvas, Sir John Soane's Museum, London 154

4.5 Wool damask and linen stays, 1740–1760, Acc. No. 1947.1622, Manchester Art Gallery, Manchester 156

4.6 Wool damask and linen stays, 1740–1760, Acc. No. 1947.1622, Manchester Art Gallery, Manchester 156

4.7 White silk satin stays, 1780–1800, Acc. No. 1947.1624, Manchester Art Gallery, Manchester 157

4.8 White silk satin stays, 1780–1800, Acc. No. 1947.1624, Manchester Art Gallery, Manchester 158

4.9 White silk satin stays, 1780–1800, Acc. No. 1949.130, Manchester Art Gallery, Manchester 160

4.10 Detail of white silk satin stays, 1780–1800, Acc. No. 1949.130, Manchester Art Gallery, Manchester 160

4.11 Beige cotton stays, 1785–1790, Acc. No. M969X.26, McCord Stewart Museum, Montreal 161

4.12 Beige cotton stays, 1785–1790, Acc. No. M969X.26, McCord Stewart Museum, Montreal 162

4.13 Pair of stays with tape straps in store, *c.* 1770s–1780s, Acc. No. 1947.1623, Manchester Art Gallery, Manchester 163

4.14 Stays for doll, 1780–1790, Acc. No. 2005-102, 8, DeWitt Wallace Museum of Decorative Arts, Williamsburg 164

4.15 Stays for doll, 1780–1790, Acc. No. 2005-102, 8, DeWitt Wallace Museum of Decorative Arts, Williamsburg 165

4.16 Stays for doll, 1780–1790, Acc. No. 2005-102, 8, DeWitt Wallace Museum of Decorative Arts, Williamsburg 166

4.17 *Tight Lacing, or, Hold Fast Behind,* 1 March 1777, publ. by Matthew and Mary Darly, etching and engraving, Lewis Walpole Library, Farmington 169

4.18 John Collet, *Tight Lacing, or Fashion Before Ease, c.* 1770–1775, publ. by Bowles and Carver, hand-coloured mezzotint, DeWitt Wallace Museum of Decorative Arts, Williamsburg 170

4.19 *The Three Graces,* 1 July 1778, hand-coloured etching, Staatliche Museen zu Berlin, Berlin 173

4.20 *Tight Lacing,* 5 March 1777, publ. by William Holland, hand-coloured etching, Lewis Walpole Library, Farmington 174

4.21 *A Speedy and Effectual Preparation for the Next World,* 1 May 1777, publ. by Matthew and Mary Darly, etching and drypoint, Lewis Walpole Library, Farmington 174

4.22 Thomas Rowlandson, *A Little Tighter,* 18 May 1791, publ. by S. W. Fores, hand-coloured etching, National Gallery of Art, Washington, D.C. 175

4.23 Thomas Rowlandson, *A Little Bigger,* 18 May 1791, publ. by S. W. Fores, hand-coloured etching, Metropolitan Museum of Art, New York 176

4.24 Thomas Rowlandson, *A Little Bigger,* 1790, pen, ink and watercolour over pencil, National Gallery of Victoria, Victoria 177

4.25 Thomas Rowlandson, *A Little Tighter,* 1790, pen, ink and watercolour over pencil, National Gallery of Victoria, Victoria 178

4.26 James Gillray, *Fashion before Ease, or, A Good Constitution Sacrificed for a Fantastick Form,* 2 January 1793, publ. by Hannah Humphrey, hand-coloured etching, Lewis Walpole Library, Farmington 181

4.27 Thomas Rowlandson, *The Contrast 1792,* 1 January 1793, publ. by S. W. Fores, hand-coloured etching, Lewis Walpole Library, Farmington 182

4.28 William Heath, *1812, or Regency à la Mode,* 1 February, *c.* 1812 [imprint erased], hand-coloured etching, British Library, London 185

5.1 James Gillray, *Progress of the Toilet. The Stays. Plate 1.*, 26 February 1810, publ. by Hannah Humphrey, etching with stipple, hand-coloured, Lewis Walpole Library, Farmington 190

5.2 James Gillray, *Progress of the Toilet. The Wig. Plate 2.*, 26 February 1810, publ. by Hannah Humphrey, etching with stipple, hand-coloured, Lewis Walpole Library, Farmington 191

5.3 James Gillray, *Progress of the Toilet. Dress Completed. Plate 3.*, 26 February 1810, publ. by Hannah Humphrey, etching with stipple, hand-coloured, Lewis Walpole Library, Farmington 192

Acknowledgements

As a fellow at the Lewis Walpole Library in the second year of my doctorate, then head librarian Maggie Powell made a concise, yet momentous remark: 'If it wasn't true, it wasn't funny.' In addition to giving me a cornerstone from which to explore and establish graphic satire as a source for dress history, Maggie's comment was emblematic of the wisdom and knowledge gained not through the Library's extensive collections, many of which are reproduced here, but through the fellowship of librarians, archivists, curators, colleagues and friends that would shape the development of this book. Thank you to the Lewis Walpole Library for granting me my first formative research fellowship, to Maggie Powell and to the continued support of Sue Walker, Cindy Roman and Kiristen McDonald. Thank you to those who opened not only your collections, but also your knowledge and expertise, including Linda Baumgarten, Beatrice Behlen, Cynthia Cooper, Hilary Davidson, Linda Eaton, Clarissa Esguerra, James Harte, Amanda Hinckle, Neal Hurst, Miles Lambert, Ned Lazaro, Eleri Lynn, Marianne Martin, Pam Parmal, Laura Parrish, Polly Putnam and Elaine Uttley. With especial thanks to Rosemary Harden, who went to heroic feats to take new photography on the Fashion Museum's last day at the Assembly Rooms.

Thank you to those scholars whose encouragement and advocacy of my research, bountiful generosity, comradery and friendship have been instrumental, including Jennie Batchelor, Sarah Bendall, Bethan Bide, Elaine Chalus, Heather Carroll, Abby Cox, Carolyn Day, Ariane Fennetaux, Hannah Greig, Karen Harvey, Mark Hutter, Marine Kisiel, Marcia Pointon, Joanna Marschner, Peter McNeil, Lesley Miller, Catriona Murray, Stana Nenadic, Giorgio Riello, Mary Schoeser, John Styles, Liz Tregenza, Sally Tuckett, Amanda Vickery, Susan Vincent, Janea Whitacre, Lucie Whitmore and Sarah Woodyard. I am especially grateful to Kate Retford and Chloe Wigston Smith for reading parts of this manuscript. And to my Georgian ladies of London, Caroline McCaffrey-Howarth and Serena Dyer, a special toast to your friendship and comradeship, which can be measured by the mile. A special thanks to Serena for her unlimited patience, listening and assistance in developing this book and my understanding of big-kid dress.

While this book was written in London, at seat 3098 in Humanities Two of the British Library to be precise, its foundations were laid in Edinburgh. In particular, it would not exist without the continued efforts and support of Viccy Coltman, who both introduced me to the eighteenth century and nurtured my pursuit of underwear and accessories all those years ago. From undergraduate dissertation to book, Viccy's astute critiques, invaluable guidance and unwavering belief are present on every page. Thank you also to Chris Breward for bringing your generosity, insight and continued collaboration over the years. Thank you to the many institutions and funding bodies who supported the research for this project and aided the development of book. In particular, thanks to the continued support of the Pasold Research Fund, the Paul Mellon Centre for Studies in British Art and research fellowships, including the William Andrews Clark Memorial Library, UCLA; Winterthur Museum, Garden and Library; and John D. Rockefeller, Jr. Library, Colonial Williamsburg. And to Frances Arnold and Rebecca Hamilton at Bloomsbury for patiently waiting for me to be ready to turn the PhD into a book and all of their support since.

And finally, my greatest thanks go to my family. To my grandmother, Gaggy, or Eleanor H. Becker, whose career in fashion publishing in the late twentieth century first introduced and inspired my love of historic fashion. To my husband, Johnny, for his perpetual love, listening and supply of life force. And to my parents, Fred and Brooks, for their unconditional love, no matter the distance and whose belief in my abilities and dreams has never faltered.

For Mom and Dad

Abbreviations

BL	British Library, London
BM	British Museum, London
DWW	DeWitt Wallace Museum of Decorative Arts, Williamsburg (Colonial Williamsburg Foundation)
FM	Fashion Museum, Bath
HD	Historic Deerfield, Deerfield
LACMA	Los Angeles County Museum of Art, Los Angeles
LOC	Library of Congress, Washington, D.C.
LWL	Lewis Walpole Library, Farmington
MAD	Musée des Arts Décoratifs, Paris
MAG	Manchester Art Gallery, Manchester
MCM	McCord Museum, Montreal
MET	Metropolitan Museum of Art, New York
MFA	Museum of Fine Arts, Boston
MOL	Museum of London, London
NPG	National Portrait Gallery, London
V&A	Victoria and Albert Museum, London
YCBA	Yale Center for British Art, New Haven

Introduction: Fashioning the modern Venus

On 27 January 1786, Horace Walpole sharpened his pen to write a letter to Anne Liddell, Countess of Upper Ossory, with whom he had been corresponding for over twenty years. After regaling her with the previous evening's entertainment and gossip, he entreated:

> I beg leave to enclose a Venus of the present hour in her *puris* non *naturabilus*. The drawing was made by a young lady at Bath and was given to me by my sister. It diverted me so much that I gave it to Kirgate with leave to have it engraved for his own benefit, and I should think he would sell hundreds of them.[1]

The exchange of drawings, prints and gifts was not uncommon for Walpole (1717–97) and members of his social circle. The circulation of visual and material culture contributed to his growing collection of treasures at Strawberry Hill and Walpole shared tokens and ephemera in kind. His closest friend, Horace Mann once remarked, that 'he cannot look around the house without seeing presents from [Walpole]' and Walpole sent drawings to Lady Ossory (*c.* 1737–1804, later FitzPatrick) on multiple occasions.[2] The drawing was a gift from Walpole's sister, Lady Maria Churchill (neé Walpole, *c.* 1725–1801).[3] Walpole identified the artist, the 'young lady from Bath', as 'Miss Hoare of Bath' in an annotation on the drawing next to the year 1785, referring to the portraitist and history painter Mary Hoare (1744–1820).[4] Compared with her known surviving works, largely pastel portraits, classicized tableaus and scenes of Shakespeare, the drawing Walpole presented to his friend is a rather unexpected departure from the typical artistic production of a young woman at the time.[5]

The pen and ink drawing is titled in Hoare's hand, 'A Modern Venus – or – a Lady of the present Fashion in the state of Nature' (Figure 0.1). The drawing depicts a full-length nude woman standing in profile with two outstanding features. Beneath a long mane of flowing curls and a diminutive face, a pair of orb-like breasts, pink nipples erect and a protruding posterior echo the contemporary

Figure 0.1 *Mary Hoare, A Modern Venus – or – a Lady of the Present Fashion in the State of Nature, 1785, pencil and ink on paper, From the New York Public Library, New York.*

fashionable silhouette of the mid-1780s. Twisting the Latin phrase *in puris naturalibus*, Walpole identifies the *Modern Venus* in a state of non-natural nudity. Upon receipt of the drawing, Ossory returned it along with a second version titled *A Modern Venus Clothed* (Figure 0.2). Having traced the contours of the *Modern Venus*, Ossory dressed her with an oversized brimmed hat over her head, a puffed handkerchief over her breast and a gown draped over her protruding behind. Though Ossory's letter that accompanied the drawing does not survive, on 10 February Walpole replied, thanking her for 'feathering his Venus'.[6] The amplified figure of this nude and her added 'feathers' portray the satirized corporeal effects of structural underwear and accessories on the body. Like sartorial bookends that underline and punctuate a look, underwear and accessories share a vital, fundamental and interconnected role in the construction of the fashionable silhouette, and therefore fashion itself, in the late eighteenth century. The comic extremity of their perceived effect in 1785 was articulated in Hoare and Ossory's drawings, which Walpole transformed from a private amusement into a publicly consumed satire when he instructed his private secretary and printer, Thomas Kirgate, to publish Hoare's original nude.[7] Whereupon in 1786, *A Modern Venus, or a Lady of the PRESENT Fashion in the State of Nature, 1786*, was engraved, printed and sold by Edward Yardley, book and printseller at No. 2 New Inn Passage, just off Clare Street, in London (Figure 0.3).[8]

Drawn, shared, dressed and printed, the *Modern Venus* represents an exchange of ink, paper, clothes and wit, emblematic of the fashionable dialogues that pervaded late eighteenth-century culture. The three decades following the end of the Seven Years' War in 1763 saw the expansion and contraction of the British Empire alongside the domestic revolutions in consumption, Enlightenment thinking, print culture and budding industrialization.[9] Within these seismic fluctuations, fashion ebbed and flowed, embodying the pervasive spirit of change. As one anonymous author mused in August 1785, 'What in all the material world is so light, so fleeting, and so volatile as Fashion. It is like the froth, which bubbling on the surface of the stream, is for ever changing its shape by insensible gradations'.[10] Since the eighteenth century, commentators and scholars alike have grappled with the definition of fashion and, in turn, the 'people of fashion'.[11] For scholars of the very elite circles of London society, like Hannah Greig, the 'people of fashion' constitute the beau monde or the ton: the sparkling metropolitan elite identified by an 'elusive yet exclusive form of social distinction'.[12] For historians of everyday dress and textiles, like John Styles, fashion is temporal, an annual cycle of change that developed in the seventeenth century and, by the late eighteenth, had quickened its pace into seasons.[13] Outwith dress history, the term 'fashion' can be applied to architecture, furniture, politics, manners and forms of knowledge.[14] Within the sartorial landscape, it permeated a range of physical and representational geographies and, as our anonymous author observes, was present in 'every age, every sex and every rank in life'.[15] He instructs that 'if you wish to see it in all its fantastical exhibitions, you must inspect the court, the

Figure 0.2 *Anne Liddell, Countess of Upper Ossory,* A Modern Venus Clothed, *1785/6, pencil and ink on paper, From the New York Public Library, New York.*

Figure 0.3 A Modern Venus, or a Lady in the Present Fashion in the State of Nature 1786, *1786, engraving*, From the New York Public Library, New York.

gardens, the theatres, the watering places, and associate with the young, the gay, the giddy, and the wanton,' and navigate through its manifestations in silk, ink, paint and print.[16]

This book locates fashion, or fashionable dress, in the conversations about it, the images portraying it and the artefacts left in its wake. Specifically, it argues that structural underwear and accessories were the key ingredients in the recipe for fashion and fashionable change. Marrying material, archival and visual approaches, it looks to the relationships between sartorial culture and its discursive and visual representations. Like the progression of the *Modern Venus*, it considers the dialogues between fashionable dress and its portrayal in print culture, in particular, its representation in satirical prints. Of the multiple revolutions waged during this brief thirty-year period from *c.* 1765 to *c.* 1795, the 'revolution' on paper and in the press is at the heart of this study. As print scholar Diana Donald has established, print culture expanded the reach of fashion beyond the glittering circles of the 'people of fashion', as fashion circulated within graphic satire as a mode of cultural currency, seeping across society like spilt ink across a page.[17] As we shall see, *The Modern Venus* offers a thorough study of the structural underwear and accessories that defined fashion in the late eighteenth century, but also an innovative and inclusive methodological approach to the field through the expansion of the visual sources we employ to study dress history. By exploring the underwear and accessories that fashioned the modern Venus, this book addresses how dress and fashion functioned and flourished as symbolic and emblematic vestments that mediated women's lives and enabled their progression through an ever-changing age.

Fashioning the breast of Venus

By the second half of the eighteenth century, the figure of Venus had become vivid in the mind's eye of the British public. As Britain's gaze turned south towards ancient Greece and Rome, art, sculpture and antiquities were carted northward into the genteel libraries, drawing rooms and galleries of townhouses and country seats, immersing the British public in the classical past.[18] With the influx of objects and interest, fuelled by a system of education that favoured antiquity, a classical literacy saturated British society, which became well-versed in the names, myths and legends of classical mythology.[19] The gods, goddesses, muses and graces were invoked in plays, poetry, pamphlets and periodicals, stepping in as archetypes for the young, the fashionable and the beautiful. The Georgian male elite, who became acquainted with Greco-Roman sculpture in person on the Grand Tour, brought back antiquities, along with descriptions, drawings, engravings and casts that were disseminated and displayed throughout Britain's public and private spaces.[20] William Hogarth articulated the influence of the antique in his 1753 *Analysis of Beauty*, visualizing his serpentine line in Plate 1 (Figure 0.4).[21] In the plate, a yard of well-known copies of classical sculpture pivots around the central figure of the *Venus de' Medici*,

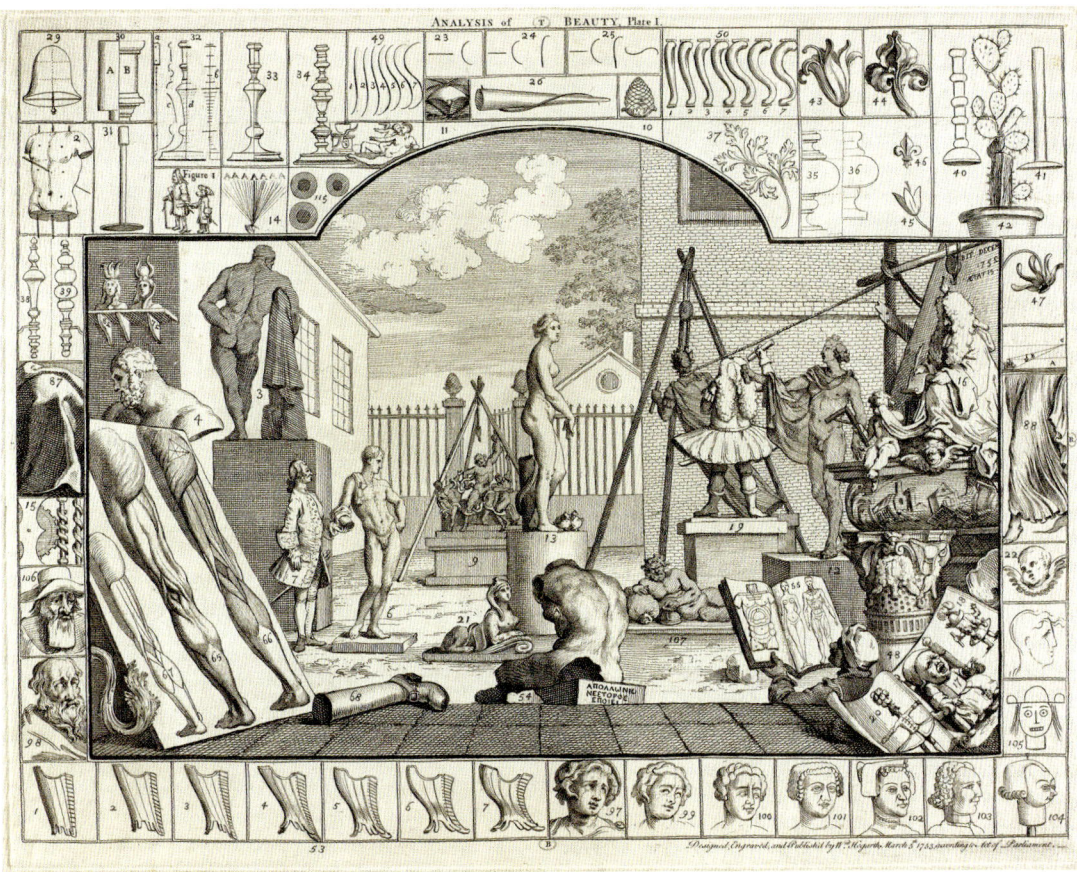

Figure 0.4 *William Hogarth,* The Analysis of Beauty. Plate 1, *5 March 1753, publ. by William Hogarth, etching and engraving, 38.8 × 50.1 cm, Courtesy of the Lewis Walpole Library, Yale University.*

bordered by Hogarth's serpentine line of beauty delineated in various forms, including chair legs, flora and the curvature of whalebone stays. The idealized proportions of the sculptures of Venus, in particular the *Medici Venus*, came to represent the flawless female form. As Viccy Coltman has argued, viewers and voyeurs alike of the *Medici Venus* described her sculpted flesh as perfection in marble: the 'perfect model of female beauty'.[22] As her prominent position in the centre of Hogarth's print attests, Venus, the goddess of beauty and love, was central to this awareness and adoption of classical archetypes in popular culture, becoming shorthand for the contemporary female beauties, or women of fashion.

In stark contrast to the idealized proportions embodied by the Greco-Roman goddess, the proportions of the *Modern Venus* drawn by Mary Hoare vary considerably! Far from being anatomically accurate or an idealized representation of the female form, the corporeal contours of the *Modern Venus* are shaped not by nature, but by fashion. As Walpole alludes to in his letter, the ballooning breasts and swelling buttocks, which give this Venus her miniscule waist and amplified features, are not natural phenomena, but rather '*puris* non *naturabilus*'. The couplet printed beneath the print, which Kirgate added to the original drawing, reads, 'This is the Form, if we believe the Fair / Of which our Ladies are, or wish they were.' Since the Renaissance, the silhouette of the dressed body bore little resemblance to the corporeal body beneath: the torso was structured and the line of the skirt extended away from the hips and legs.[23] Like the style of drawing from which the term derives its name, the evolution of the female silhouette in the eighteenth century has been well traced.[24] Throughout the eighteenth-century, wide-skirted mantuas, sacques and court dress displayed the finely woven, painted and embroidered textiles to their best advantage (Figure 0.5). By the latter 1760s, fashion had found new venues for its display in 'the

Figure 0.5 *Robe à la Française, 1740s, British, hand-painted silk, Acc. No. 1995.235.a,b, Metropolitan Museum of Art, New York.*

gardens, the theatres, [and] the watering places' of the growing metropolis beyond the stricter sartorial codes of court, birthing new modes of fashionable dress and shifting the volume of the silhouette.[25] The polonaise, looped, English and Italian styles transferred emphasis from a horizontal plane across the hips that emphasized the quality of the textiles towards an architectural body, formed of sculptural pleats and gathers around the rear.[26] William Redmore Bigg's 1784 moralizing genre painting, *A Lady and her Children Relieving a Cottager,* is a rare delineation of this style as painted portraiture favoured depicting its sitters as timeless, adopting classicized drapery and historicized costume (Figure 0.6). The fashionable dress of the lady, whose charity, as Beth Fowkes Tobin argues, is magnanimously bestowed both on the poor white woman and the liveried Black serving boy, acts as a timestamp that temporally connects the painting with the contemporary concerns of charity and abolition.[27] Drawn the following year, the figure of the *Modern Venus* reflects an exaggerated version of the fashionable

Figure 0.6 *William Redmore Bigg,* A Lady and Children Relieving a Cottager, *1781, oil on canvas, 75.2 × 90.5 cm, Philadelphia Museum of Art, Philadelphia.*

silhouette of the mid to late 1780s, which represented the final peak of architectural artificiality before fashion plummeted towards the natural curves of body of the *Medici Venus* in the clinging gowns of the 1790s.[28] However, the garments that facilitated these fantastic forms were not the gowns themselves, but rather the structural underwear worn beneath and the amplifying accessories worn above.

As the beginning and the end of a sartorial ensemble, underwear and accessories were critical components of an eighteenth-century wardrobe. Structural underwear created the shape of the silhouette, fashioning the frame over which a gown was pinned in place. Accessories, like the fluctuating grammatical role of punctuation in a sentence, not only completed, but emphasized and transformed an outfit. Etymologically, the terms 'underwear' and 'accessories' are anachronistic conveniences, only appearing in relation to dress and fashion in the late nineteenth century.[29] Throughout the eighteenth century, what can comparatively be considered underwear is a linen, though sometimes cotton, shift or a loose-fitting, sleeved, short dress reaching just above the knees, worn with nothing, apart from stockings and garters, underneath (Figure 0.7).[30] The term 'linen'

Figure 0.7 *Shift, c. 1780, American, linen and cotton, Acc. No. 2005.369, Metropolitan Museum of Art, New York.*

itself became synonymous with the undergarments it was used to construct.[31] The shift acted as the protective layer that formed a launderable boundary between the greasy, oily secretions of the skin and pores and the scratchy, irritable, expensive and often nonwashable textiles that composed women's gowns.

Above the shift, the torso was structured through baleen, or whalebone stays, the focus of my final chapter, which lifted and compressed the bust and supported the lower back. For the first three quarters of the century, the line of the skirt was widened away from the body through cane or baleen hoops and panniers that expanded the lower proportions of the body (Figures 0.8 and 0.9). However, volume below the waist shifted in the mid-1770s from the hips towards the rear, through the support of a padded rump, or bum, the subject of Chapter 2. Tie-on pockets and petticoats were worn above these lower foundations, and finally the gown and stomacher were pinned in place, completing the fundamental layers of the dressed body.[32] When Lady Ossory traced and returned the augmented drawing, *A Modern Venus Clothed*, she added not only the outline of the gown which fills out the line of the skirt, but an enormous hat and handkerchief. Accessories, or the supplemental articles of dress that complement and complete an outfit, also only began to be used as a term in relation to dress and fashion in the late nineteenth century. Contemporary language lacked a categorial term for the supplemental articles of dress. In his description of London milliners, the branch of the sartorial trades responsible for these addendums of fashion, Robert Campbell fittingly remarked, that milliners make up 'as many *Etceteras* as would reach from *Charing-Cross* to the *Royal Exchange*', filling the two-mile distance with as many articles, ranging from trims, ribbons and ruffles, which could be attached to a gown, to made-up pieces, including articles for the head and hands, the subjects of Chapters 1 and 3 respectively.[33]

When viewing the *Modern Venus* and *A Modern Venus Clothed* as a diptych, it is not the gown itself that defines her amplified figure, but rather the underwear below and the accessories above that construct the present mode. Comparing the amplified constructions of the sartorial body with the form of the natural body was a common motif within contemporary graphic satire. For instance, *A Pig in a Poke*, published 6 February 1786 by James Phillips, portrays two depictions of the same woman back-to-back, both modelled in the pose of the *Venus de' Medici*, a miniature statuette of which stand on a plinth to the left of the room (Figure 0.10). Like the *Modern Venus,* one is nude and the other clothed. On the left, the woman is fully dressed from top to tail in the amplifications of the current fashion: a large feathered and festooned hat, a puffed handkerchief over her breast and a swelling rump lifts the back of her blue gown. On the right, her unsympathetically drawn nude body is displayed withered and nearly skeletal. Stripped of the luscious volume that her clothes create, her false bum, yellow petticoat and blue gown are scattered at her feet. Two months later, this motif was

Figure 0.8 *Stays and hoop petticoat, c. 1750–1780, English, linen, cane, baleen, twill, Acc. Nos. M.2007.211.353 and M.2007.211.981, Los Angeles County Museum of Art, Los Angeles.*

Figure 0.9 *Stays and hoop petticoat*, c. 1750–1780, English, linen, cane, baleen, twill, Acc. Nos. M.2007.211.353 and M.2007.211.981, Los Angeles County Museum of Art, Los Angeles.

Figure 0.10 A Pig in a Poke, *6 February 1786, publ. by J. Phillips, hand-coloured etching, 25.6 × 36.1 cm, British Museum, London.*

employed again in *Eve and her Granddaughter in the Modern Eden*, published by William Holland on 1 April 1786 (Figure 0.11). Set within a landscape reminiscent of a country parkland, a nude Eve, right hand covering her *mons pubis* for modesty, gestures with disbelief to her granddaughter on the left, who is portrayed as a chaotic, sartorial menagerie of ribbons and ruffles, with a caged bird crowning her hat and a cat with her kittens resting on her colossal bum. Like the *Modern Venus*, her enormous bare breasts are displayed, protruding from her low-cut gown, a stark contrast to the delicate apples of Eve. The juxtapositions of these three pairs of women playfully emphasize the role of fashion as both a method of creating or distorting beauty and the body.

However, when this dichotomy is employed in depictions of women of non-white races, the contrast is far more loaded and cutting. In the depiction of North American Indigenous women or women of the African diaspora, nudity compared to clothed is not a symbol of fashion versus nature, but 'savage' versus civilized.[34] For example, in allegorical depictions of Britannia and her rebellious colonial daughter America, like *The Female Combatants, or, Who shall*, published 26 January 1776, Britannia is dressed in either fashionable garb or classical drapery whereas America is often portrayed

Figure 0.11 Eve and Her Granddaughter in a Modern Eden, *1 April 1786, publ. by W. Holland, engraving, 28.2 × 33.5 cm, Courtesy of the Library of Congress, Washington, D.C.*

with quasi-Native American features including bare breasts, tattoos and her body solely covered in a skirt made of feathers (Figure 0.12). Likewise, to the modern viewer, the corporeal contours of Hoare's *Modern Venus* cannot be seen without drawing a parallel to the representations of Sara Baartman published over twenty years later. Also known as Saartje, Sartjee and Sarah Bartmann, Baartman was born in present-day South Africa in the 1770s and died in France in December 1815 or January 1816.[35] Contemptuously advertised as the 'Hottentot Venus', Baartman's nearly naked body was first exhibited for popular consumption in London in 1810 and, as Robin Mitchell has argued, signified for the white paying public 'an early colonial [trope] of savagery and otherworldliness'.[36] Posthumously, her body was cast in bronze under an auspice of scientific posterity that was laced with prejudiced curiosity. Portrayed in profile to highlight the curvature of her hind parts, her image was widely circulated in the British and French print markets, cementing a visual legacy of exoticism,

Figure 0.12 The Female Combatants, or, Who Shall, *26 January 1776, hand-coloured etching and engraving, 22 × 17 cm, Courtesy of the Lewis Walpole Library, Yale University.*

racism and the commodification of the 'other'.[37] As Saidiya Hartman has established, prior to and including Baartman, Venus as an archetype and synecdoche of Black women was a 'ubiquitous presence' throughout the Atlantic world, whose narratives and lives were shrouded and silenced.[38] Through the racist hegemonic structures and constructs of eighteenth-century society, Black women were simultaneously exoticized and diminished, erased from archive, record and representation despite their complex and pervasive presence throughout society.[39] Though specific fashions, like 1780s frizzed hair and the madras headwrap, have demonstrated the global influence of African and Caribbean style in London, the privileged seat of fashion overwhelmingly favoured whiteness as its palette.[40] As Charmaine Nelson has argued, marble's absence of colour from which sculptures of Venus were carved reinforced a racially constructed ideal of beauty dominant throughout the eighteenth and nineteenth centuries, one that remained a requisite of fashion.[41] Created within these racist constructs, the representations and discourses on the modern Venus as a symbol of late-eighteenth fashionability explored and addressed within this book overwhelmingly portray white, young, moneyed, straight women. For in the eighteenth century, to be fashionable was to be white.

This fashionability of whiteness extended beyond skin to textiles. When Lady Ossory returned *A Modern Venus Clothed*, she covered the voluptuous, exposed bosom within the folds of a handkerchief, the accessory that defined the upper part of what today is commonly known as the pouter pigeon silhouette. Named after the English fowl, whose jutting breast feathers and tail form a similar profile, the pouter pigeon silhouette reached its peak in the mid to late 1780s (Figure 0.13). The nickname first appeared in print in 1785 in relation to the amplification of the bosom, lifted by the stays beneath and augmented by wearing a handkerchief above.[42] While the handkerchief was not new, worn by both men and women from across the socio-economic spectrum throughout the century, its position as a fashionable appendage took prominence in the 1780s.[43] Worn about the neck, the large, folded square or triangular textile could be either pinned and tucked into the front of the stays, or was later worn crossed over the torso and tied about the waist.[44] Though handkerchiefs were made from a variety of textiles, including linen, silk and cotton, with some decoratively printed for commemoration, the fashionable buffont, the term borrowing from the French and appearing in the late 1770s, was most frequently made of muslin, lawn or gauze, ornamented with whitework embroidery, netting or lace (Figure 0.14).[45] Buffonts were advertised from four shillings and six pence to two shillings and six pence, slightly less than other articles of fine cottons like aprons and caps, their cost reflecting the calibre of the textile rather than its maker's labour.[46] However, Elizabeth Motley Austen (née Wilson, 1751–1817) bought '2 worked muslin handkerchief's' for ten shillings on 4 November 1778 and Lady Mary De La Warr (née Wynyard, 1735–84) bought 'a boufan' for her daughter, Charlotte on 6 February 1778 for seven shillings and six pence.[47] Once the ban on imported cottons had been repealed in 1774, fine cottons became increasingly incorporated into fashion, favoured for their lightness and translucence.[48] As seen in a portrait of

Figure 0.13 Cock and Hen Pouters, *24 February 1787, publ. by S. W. Fores, hand-coloured etching and engraving, 12.8 × 17.8 cm, Courtesy of the Lewis Walpole Library, Yale University.*

Margot Wheatley, painted as part of a pair with her husband William Wheatley in 1786 by Francis Alleyne, the near translucent quality of the fabric simultaneously covered her neckline, but allowed the decolletage to be seen beneath, while also adding the perception of volume above the natural curvature of the breast (Figure 0.15). This voluminous effect was achieved through clear-starching or crimping, manual processes that, like laundering, were continually required to maintain both the whiteness and desired shape of the fabric.[49] Like Wheatley's cap and her husband's cuffs, the manual effort required to keep white white and delicate textiles starched was a marker for social status throughout the early modern period.[50] To this effect, milliners advertised 'buffonts cleaned and dressed', instruction manuals were published in ladies' cookery books outlining methods for clear-starching and portable machines were advertised 'for crimping BUFFONTS of all sizes … to remedy the inconvenience of sending Buffonts to town to be crimpt'.[51] In addition to knowledge of dressing hair or millinery, lady's maids were sought who '[understood] clear-starching and cleaning of buffonts' or 'buffont crimping', emphasizing that in the 1780s, the desired volume was equally as important as the whiteness and fineness of the textile.[52]

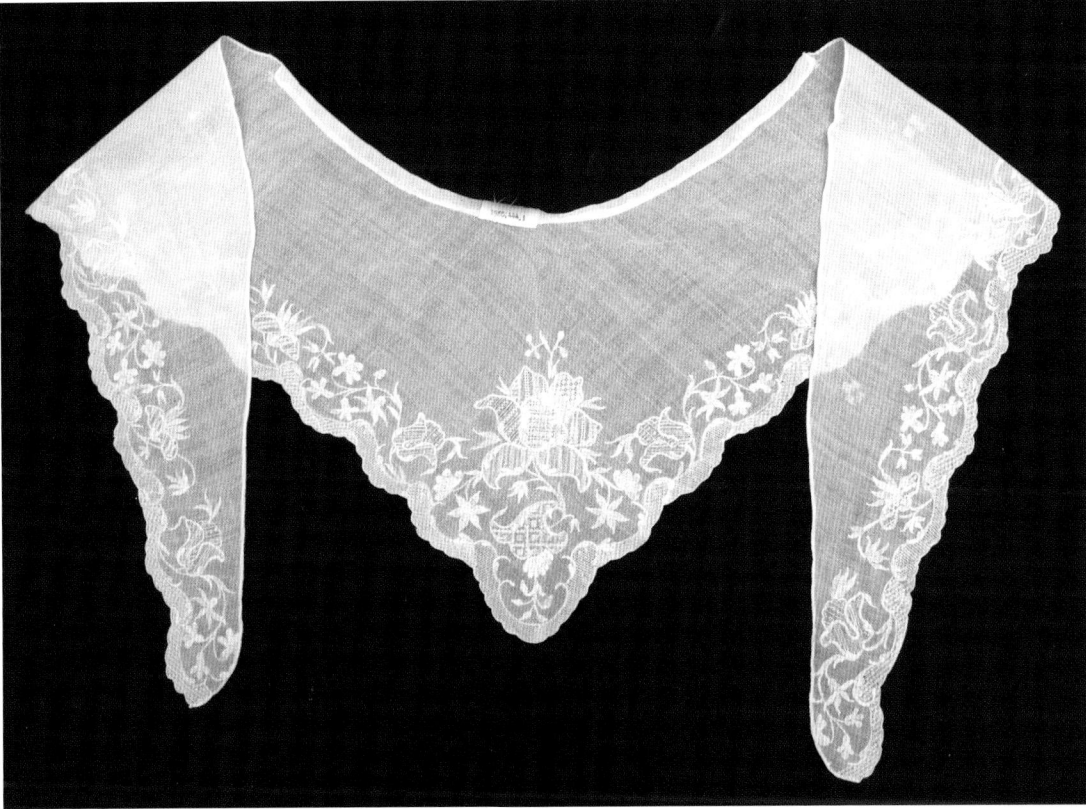

Figure 0.14 *Handkerchief, 1775–1800, British, muslin, Acc. No. 1980.444.1, Metropolitan Museum of Art, New York.*

The amplified effect was not lost on the spectators of fashion, who propagated the newspapers with commentaries and diatribes on the reigning fashions of the day, and whose snide remarks and comic asides were visualized on the pages of satirical prints. In a column titled the 'Levities of Fashion', published in 1785, the anonymous author, quipped:

> The stomager [sic.] or chest-piece is also a levity in Fashion. This is something like a porch which opens with an inviting aspect to every stranger. It is cut with such a fine oval and ample sweep, as to convey no inadequate idea of that easy protuberance, that delicious swell; which is not the least perfection in the model of feminine shape.[53]

Within satirical circles, the pleasing effect of emphasizing the heave and 'delicious swell' of the breast inspired the name a 'merry-thought' to be used, the light and airy textiles conceived to be held aloft with wire, or even 'by the admission of elastic globes replete with gas'.[54] The use of helium to inflate the breasts was visualized in *A new Conveyance to the Regions of Folly, or the Ladies Balloon Dress for the Year 1786*, where the erotic appeal blended with the perceived scale of the pouter pigeon silhouette (Figure 0.16). Mimicking the 'dress of the year' format of fashion plates, the print portrays a woman

Figure 0.15 *Francis Alleyne,* Margot Wheatley, *1786, oil on canvas, 36.8 × 29.2 cm, Courtesy of Yale Centre for British Art, Yale University.*

Fashioning the Modern Venus   21

Figure 0.16 A New Conveyance to the Regions of Folly, or the Ladies Balloon Dress for the Year 1786, *17 April 1786, publ. by W. Wellings, hand-coloured etching, 23.7 × 16.6 cm, Courtesy of the Library of Congress, Washington, D.C.*

in a pink and green striped gown hanging suspended from a canopy, which resembles the top of a hot air balloon.[55] The flight of Vincenzo Lundardi's hot air balloon in 1784 had caused balloon-mania to sweep through fashion like a contagion.[56] As one columnist reported in August 1784:

> The *balloon influenza* rages with more violence than ever: added to balloon hats, balloon bonnets, balloon caps, balloon ribbons, and balloon pins, the ladies now have *double balloon ear-rings,* and *balloon side curls*; so that there are no less than seven balloon articles appertaining to the decoration of the most *beautiful balloon* in nature – the head of a pretty woman![57]

While hats and caps were the most common and easily adaptable fashionable incarnations of balloon-mania, in the print, the woman herself 'was *ballooned* from top to toe', with a rope tied to each nipple and two attached to her bum.[58] Suggestively, a fop, potentially Lunardi himself, straddles the swell of her bum. Waving a union jack flag that flutters in the wind, the woman is presented as a whimsical, eroticized convergence of fashion and patriotism, as British fashion flies ever further into 'the Regions of Folly'. The extremity of this print, whose body echoes the extremity of the *Modern Venus*, was accompanied by a flock of earth-bound pigeons, restricted by the size of their puffed buffonts from eating soup, kissing a beau or keeping a healthy social distance from their companions.[59] Like the modern Venus, the women of 1786 were portrayed on the printed page, '*Full cropp'd before* just like a pouting pigeon, / *Dove tail'd behind,* and *bustling* like a widgeon; / From neck to heel observing HOGARTH'S line /All *in* and *out* – a perfect *serpentine*', corporeally embodying Hogarth's serpentine line of beauty delineated above in Figure 0.4.[60]

This concern with the scale of the buffont was not limited to satire. German diarist Sophie von La Roche, who made numerous observations on English dress during her travels to London in 1786, noted scornfully on 7 September that the metaphorical 'goddess of fashion suffers from quotidian fever, which … at a certain degree of heat turns to madness'.[61] Evidence of this madness was four women who, upon entering a box at the theatre, were 'received by the entire audience with loud derision' due to their 'wonderfully fantastic caps and hats perched on their heads' and 'their neckerchiefs were puffed up so high that their noses were scarce visible'. In the format of a pantomime call and response, four members of the cast appeared shortly after their entrance, 'dressed equally foolishly, and hailed the four ladies in the box as their friends', resulting in the ladies' eventual departure from the theatre.[62] Much like the evicted women, the style of wearing very large buffonts soon too departed. In the society news on 1 May 1787, a newspaper reported optimistically that the 'pouting handkerchief for the neck is very much on the decline; a large bouquet of natural or artificial flowers adorns now the bosom of our belles, and they could not have devised an ornament more becoming', indicating that once again, the wheel of fashion was turning.[63] Though handkerchiefs would continue to be worn through the end of the century, their scale deflated as did the scale of the overall silhouette. When once the commentators of fashion were horrified by the amplification of the body, within a matter of years, they then became equally aghast at its natural exposure, when the deflated breast was laid bare through muslin's clinging form, and bared breasts were actually on display.[64]

Fashion and print

The rise and fall of the handkerchief, or buffont, present a microhistory of fashionable dress for the year 1786. Widely worn and emblematic of the prominent position that one small accessory could occupy, its presence on the fashionable body was conspicuous and pervasive. Unlike the material volume and lightness which were captured in oil by the delicate brushwork of portraitists, like Francis Alleyne, the fragile extant examples that are now preserved in museum stores lie flat, carefully conserved and protected from further damage and discoloration. Despite their plentiful survival within collections, our understanding of the handkerchief's presence on the eighteenth-century body is largely reliant on description, like that of von La Roche, and through its visual portrayal. Visual culture is a vital lens that can help us see and understand garments, how they appeared and were worn, even when extant examples exist. The study of dress has long relied on painted representation to reconstruct the 'the ephemeral but vital arts of the tailor, dressmaker and hairdresser' and replace the lost body that once occupied extant material objects, offering tantalizing glimpses into the dress of the past.[65] Carefully agreed upon constructions between sitter, painter and patron, the image on the painted canvas follows its own sartorial and artistic conventions – portraying what was then popular to be painted wearing, but not necessarily what was worn.[66] Arguably, the fashion for half-length portraits of women with precise confections of hair and headwear and a puffed handkerchief at the breast, like Mrs Wheatley's, participates within its own fashionable convention. But breaking from well-trodden paths of art historical scholarship on the Romney's, Gainsborough's and Reynolds's, this book posits: what of those garments that painted portraiture excluded, those either too ephemeral or short-lived to be immortalized in oils, or too far beneath the formality of the genre to be deemed polite? It asks why do we favour the portrait of Mrs Wheatley over the lady suspended by her bosom and bum like a hot air balloon, or the *Modern Venus* herself, in our quest to understand eighteenth-century dress?

Traditionally, satirical prints have been viewed with mild concern to scathing contempt when considered in relation to clothing. Influentially, Doris Langley Moore asserted that due to their often exaggerated and distorted effects, 'parodies of fashion must be ruled out', prioritizing fashion plates instead.[67] By contrast, advocates for the medium, including print scholars like Donald, have argued that satires have 'a scale and panache which [convey] the fashionable "look" far more effectively than the frozen and timid manner of contemporary fashion plates … [and] pocket book illustrations'.[68] Somewhere in between these opposing opinions, like the preferred temperature of Goldilocks' porridge, Lou Taylor tepidly endorses the use of satirical prints as a 'gauge of period reaction to dress [rather] than … their "reliable" depiction of style'.[69] Rather than hinging only over reliability or accuracy, this book approaches graphic satires as rich and fruitful sources that were active players within the construction of fashion in the late eighteenth century. Building on the work of Peter McNeil, whose research into print culture, the macaroni and fashion has been instrumental in reframing the relationship of satirical prints and dress, not as deterrents to fashionable excess, but instigators of fashionable innovation, this book continues to develop the vibrant cyclical dialogues and exchanges between style and satire, establishing a symbiotic relationship between women's fashion and print culture.[70]

As this book argues, the world of fashion and the world of print are expressly entwined. Over the second half of the eighteenth century, the publication of newspapers and periodicals grew considerably, providing ever more column inches for fashion news, as well as those seeking to report or comment on the latest levity or fashionable whim, both pleasing and vexing to the public eye.[71] Though fashion reports and commentaries had been a fixture of periodicals since the beginning of the century, with cautionary didactic tales peppering the pages of *The Spectator* and *The Tatler*, their presence proliferated in the last thirty years of the century.[72] 1770 saw the publication of *The Lady's Magazine, or Entertaining Companion for the Fair Sex*, the first British monthly fashion magazine, which acted as a departure from the pocket book format that had been and would continue to print fashionable news and plates.[73] Published monthly, *The Lady's Magazine* brought fashionable news, embroidery patterns and the occasional fashion plate to its subscribers, extending the reach of fashion outside the metropolis. Alongside this growth in fashion-focused periodicals and newsprint, the publication of and demand for satirical prints flourished.[74] On the etched, engraved, mezzotint or stippled pages, fashion played a key role as a subject as well as a scaffold within graphic satire, employed as the vehicle to convey meaning or commentary about the social or political anxieties of the day beyond the mere ridicule of fashion itself.[75] Dress provided a language of material motifs of which the viewing public was fluent, a cultural currency which was bartered back and forth between the producers and consumers of fashion and its image. The treatment of dress within prints varied, dependent on the artist, publisher and socio-political context, for example there was a noticeable dip in fashion prints during the early 1780s due to the continued war between Britain and colonial America. For sartorially eloquent artists, like John Collet, for whom attention to detail in dress became one of his iconographic signatures, the rendering and employment of dress function as both a reliable depiction of garments worn and a tool within the 'loaded', opinionated field of satirical commentary, giving added weight and significance to the material life represented.[76] This, to borrow a phrase, 'material literacy' of graphic satirists can be attributed to their proximity and close relationship with the production and dissemination of fashion.[77]

The routes and trajectories of fashion and its printed image were often in tandem. Fashionable dress and those that wore, or aspired to it, provided not only inspiration and comic material for satirical prints, but a language of motifs understood by the viewing public. The speed of satirical prints kept up with the pace of fashion, unlike fashion plates, whose images often lagged well behind the current mode. For example, Matthew and Mary Darly, who traded largely in fashion satires, were able to take a caricature of an attendee's dress at a masquerade in the evening and pin it up for sale in their printshop window at 39 Strand by the following morning.[78] The consumption of prints, which could be purchased for one to two shillings, plain and hand-coloured respectively, extended beyond those whose fashions they satirized or even whose pockets could pay for them.[79] Prints were displayed in printshop and bookshop windows, coffee houses and pinned up for sale and display in the streets (Figure 0.17).⁸⁰ As will be addressed in Chapter 4, the geographies of production for fashionable dress and satirical prints were enmeshed, occupying adjacent streets and neighbourhoods within a small radius within the metropolis. Though the heart of production for these two industries was heavily metropolitan, the geographical boundaries of fashion were, as Marcia Pointon's observes, 'porous'.⁸¹ Satirical prints and fashionable knowledge were widely circulated beyond the limits of the capital, disseminated across provincial Britain and exported to Europe and colonial and Early America.⁸² By the 1760s, well-established maritime routes criss-crossed the seas, transporting raw materials, letters, goods and enslaved labour that made up a network of global trade. Framed as a 'highway rather than a barrier', the Atlantic facilitated the movement of fashion between London and her port cities, ferrying the concepts of fashion conveyed in letters, news clippings and prints, alongside the fashionable articles themselves, cratefuls of dress and textiles, 'just imported' from London.⁸³

Figure 0.17 Miss Macaroni and Her Gallant at a Print-Shop, *2 April 1773, publ. by John Bowles, mezzotint, 35.0 × 25.0 cm, Courtesy of the Lewis Walpole Library, Yale University.*

Returning to the *Modern Venus,* the missing stage of that progression is arguably the first: the material artefacts that inspired Mary Hoare's nude. The clothes that Hoare saw, or even may have worn herself, do not survive. Nor do archival records or descriptions of the dress that created so voluptuous a figure. Though, as demonstrated above, it is possible to work backwards from representation – to contextualize the handkerchief, or buffont that constructed the puff of the modern Venus's breast – it is necessary to, whenever possible, be grounded in the material, for only when intimately familiar with the material can we understand the nuances of fashion and dress within its various discursive and visual incarnations. As such, this book contributes to a long and distinguished tradition of object-based research.[84] Ariane Fennetaux and Barbara Burman in their work on pockets have argued that 'by refocusing our gaze on what is small and apparently tangential, we see more not less', a sentiment particularly relevant to the study of underwear and accessories, and their 'commitment to objects' is upheld here.[85] Disciplinarily, this book answers Michael Yonan's call for a greater rapport between object and image, positioning the history of dress as a bridge between history of art and material culture studies through the emphasis placed on representations of dress and their relationship with the artefact.[86] The employment of the modern Venus as a model is two-pronged. First, it uses the exchange as a visualization of the significance of underwear and accessories in defining fashion in the late eighteenth century. Borrowing Susan Vincent's anatomical approach, the chapters of this book each addresses a piece of the modern Venus, the underwear and accessories that together composed the fashionable silhouette from *c.* 1765 to *c.* 1795.[87] Second, it considers the intimate relationship portrayed in the exchange between the sartorial and the satirical. Though this book is not exclusively about satire, it argues that by embracing and enveloping our study of underwear and accessories within the satirical realm, we can achieve a better understanding of how the ephemeral and underlying articles of dress functioned within society. Like the necessity of salt to reveal flavour, graphic satire establishes the fundamental role these garments played both as elements of fashion and as weighted facets emblematic of the anxieties and concerns of this charged revolutionary period.

The progression of Venus

As coiffeurs grew to new heights and widths over the decades, headwear climbed to accommodate them. Chapter 1 addresses the profusion of styles of brimmed hats as representational of fashionable change in contrast to the continuity of a boned, collapsible hood, known as a calash. As hairstyles rose and rounded, hats and headwear were produced at an insatiable rate, fashioned, delineated and disseminated in the new medium of the fashion magazine. Advertised as a parade of fashion, hats embodied the current moment, capturing Coxheath patriotism, Lunardi's flight, and the latest notable member of the bon ton. Due to their quick succession, enabled by the process of making, remaking and adaptation, comparatively few brimmed hats survive outwith visual representation, a sharp contrast to the calash's abundant material survival. Despite its profuse survival in museum collections, the calash has never before been discussed in detail. This chapter will approach the calash in terms of its mobility, tracing a path from its collapsible material structure evident in extant examples to the physical and social mobility of its wearer. Progressing from a paper procession of heads to the practical and social mobility of the calash, this chapter highlights how hair and headwear aided women's navigation of their social and geographical landscapes.

Chapter 2 poses the question of how to address a material artefact that nearly only survives in the satirical record. Appearing in the mid-1770s and signalling the move away from the wide-silhouetted hoop, the cork rump, termed a bum in the 1780s, was a bustle that shaped and lifted the looped skirt style of the latter eighteenth century. Until now, previous scholarship that has acknowledged cork rumps and bums has done so briefly, treating it as a fleeting extremity of fashion, an exaggeration of the satirist's pen, which is then quickly dropped in favour of the pronounced lack of emphasis on the backside of the neoclassical silhouette. This chapter aims to amend this oversight by challenging the extent to which dress history can be informed by graphic satire. First, it establishes the cork rump's material footprint; then, it delves into the rump's prolific satirical representation. By tracing the cork rump and bum's satirical lifecycle, this chapter establishes how sartorial motifs were referenced, manipulated and exploited in printed discourse, and how satirical prints influenced and were influenced by perceptions of dress.

Chapter 3 examines fur and silk muffs. Typical of the voluminous shapes of the 1780s, the fur muff was an indispensable element in the sartorial recipe for the silhouette. Its material, size and scale became an iconographic trope of monstrous fashionability. While fur dominated print culture and women's wardrobes alike, the chapter turns to the fur muff's overlooked sister, the silk muff. Examining silk muffs that were embroidered, mostly by their wearers, this chapter establishes both the practical and social networks cultivated to facilitate the dissemination of embroidery patterns, but also the artistic and personal significance the haptic practice of embroidering a muff fostered. The chapter situates the embroidered muff as a receptacle of meaning and a medium of artistic output. The silk muff's role as a portable canvas becomes evident in an examination of printed silk muffs, establishing the silk muff as a touchable means of feminine self-fashioning, connoisseurship and patronage.

Chapter 4, the final chapter, tackles the narratives around stays and the practice of tight lacing, which appeared in the 1760s and has dominated the discourses around stays and corsets to this day. Though thorough chronicles of the stay's evolution have been diligently written, this chapter addresses not an overarching stylistic evolution, but a distinct period of material change and its aftermath. This chapter examines the change to the construction of stays in the 1770s and 1780s as emblematic of both a material shift and a shift in meaning. Focusing on previously unaddressed constructional adaptations in relation to the stay's representation in graphic satire, in particular the trope of tight lacing, this chapter addresses the stay as embodying a vast range of social and political anxieties. In satirical prints, the stay became one of the most abundantly used sartorial iconographic motifs. This final chapter examines the entwined relationship between material artefact and its satirical representation of one of the most socially and culturally significant, yet contested garments of the eighteenth century.

The Modern Venus realizes a prediction foretold by that anonymous commentator in August 1785. Following a list of underwear and accessories, including hats, bums and handkerchiefs, he penned, 'such are a few of those exterior levities most in Fashion. How this sovereign arbitress of human destiny affects the minds, the sentiments, and the hearts of our fair country women, may probably be the subject of some future lucrabation'.[88] The author invites us to lucrabate, or to study or meditate, upon the 'levities most in Fashion' and their effects on 'the minds, the sentiments, and the hearts' of British women in the late eighteenth century. Following his invitation, this book addresses and explores how those levities, specifically underwear and accessories defined the pace of fashionable change in the late eighteenth century. Spanning a thirty-year period from *c.* 1765 to *c.* 1795, it establishes how underwear and accessories – those garments traditionally cast as peripheral, underlying and ephemeral – became emblematic of fashion itself. In a period defined by significant political, social and cultural change, the fashionable silhouette expanded and contracted dramatically, propelled by fashion's underlying relationship with print. While this book champions the position of underwear and accessories in defining fashion, it simultaneously champions the position of print culture in shaping it. Not merely a passive observer or recorder, print culture mediated fashion through its descriptions, reports, patterns and representations. This book looks beyond the fashion plate to elevate graphic satire as a key primary source of dress and fashion history. Bridging the sartorial and the satirical, *The Modern Venus* foregrounds the connection between satirical prints and dress as a catalyst that fuelled fashion's course. It is through this fundamental relationship that we find the modern Venus, the archetype of fashion and fashionable change, whose form we begin to trace from the head down.

1

Head first: Brimmed hats and calashes on the tides of fashion

In his 1747 *London Tradesman*, Robert Campbell observed that 'Ladies Heads [are fashioned] in as many different Shapes in one Month as there are different Appearances of the Moon.'[1] Never was this astrological observation more true than twenty years later when women's hair climbed to new heights and widths, and an outpouring of hats, caps and decorative headwear were made to match.[2] The latest ladies' headdress was reported in magazines, complained about at the theatre and portrayed as a parade on paper in fashion plates produced for periodicals, almanacs and pocket books. Graphic satirists took no time to seize upon the towering coiffeurs of the 1770s and wide, frizzed styles of the 1780s, producing a body of satires focused entirely on the enormous coiffeur (Figure 1.1). Even when wrapping their sitters in classicizing, draped constructions of satin and gauze, portraitists carefully delineated the fashionable hairstyle of the day, often only to change the style at the sitter's bequest a few years later.[3]

Of dress and accessories, the rapid progression of hair, headwear and hats is perhaps the fastest rate of fashionable change, setting the pace of fashion from the head down. One fashion report observed that hats and headwear 'change with inconceivable rapidity'.[4] Returning to the anonymous author of the 'Levities of Fashion', in his attempt to pin down the changing winds of fashionable dress, he observed that the 'insensible gradations' of fashion are:

> like the vivid visits of a rainbow, the variation of whose colours defy the accuracy of human attention – it is like the delicate and interesting humours of a lovely woman, which though never the same for a moment, increasingly possess a charm which captivate [sic.] the heart.[5]

Following his metaphorical musings, he turned his attention to three hats that 'were sported in succession with infinite glee and variety'. The magnitude of hats produced and worn, both in quantity and scale, became a particular focal point during the period, as headwear was produced of ever-

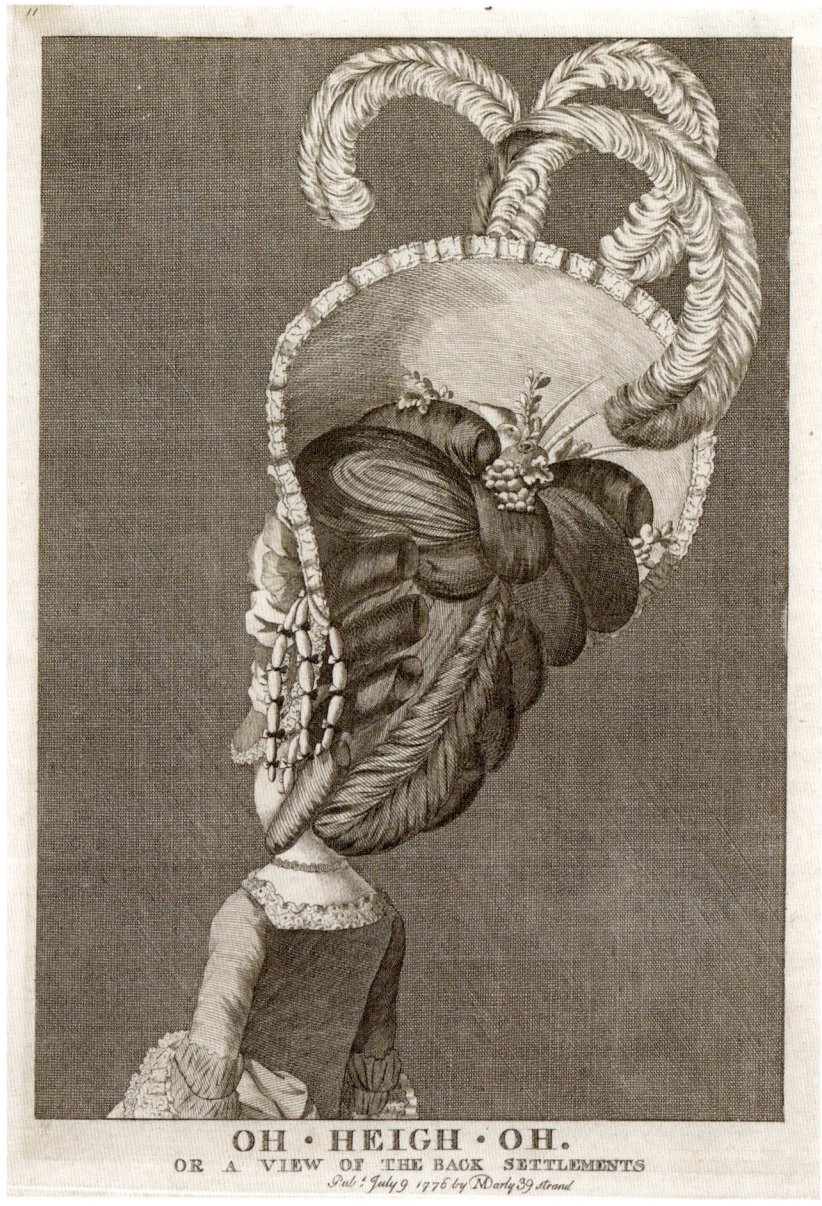

Figure 1.1 Oh Heigh Oh, or, A View of the Back Settlements, *9 July 1776, publ. by Mathew and Mary Darly, hand-coloured etching and engraving, 35.1 × 24.8 cm, Courtesy of the Lewis Walpole Library, Yale University.*

expanding size, shape and levels of ornamentation. It is not the intention of this chapter, nor the style of this book, to list every fashionable variation, but rather to let the frothy tide of fashionable brimmed headwear wash over us, before focusing on one stalwart that arguably sailed above these infinite permutations, successfully surviving the tides of fashionable change.

Paper heads

Over the late eighteenth century, women's heads became sites of significant coiffeurial construction.[6] Frisseurs, or hairdressers, sculpted natural and false hair over cushions of wool, horsehair and wire to create teased, frizzed and curled edifices.[7] Between June 1772 and September 1782, Elizabeth Motley Austen (née Wilson, 1751–1817) bought ten cushions for her hair for three to four shillings each, along with pomatum, powder, lavender water, curls and a cignon, and the services of her local frisseur, Arkell.[8] Structural additions and stylization were held into place with pomatum, a scented pomade made of animal fats and flour, which could be either purchased ready-made and scented or made up at home using recipes from didactic hair and beauty treatises like *The Toilet of Flora* (1779) and *Plocacosmos* (1782).[9] Volumizing white, grey or coloured hair powder, whose primary ingredient was starch, was dusted on top.[10] Stylistically, 1770s coiffeurs were predominantly tall and narrow in shape.[11] Typified by a flat edifice in front, flanked by curls and finished with a chignon down the back of the head, the coiffeur was an incorporation of natural and false hair. Plumed with ostrich feathers, the height of women's hair crested in the 1770s.[12] As the female silhouette rounded into a serpentine juxtaposition of globes in the early 1780s, so too did the coiffeur. Rather than reaching upwards into a sculpted narrow peak, the hair was frizzed into a lower and broader orb, commonly known as the 'hedgehog' style.[13] Though women's wigs were made and worn, the majority of hairstyles were a confection of natural hair, false hair, products, pins and cushions, innately connected to their mortal hosts and thus surviving primarily on paper.

Fashion plates, first engraved annually for pocket books and almanacs in the 1750s, and published within monthly serials with the advent of *The Lady's Magazine, or Entertaining Companion for the Fair Sex* (1770–1832) in 1770, disseminated these styles, as Campbell predicted, like the changing phases of the moon.[14] As hair grew, a plethora of soft headwear, including poufs, caps, turbans and bonnets, along with the more fanciful appendages of the 1770s, were fashioned. As *Lady's Magazine* fashion correspondent Charlotte Stanley bemoaned in March 1776, 'I have seen several ladies, very handsome, so disguised, and features quite distorted, by the horrid drag of their hair, to a height absolutely half as tall as themselves, and so loaded with gause, flowers, fruits, herbs, ribbons, pins &c'.[15] Stanley and her fellow correspondents became the first arbiters of a new genre: fashion news.[16] Printed sporadically through the 1770s and 1780s and appearing with seasonal regularity by the 1790s, fashion reports became one of the features of the periodical, accompanied by the even more sporadically printed fashion plate.[17] With the object of bringing the latest fashions beyond the boundaries of the cosmopolitan capital, fashion was disseminated in print discursively and visually in the new-found medium of the fashion magazine.[18]

Significantly more than full size dress, fashion plates of the late eighteenth century centred on hair and headwear, printing a procession of paper heads. In British publications, 'Fashionable Head

Figure 1.2 Twelve Fashionable Head Dresses of 1778, 1778, engraving, 11.6 × 14.2 cm, Museum of Applied Arts and Sciences, Ultimo, Powerhouse collection. Gift of Mr H Matthews, 1982. Photographer Stuart Humphreys.

Dresses' by month or by year became the reigning format, featuring ten to twelve busts of women on a page in a variety of hair styles, caps, hats and headwear (Figure 1.2). This assemblage of floating busts contrasted the French format, where, in publications like *Gallerie des Modes* (1778–87), which was specifically dedicated to engravings of fashion, heads were individually framed like *tête-a-têtes* and miniatures, titled and printed in grids of four or sixteen a page.[19] Like trading cards, they were cut, pasted and collated into albums and scrapbooks, like those made by Sarah Sophia Banks, Barbara Johnson and Anne Damer.[20] These haptic practices extended playfully to paper dolls, whose heads were dressed with interchangeable coiffeurs rather than bodies dressed with full-length gowns (Figure 1.3). Echoing the framed style of fashion plates, a set of watercolours on pasteboard sold by prominent Paris publisher Philippe-Denis Pierres features a framed nude quarter-length woman with a set of

Figure 1.3 *Eight of Twelve Interchangeable Coiffeurs, c. 1780s, watercolour on paper and pasteboard case, Collection 121, 73 × 319.2, Courtesy of the Winterthur Library: Joseph Downs Collection of Manuscripts and Printed Ephemera.*

twelve different coiffeurs, providing their owner with a selection of appearances at their fingertips.[21] This haptic interchange on paper, which reflected the changeability of hair itself, evokes the fleeting temporality of fashion. As Serena Dyer has argued, the temporality of fashion plates acts as 'time capsules and epitaphs of their cultural context'.[22] Together they can be read as a miscellany of polaroid pictures capturing the present pulse of fashion – how widely worn or representative these fashions were is arguably another matter entirely.

The ephemerality of hats is especially apparent: a quick succession of straw, chip, beaver and silk, each diligently described and delineated in the sartorial press.[23] While the shallow-crowned chip and straw bergère, or shepherdess style, which had dominated over the middle decades of the century, continued to be worn, if at a more and more severe angle, an outpouring of other brimmed hats appeared alongside (Figure 1.4).[24] Responding to and commemorating the events of the day, each new hat was christened after the latest person, place or thing of note, for example: the Rutland, the Perdita, the Cumberland, the Boston and the Theodore.[25] After Vincenzo Lunardi's flight, first in France in 1783 and in Britain in 1784, the Lunardi, air balloon or parachute hat, a chip brimmed hat with wide pleated fabric crown, was widely advertised, satirized and complained about at the theatre. Five years earlier, when the patriotic 'Amazons' of Coxheath dressed in 'scarlet riding habits *epaulet*,' led by the general of fashion herself, Georgina Cavendish, the Duchess of Devonshire (1757–1806), their hats too were dressed *en militaire*.[26] Beaver and silk riding hats were cocked and adorned with feathers, cockades and shining gold loops and buttons to align with the militarized styles (Figure 1.5). At a regimental ball in Hartford on 21 January 1780, Lady Cranborne wore a 'gown of scarlet sattin with buff ornament … [and] a Devonshire Hatt, turned up before with a cockade and diamond button

Figure 1.4 *Bergère, c. 1770, French, straw and silk, Acc. No. 2017.16, Metropolitan Museum of Art, New York.*

Figure 1.5 *John Singleton Copley,* Frances Tucker Montresor, *c. 1778, oil on canvas, 77.15 × 63.82 cm, Courtesy of the Diplomatic Reception Rooms, U.S. Department of State, Washington D.C.*

and loop, with several scarlet and Buff feathers'.²⁷ Of the members of the bon ton whose names were ascribed to garments, the Devonshire name carried significant fashionable weight by the early 1780s and was widely monopolized upon by milliners. It was attributed to a hood imported to Jamaica in 1780, a chip hat in 1781, a cap in 1783 and a 'straw [hat], lined with any coloured sarcenet, very large and worn quite round; sometimes with a large bow behind and before; but the most fashionable with only a broad band and buckle in front' in 1784.²⁸ By early 1786, when Lady Ossory placed a large, wide-brimmed hat on the head of the *Modern Venus,* the style was pervasive: an evolution of the riding hat, whose scale complimented the amplified proportions of the body beneath. The style was heavily satirized in prints and portrayed frequently in painted portraiture by John Hopner, George Romney and Thomas Gainsborough, including his *Mr and Mrs Willian Hallet* in 1785 and the *c.* 1786 portrait of the Duchess herself, which later inspired the term the 'picture hat' or 'Gainsborough hat' with the Sheridan revival in the nineteenth century (Figure 1.6).²⁹

One Scottish observer, under the pseudonym, 'MEMORY MODISH', noted 'an antiquarian observed to me, what an opinion our great-grandchildren might be led to form of the size of the ladies [sic.] heads towards the close of the 18th century, if any of the fashionable *Hats* should happen to be preserved in the cabinets of the curious'.³⁰ Within modern-day cabinets of curiosities – the museum store – these hats are hard to come by. Though a number of straw and chip bergères survive, as does the primary focus of this chapter, the boned hood called a calash, in rather astounding quantities, the large brimmed hats that attracted such attention in the newspapers, printshop windows and on the painted canvas are nowhere to be found.³¹ However, where something large cannot be located, something small stands in its place. Upon opening a drawer in the stores of the DeWitt Wallace Museum of Colonial Williamsburg, one wonders with curiosity at the sartorial curios beheld within. Over thirty articles of the most fashionable dress compose the wardrobe of a doll, dating from the 1780s (Figure 1.7).³² Amidst a selection of perfect miniature gowns, linen and accessories are two brimmed hats, along with a turban, a narrow hood and two muslin caps.³³ Both brimmed hats are made of braided straw, each measuring roughly two inches (5 cm) in diameter (Figures 1.8 and 1.9). The straw is trimmed with cream silk ribbon around the brim and crown and a wide navy ribbon is tied in bows around the base of the crown. The second, using the same straw foundation, is covered in black ribbed silk and cocked at the side with a silk loop and black silk button. A plume of dressed black feathers balances the hat on the other side of the brim. Though the brim-to-crown proportions are smaller than those portrayed on the painted canvas, their survival is a rare testament to the changefulness of fashion. The swift adaptation of styles, made up and taken apart with the addition or subtraction of a feather or the change of ribbon or gauze, has made these quick concoctions of straw and sarcenet, like the coiffeur itself, plentiful on paper, but scarce within material collections. Their lack of survival speaks to their ephemerality, quickly changing like the froth on a bubbling stream.

Figure 1.6 *George Romney, Mrs. Bryan Cooke, c. 1787–91, oil on canvas, 127 × 100.3 cm, Metropolitan Museum of Art, New York.*

Figure 1.7 *Wooden doll with wardrobe, English c. 1780s, wood, gesso, paint, and glass, Acc. No. 2005-102,1, DeWitt Wallace Museum of Decorative Arts, Williamsburg, The Colonial Williamsburg Foundation. Museum Purchase.*

Figure 1.8 *Straw and silk doll's hat, c. 1780s, silk and straw, Acc. No. 2005-102, 8, DeWitt Wallace Museum of Decorative Arts, Williamsburg, The Colonial Williamsburg Foundation. Museum Purchase.*

Figure 1.9 *Black silk brimmed doll's hat, c. 1780s, silk, straw, brass, feathers, Acc. No. 2005-102, 8, DeWitt Wallace Museum of Decorative Arts, Williamsburg, The Colonial Williamsburg Foundation. Museum Purchase.*

Navigating the calash

As brimmed hats broke like waves, one after another, a boned, folding hood, called a calash sailed gently over the churning seas below. Crafted to pass above and envelope the fluctuating volumes beneath, the calash was worn from the mid-1760s into the 1790s, making a brief revival in the nineteenth century.[34] Its name derived from a popular pleasure carriage, the calash or *calèche*, whose jointed leather hood could be lifted and lowered over its passengers. As amateur historian John F. Watson noted in 1830, the '"calash bonnet" was always formed of green silk [and] worn abroad, covering the head, but when in rooms it could fall back in folds like the springs of a calash or gig top'.[35] In contrast to brimmed hats, it survives plentifully in museum collections; however, extant scholarship about the calash has remained a passing paragraph in fashionable chronologies of the eighteenth century, often reiterating Watson's brief remarks.[36] The remainder of this chapter broadens our understanding of the calash within the cannon of fashion history by tracing its mobility and manoeuvrability within eighteenth-century society.

The calash's collapsible design has no doubt contributed to its copious survival in collections today. In a typical example from the 1770s, five split cane or reed arches support the structure of a green silk taffeta calash, lined with a rose pink silk (Figures 1.10 and 1.11).[37] The silk taffeta ruches along the bones and is gathered at the back to form a structured hood, which, when raised, forms valleys of silk between each arch that reaches 13½ inches (33.29 cm) high.[38] Joined by a centre seam,

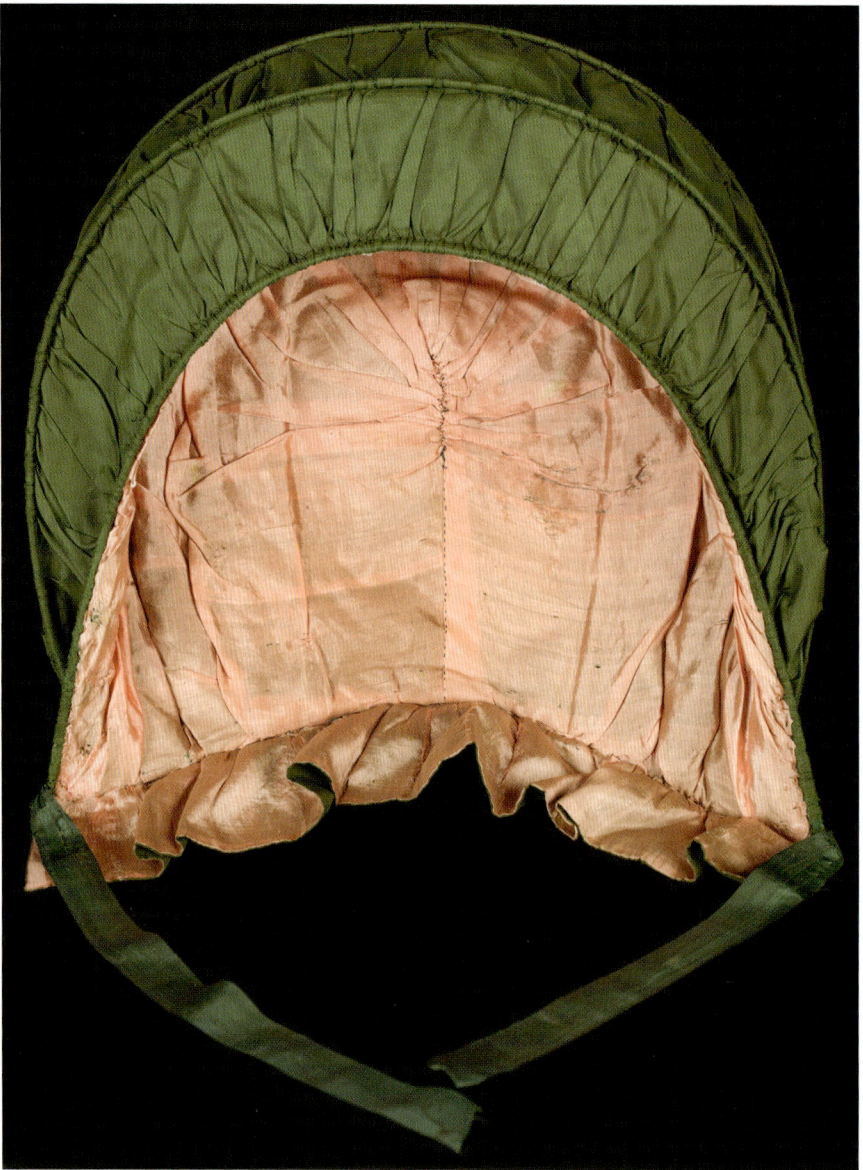

Figure 1.10 *Green and pink silk calash, c. 1775–80, English, silk and reeds or whalebone, Acc. No. 1960-723, DeWitt Wallace Museum of Art, Colonial Williamsburg Foundation, Williamsburg, The Colonial Williamsburg Foundation. Museum Purchase.*

fanned pleats meet to form the back panel.[39] The calash is finished below the neck bone with a flap, or 'apron', of matching lined silk and green silk ribbons at each end of the neck bone, which would have enabled its wearer to tie the calash in place. Calashes were most frequently made of silk, but could also be made with starch-glazed cotton, whose silk-like lustre would have given consumers a less expensive alternative.[40] The silhouette when raised would have created a high, yet relatively shallow and narrow cavern, not drawn very far away from the face.[41] The arches of the hood are not fused

Figure 1.11 *Green and pink silk calash, c. 1775–80, English, silk and reeds or whalebone, Acc. No. 1960-723, DeWitt Wallace Museum of Art, Colonial Williamsburg Foundation, Williamsburg, The Colonial Williamsburg Foundation. Museum Purchase.*

with the neck-bone in a fixed perpendicular, or upright position, but rather are attached loosely with thread either drilled through or wrapped around the adjoining bones, ensuring the calash's easy mobility.[42]

In contrast, a calash from the 1780s reflects the change in coiffeurial style, from tall and narrow to round and wide (Figures 1.12 and 1.13). Made of a brown silk exterior, with a bright pink silk lining, the calash is structured with four flat bones of cane or whalebone. It measures 14 inches (38 cm) in height and 15 inches

Figure 1.12 *Brown and pink silk calash, 1780–1790, Acc. No. 1.12.771, Fashion Museum Bath © Fashion Museum Bath/Bridgeman Images.*

(40 cm) in width at the widest point. Unlike the green calash, the bones are even in length, creating a uniform height. A matching brown apron skirts the neckline and the first boning casing has been set back from the front, creating a trim around the opening. A dark brown silk ribbon bow tops the centre front of the calash, and matching silk ribbons flank each side.[43] In addition to the added decorative elements, the

Figure 1.13 *Brown and pink silk calash, 1780–1790, Acc. No. 1.12.771, Fashion Museum Bath © Fashion Museum Bath/Bridgeman Images.*

construction of the design is also more complex. While the green calash has been finished in the back by bringing the single piece of fabric together in fanned pleats, the length of brown silk that forms the body of the Bath calash has been gathered in the back and pleated around a flat oval back piece, which is stiffened by a supplementary piece of boning and creates a concentric oval mirroring the hood's outer shape.

The close relationship between hair and the calash was heralded in popular poems and songs, like *The Calash*, 'a favourite Song at all the Watering Places, Camps, &c.' of Britain, published in the *Morning Chronicle and London Advertiser*, 9 August 1779:

HAIL! Great *Calash*! O'erhelming veil,
By all indulgent Heaven
To sallow nymphs, and maidens stale,
In sportive kindness given,

Safe hid beneath thy circling sphere,
Unseen by mortal eyes,
The mingled heap of grease and hair,
And wool, and powder, lies.

From the bald head should pad and tete,
And loads of horse hair fall,
Fear not the loose disorder'd pate,
Calash will hold it all.

Hail! Great *Calash*! O'erwhelming veil,
By all indulgent heaven
To sallow nymphs, and maidens stale,
In sportive kindness given.[44]

As the rondo suggests, the calash accommodated 'the heap of grease and hair, And wool and powder' that was encircled beneath. Unlike un-boned hoods, caps or hats, which rested directly on the hair, the top and sides of the calash rose above the carefully sculpted coiffeur. As numerous scholars have established, a well-styled coiffeur acted as a vehicle for cultural and gendered performance through which women communicated their character and position in society, heightening the necessity to keep one's powdered curls intact.[45] As the song alludes, preserving the neat appearance of one's hair was a principal concern, and the disgrace of a coiffeur falling apart was safeguarded by the calash.[46] The rondo teasingly jests that in case one's hair comes undone, 'From the baldhead should pad and tete, / And loads of horsehair fall,' the calash will conceal the shame and embarrassment of an exposed bare head (pate): 'Fear not the loose disordered pate, / Calash will hold it all'.[47] By protecting both a woman's hair and by extension her public self, the calash operated as a shield, whose shape and construction evolved with the changing styles of the hair beneath. Yet, this act of protection was not always positively cast.

Figure 1.14 *'Fashionable Dresses in the Rooms at Weymouth 1774,'* The Lady's Magazine or Entertaining Companion for the Fair Sex, *1774, engraving, 14 × 8.8 cm, Wellcome Collection, London.*

Though the calash inspired multiple published poems, the most extensive poetic reflection on its arrival within fashion was published in three instalments in *The Lady's Magazine, or Entertaining Companion for the Fair Sex* of 1784.[48] *The Lady's Magazine* had depicted a calash in a fashion plate ten years prior, but only expounded upon its mythical origin ten years later (Figure 1.14). Unlike other sartorial it-narratives, like *Memoirs and Interesting Adventures of an Embroidered Waistcoat* (1751), which provides a fictional first-person account of its wearer's amorous conquests, travels and business encounters, *The Triumph of the Calash* acts as a fictional object biography.[49] In rhyming verse, it traces the calash's mythical conception back to the classical story of Judgement of Paris, in which the Trojan prince Paris declared Venus the most beautiful goddess over Juno and Minerva.[50] *The Triumph of the Calash* identifies the calash as a product of Juno and Minerva's outrage and revenge upon the female sex.[51] Having been slighted by Paris, Juno prophesizes her revenge, not taken out on Paris or the Trojans, but instead on the women of the eighteenth century:

> But when Great Britain mighty Rome outvies,
> When science brightens, superstition dies,
> May her fair daughters (fairer they shall prove
> Than Venus's self, the boasted queen of love;)
> Their lovely limbs by monstrous arts deform,
> While o'er the rais'd head waves the feather'd storm;
> And from behind the streaming pendants fly,
> Like meteors blazing in a troubled sky.
> Then shall the great Calash expand its size,
> And with its bulk astonish human eyes;
> The fam'd Calash shall faults and beauties hide,
> The men's aversion, as the woman's pride ....[52]

The author, unidentifiable by her name J——— W———, pens that Juno's vengeance shall be enacted when fashions, contemporaneous to the poem's publication, are in style – including feathered, ornamented hair, and bodies 'deformed', presumably by cork rumps. Amongst these fashions, the calash is contrived to 'intercept the glance that flies' from young men, like Paris, inhibiting their gaze on female beauties.[53]

Following the orders of a slighted Juno, Minerva, the calash's mythical designer, instructs a fictional eighteenth-century milliner named Flirtilla in a dream, commanding:

> Receive this model of a lady's head,
> And mark the silken sides around it spread;
> Observe its bulk, and vast rotund behind,
> At once to shade, to shelter, and to blind;
> Let it o'er-hang the face, and meet before,
> Employ – let's see – ay – thirty ells – or more;
> Then be Minerva's great command obey'd.
> Thy hands shall make it, as my hands have made;
> Britannia's daughters shall thy genius bless,
> And milliners grow rich as duchesses.[54]

Linguistically mimicking a Latin name, 'Flirtilla' alludes to milliners' flirtatious and promiscuous reputations, as they were frequently reprimanded in trade dictionaries, such as *The London Tradesman*.[55] A subsequent couplet of the poem boasts of Flirtilla's future fame as the first milliner to make and sell the calash, 'Now all ye curious milliners for shame, / Hang down your heads, nor rival me in fame.'[56] Flirtilla's projected success reflects the popularity of the calash at the time of the poem's publication.

The calash's fashionability can be seen in its widespread advertisement across the burgeoning empire, fashioned by the nimble fingers not of goddesses, but of milliners. As Campbell's *London Tradesman* ascribes, the millinery trade was responsible for '[making] up and [selling] Hats, Hoods, and Caps of all Sorts and Materials', as well as producing and selling a vast variety of fashionable addendums and ornaments, including calashes.[57] In London, 'Calashes, Large, full and, handsome', were advertised for ten shillings, alongside children's calashes for six shillings by the Millinery Warehouse at No. 48 Jermin Street, St. James's.[58] Similarly, in Manchester, Ann Kay, Milliner and Black-Worker, sold 'CAPS, HATS BONNETS, CLOAKS, CALASHES, and also every other Article, under the Denomination of Millinery', from 'a House nearly opposite Mr. Finney's Grocer, in Hanging-Ditch'.[59] Across the Atlantic, Jane Hunter, one of the seven milliners active in Williamsburg, Virginia between 1760 and 1790, advertised in October 1766:

> JUST IMPORTED … a GENTEEL assortment of MILLINERY GOODS, *viz*. Fashionable caps, Italian caps, egrets and fillets, breast flowers, turbans and tippets, best French bead, pearl, and yard and yard and half wide book muslins, fine thick muslin, plain and spotted gauze, fashionable ribands and trimmings, black mittens, French and glazed kid and lamb gloves and mittens, white fans and white wire, calash bonnets, &c …[60]

In December 1773, a second milliner, Mrs Hughes advertised that she makes 'Ladies Sacks and Gowns, *Brunswick* Dresses, Cloaks, Cardinals, Bonnets, Calashes, &c.'[61] The latest designs and samples of ready-made accessories reached colonial shops within a matter of weeks from London as colonial milliners, as well as tailors and mantuamakers, profited from the trans-Atlantic trade network and were well-versed in the steady stream of communication and goods from London.[62] When Jane Hunter returned to England from Virginia in 1769, her sister Margaret Hunter continued to run the millinery business, receiving the latest fashionable news from England from Jane.[63] Similarly, Mrs Brodie, a mantuamaker, made her active connection with London even more transparent, noting 'her Partner still continues to carry on the Business in London, by whose Assistance, and that of the Queen's Mantua-Maker, she is every three Months to be supplied with the Fashions'.[64] That calashes were available in colonial shops as early as 1766 demonstrates both their popularity and the relative speed of trans-Atlantic fashionable communication. Echoing the *Triumph of the Calash's* nautical couplets, the calash sailed across the Atlantic. As the poem states, 'the Calash round those fair features rear'd; That like a broad sail bulging in the wind, Conceals the neck, and lovely locks behind,' suggesting the encompassing circumference of this 'vast orb', encircling the back of the neck and head. Though only a brief allusion, the choice of the word 'rear'd' and the maritime imagery invoked suggest that the calash metaphorically rises like a hoisted sail, highlighting its material constructed collapsibility.

A moveable object: The calash in motion

The calash's collapsible nature resonated in eighteenth-century opinion as being movable and even mechanical.[65] While a 1778 fashion plate of the 'dress of the year' presented the calash as an item of fashion, in the 1778 *The Miscellaneous works of Mr. Philip Freneau containing his essays, and additional poems* by colonial American poet and essayist, Philip Freneau, it is presented as an apparatus (Figure 1.15). The author poses a comic, sartorial debate between a 'Christopher Clodhopper, yeoman' and a fashionable Philadelphia lady, 'Pricilla Tripstreet', arguing over the taxation and triviality of the calash.[66] Clodhopper condemns the calash as an 'unwieldy machine', warning that it is especially dangerous in the wind due to its sail-like design.[67] Tripstreet, however, rebuffs his concerns by positively embracing its technological potential, suggesting bespoke nautical improvements made by her sea-faring husband:

> … to obviate all possibility of my being blown off a horse, or out of an open carriage, or off my feet into the river by the sudden gusts or flaws … he intends to provide my calash with what he calls single, double and balance-reef *eyelet holes*, with *reef-knittles* … knotted therein, ready for use upon any emergency, together with certain things he calls *sheets, tacks, clew-garnets, clew-lines* and *reef-tackles* running through a set of small pullies ….[68]

Outfitting his wife's calash with the technical devices used to adjust a ship's sails in high winds discloses a comic, yet revealing perception of the calash as a nautical artefact – that it was viewed not merely as an article of clothing, but an artful apparatus which could be altered and adjusted dependent on weather, or, as will be later addressed, even social, conditions.[69]

The calash's mobile ability to expand and contract groups it amongst other movable objects, including personal accessories such as fans, umbrellas and parasols, as well as mechanical furniture.[70] Numerous scholars have questioned 'the affinity between fashion, body, artefact and space', drawing comparisons particularly between dress and eighteenth-century furniture.[71] Mimi Hellman offers a useful approach from which to consider the broader parameters surrounding the calash and its relationship with its wearer. Hellman probes how the use and observance of furniture within elite interiors instructed and, in fact, dictated the modes and behaviours of the occupants – producing the effect of corporeal politeness.[72] She argues that 'decorative objects conveyed meaning not simply through possession but also through usage, through a spatial and temporal complicity with the cultivated body', which, in turn, made 'the practice of consumption … visual and kinetic; objects were not simply owned, but indeed *performed*'.[73] The kinetic handling of moving objects, ones that required knowledge of their workings and a corresponding corporeal awareness, had a specific effect on the bodies with which they came in contact.[74] Building from Hellman's argument, if a movable object can

Figure 1.15 *Dress of the year 1778*, 1778, 12.5 × 7.5 cm, Collection of the Author.

prescribe a person's movements and behaviours, how we consider the relationship between object and body is altered. Hellman approaches furniture as a prosthetic, 'an artificial extension of the body that enabled its management of physical and social spaces'.[75] She aligns the effect of furniture with the effect of garments on the body – designed to position and hold the body in a specific manner, like high set armholes that keep the shoulders back and posture upright.[76] However, if we apply Hellman's concept of spatial prescription to items of dress beyond those that physically shaped the body, like the calash, it is far more useful to consider the affect not of that of a prosthetic, but of a conveyance or tool which helps to move its wearer through space and society. Broadening out from the material movement, or mechanism of the calash's construction to that of the movement of its wearer, this discussion turns to how the calash enabled its wearer to manoeuvre both geographical and social spaces. To do this, we must retire the material artefact and look instead to the calash's visual representation in graphic satire to map the calash as an instrument of women's mobility.

Enter Miss Calash: The calash in graphic satire

Querying the calash's reputation is appropriate in graphic satire as its name was assumed linguistically to personify its wearer.[77] Distinct from other trope characters associated with a specific fashion, like Chloe and her cork rump, whom we will meet in Chapter 2, Miss, Mrs or Lady Calash is not limited to depictions of the fashionable belles of the beau monde. While Miss Calash conforms to the young, fashionable satirical norm, her other aliases represent a range of women, varied in age, appearance and class distinction. They also appear across a range of spatial and social settings, indicating the movement of their wearer within the practices of eighteenth-century leisure and sociability. The calash's physical collapsibility is mirrored in the wearer's represented mobility. This discussion of the calash in graphic satire will trace the calash's representation around the geographies of the promenade and the social custom of visiting in order to gauge how the calash affected its wearer's mobility, positing how an accessory can influence the navigation of eighteenth-century exteriors.

Miss Calash

Miss Calash is first depicted in *Miss Calash: Drawn by Miss Calash 1778,* published on 14 October 1778 by William Richardson (Figure 1.16).[78] A solitary young woman stands in profile against a plain background, wearing a fashionable gown with a lace furbelow around her skirts, a trimmed apron and elbow length gloves. From what is visible, the viewer can see that her hair has been teased and fashioned into a high coiffeur with curls falling around her neck and a decorative ribbon around the edifice. Her physique and dress illustrate the traditional satirical representation of fashionable women of the late 1770s – petite frame, features and tiny feet. But here her minuteness is overtly pronounced because she is physically dwarfed by an enormous calash, which protrudes from her diminutive waist. Vastly over-exaggerated in size, the calash measures over half of her body height.[79] Its volume is visually counterbalanced by her skirts and the shadow it creates on the ground, dividing her body in half on the page.[80] Portrayed like the sail of a ship billowing in the wind, the calash is equipped with technical improvements. Echoing Mrs Tripstreet's nautical modifications, the calash is hoisted up, or 'drawn', with a rope from the wearer's waist through a pulley system attached at the top. In addition to its mechanical advancements, the title, *Drawn by Miss Calash*, also plays on the calash's namesake, the carriage, which was drawn by horses. Like Freneau's poem, which was published in the same year, we are presented again with the contrast of technical innovation juxtaposed against feminine fashion, the result of which transforms the accessory into an apparatus. The application of engineering gear to augment the folding design of a woman's accessory would have been a comic opposition, pitting the masculine associations of mechanical technology against the feminine realm of accessories and fashion.[81] Yet, this repeating theme exposes a revealing insight into contemporary perception – that in some way,

Figure 1.16 Miss Calash: Drawn by Miss Calash 1778, 14 October 1778, publ. by William Richardson, etching, 32.5 × 20.2 cm, British Museum, London.

the calash's collapsible construction was, at least partially, considered to draw from each, bordering the opposing worlds of frivolous, feminine fashion and practical, masculine innovation. In both Freneau's fictional debate and Richardson's print, the innovations appear to benefit the wearer by harnessing the wind and aiding her to navigate her course.

In contrast to the stark profile of the previous print, the mezzotint entitled *Miss Calash in Contemplation*, published two years later by Carington Bowles on 15 May 1780, presents Miss Calash in an entirely different nature of print (Figure 1.17).[82] The lushly hand-coloured mezzotint leaves

Figure 1.17 Miss Calash in Contemplation, *15 May 1780, publ. by Carington Bowles, hand-coloured mezzotint, 35 × 25 cm, Courtesy of the Lewis Walpole Library, Yale University.*

all trace of the mechanical, and obviously satirical behind. Here, Miss Calash is portrayed wearing a large, white calash around her frizzed coiffeur. The calash is carefully detailed, with three visible indentations signifying boning and a ruffle trim around the front of the face. Hanging just off centre from the top is a thin white cord, the end of which is tucked between her folded arms. Surviving calashes often retain a ribbon, sewn about half-way up the first bone at the side of the face, which would have allowed the wearer to both draw up the calash, and hold it in an upright position.[83] Unlike the previous representation of Miss Calash, who was satirized by the addition of mechanical augmentation and severely over-exaggerated scale, here, the calash, though large, is not dramatically out of proportion. Her dress is also fairly restrained, comprised of a blue tasselled shawl worn over a yellow gown and pink petticoat. The book in her right hand and the subtitle of the print indicate her wandering mind: 'This Lady reads, then Tripping Thro' the Grove. – Turns all her thoughts to rural bliss and love,' portraying Miss Calash as a romantic rambler, whose mind is occupied with thoughts of love and countryside simplicity.

Published as part of a series of prints by Carington Bowles, described as 'Ladies in fashionable Dresses and enchanting Attitudes' in the 1784 catalogue, the print borders what can be considered graphic satire, in that there is little of the satirical.[84] Rather than satirizing fashion or using dress as a vehicle to satirize, Bowles's prints act more as eighteenth-century pin-ups.[85] A similar set, often with the same or a variant titles and lifted compositions, was subsequently produced by R. Sayer & J. Bennett, of which, *A Lady in Waiting*, first published 14 October 1780 and reissued in 1787, is also portrayed wearing a calash (Figures 1.18 and 1.19).[86] Both sets of women in the series are each portrayed through a voyeuristic lens, often alone and in alluring positions, inviting the viewer's gaze. In Figure 1.17, the outlines of her legs are visible beneath the pink petticoat, transforming her contemplative pause into a suggestive stance. The second calash-wearer in Figure 1.18 is depicted seated, her right arm holding the ties of her calash while her left points to the orb above her head, tilted down to the right, coyly looking away.[87] Like *Miss Calash*, the outline of her legs and prominent posterior are suggestively visible to the viewer. Unlike the figure portrayed in Figure 1.16, whose body appears simplified and static, conforming with the stylized body of the 1770s fashion satire, these series of posture mezzotints present their subjects in more realized bodies, carefully depicting corporeal proportion, shadow, expression and even the flush of the cheeks. Though these effects can partially be attributed to differences of method – etching versus hand-coloured mezzotint, of which the latter favours colour over line – they nonetheless render both Miss Calash and Sayer & Bennett's waiting lady as accessible to the viewer, partially through the presentation of their appearance and partially through their seemingly fluid engagement within the setting of the print.

Unlike the devoid background of *Drawn by Miss Calash*, *Miss Calash in Contemplation* is depicted within a lush landscape. A picturesque, craggy stone archway spotted with vines frames the central

Figure 1.18 A Lady in Waiting, *14 October 1780, publ. by R. Sayer & J. Bennett, mezzotint, 35 × 24 cm, British Museum, London.*

figure. She stands on the bank of a small waterfall, and beyond, a path can be seen cutting through a wood. While at first the setting, and subtitle of the print, suggests a depiction of the idyllic pastoral, the manicured structure of the landscape denotes instead the grounds of a pleasure garden, like Vauxhall, whose grounds were augmented with grottos, groves and water features. Likewise, the second woman is also featured outdoors, sitting between two clusters of trees on a grassy bank. In

Figure 1.19 A Lady in Waiting, *14 October 1787, publ. by Robert Sayer, hand-coloured mezzotint, 15.2 × 11.2 cm, British Museum, London.*

contrast to Miss Calash, whose manicured landscape is merely suggestive of a geographical location, her position is identifiable as the south bank of the Thames, as an outline of St. Paul's Cathedral is visible in the right background of the print. Both of these women, in addition to their alluring qualities, are portrayed as members of the late eighteenth-century ambling public, positioning the calash as a mobile garment.

The calash's promenade

The fashion for walking and the geographies that arose to accommodate and promote it became prominent features of eighteenth-century commercialized leisure (Figure 1.20). Peter Borsay has identified the act of promenading as the corresponding result of advancements in provincial (and urban) architecture and landscape that 'created an appropriate physical setting for a parallel transformation in their social life'.[88] This transformation promoted pedestrian movement along public walks and in pleasure, as well as private, gardens.[89] Pleasure gardens, notably Vauxhall and Ranelagh, became frequented attractions, in which paying clientele could promenade within an immersive garden landscape, partaking in culinary, visual and auditory amusements and entertainments.[90] Yet, perhaps one of the most appealing entertainments was observing the promenaders themselves.[91] Walking around the garden paths and the rotundas, which fostered a circular progression rather than linear, encouraged the performative nature of walking – not intended to travel a distance, but to amble within an almost suspended state of time.[92] Attendees of the fashionable world were reported in newspapers, and as long as one could pay for admittance, it was perceived possible to 'catch a glimpse of the glitterati'.[93] Within this arena of mobile display, pleasure gardens and promenades encouraged and cultivated the practice of to see and be seen, profiting in voyeuristic consumption, to which dress played a significant role.[94]

Taking up the call to consider the intersection of dress, the body, movement and the physical environment, eighteenth-century dress historians have often featured the shoe within this 'preoccupation with walking as a leisure activity'.[95] While footwear's affiliation with walking is inherent, we can also view the calash as ambulatory, as it was specifically designed to be worn while walking out of doors. Prescribed as protection from the sun and 'catching cold in the head' in multiple publications in the 1770s, the hooded design functioned as a fashionable barrier from the outdoor elements.[96] Returning to *The Triumph of the Calash*, Minerva declares that due to its ribbed canopy, 'the fair [sex] may safely court the hill or shade, Nor rain, nor hail, prevent their *promenade*'.[97] When worn erect above the head while walking, the calash shielded the eyes from sunlight and protected a dressed coiffeur from a light breeze or drizzle.[98] That they were often finished with a glaze would have aided in creating a waterproof covering. The poem continues that 'for this shall intercept the glance that flies, in mutual intercourse from eyes to eyes', suggesting that the calash's high walls around the face not only acted as a barrier from the elements, but allowed the wearer an element of control in the voyeuristic nature of the promenade.[99]

A social mix of clientele fiscally supported the running of pleasure gardens, and public walks were free to the public.[100] However, promenading excluded those who could not afford to partake in leisure during the day and during the week, as well as those who could not afford the appearance considered fashionable enough to be 'seen'.[101] Within this narrower spectrum of society, which ranged from the higher echelons of the bon ton to those aspiring to fashion, dress was a distinguishing factor, and encouraged a climate of sartorial gawking and judgement. As Bernard Mandeville demonstrated in his

Figure 1.20 A Morning Excursion, *publ. by Bowles and Carver, 16.2 × 21 cm, Collection of the Author.*

1724 *Fable of the Bees*, casting aspersions on those struggling to achieve fashionability was not a new practice: 'fine feathers make fine birds, and people where they are not known, are generally honoured according to their clothes and other accoutrements they have about them: from the richness of them we judge of their wealth, and by their ordering we judge of their understanding'.[102] The correct deployment of fashion underlines numerous graphic satires, particularly those which address the apparent fluidity and mobility of class through fashion. As Peter McNeil and Giorgio Riello have observed, 'many of the puns of fashion caricatures revolve around such class-based encounters in public space ... whilst social mixing was carefully avoided by the elite, caricatures insisted on the misplacement of elite dress within the vulgar public space, and the wearing of formally elite dress by the lower orders'.[103] Though their observation is particularly directed at satires of those walking on the streets, within the promenade, which revolved around sartorial display, satirists and viewers cast an even more critical eye.

58 The Modern Venus

Figure 1.21 Capt. Calipash & Mrs. Calipee, *28 October 1777, publ. by Mathew and Mary Darly, crayon manner, 34 × 23 cm, Courtesy of the Lewis Walpole Library, Yale University.*

Arm in arm, a stout couple promenade across the page of *Capt. Calipash & Mrs Calipee*, published by Matthew and Mary Darly on 28 October 1777 (Figure 1.21). Though the characters do not bear the name calash, they have been dubbed with phonetically similar titles, 'Capt. Calipash' and 'Mrs Calipee', familiar to the eighteenth-century viewer as the fatty, gelatinous flesh attached to the bottom (calipash) and upper (calipee) shells of a turtle, the culinary ingredients in the exclusive turtle soup.[104] Their rounded figures echo their aquatic names; Capt. Calipash's stomach resembles a turtle's shell, flipped vertically, and Mrs Calipee's nose, mouth and double chin poke out of her barrel-like calash as a turtle pokes its head out of its shell. The calash, which creates an upturned cylinder around her head, is held by a loop in her left hand, while her right holds the arm of her husband. As with many of the Darlys' caricatures, the depiction mocks those endeavouring to be fashionable – simultaneously in their clothes and activities, as well as the scale of their bodies.[105] Physiognomically, those the Darlys portrayed as members of the fashionable elite are typically slender with exaggeratedly small features, as seen in Figure 2.7. Here, however, seen in profile, Mrs Calipee's stays project outwards at the waist, suggesting the expansive girth of her belly, and even her feet are uncharacteristically large for satire. The jumble of accessories – the captain wearing a walking stick and sword together, while his wife wears an unfashionably long apron down to the hemline – suggests that the couple are fumbling the etiquette of fashion, a blunder not to go unnoticed, as Mandeville warns. It was not enough to own fashionable garments, but a person's fashionability was expressed in their ability to successfully wear garments *à la mode*, which our turtles are not.[106]

In addition to reflecting their corpulent, slowly moving bodies, the turtle-based names of the couple also denote themes of importation and foreignness. Not imported from abroad, this pair, the print suggests, are imported from the countryside: country interlopers attempting to partake within the metropolitan pastime.[107] Likewise, the captain's position in the navy, as signified by his title, hat and the distinctive frogged lapel of his uniform, serves as another indication that they may also be attempting to socially ascend. As Sir Walter Elliot in Jane Austen's *Persuasion* (1818) noted with disgust, the navy was considered 'the means of bringing persons of obscure birth into undue distinction'.[108] Here, the calash is portrayed as an aid for not only negotiating the promenade, but also an attempt to manoeuvre the social spectrum. However, as the Darlys so sharply articulate, owning fashionable accessories, like the calash, and wielding them successfully were two disparate realities.

Though the Darlys' pair of promenaders is mocked for their inability to achieve the nuances of fashion, others were satirized for the places in which they employed their calashes. A second Darly print published two months earlier on 11 August 1777, *The Ton at Greenwich. A La Festoon Dans le Park a Greenwich* portrays a woman more confident in her mode of display. She wears a flowered gown, which has been 'festooned' around her cork rump by cords (Figure 1.22).[109] In front she wears

Figure 1.22 The Ton at Greenwich, a Lá Festoon dans le Park a Greenwich, *11 August 1777, publ. by Matthew and Mary Darly, etching, 32.5 × 21.5 cm, British Museum, London.*

a quilted apron and a trimmed handkerchief floats from her shoulders in the breeze. The same breeze fills her large calash like a sail, which she holds by two ribbons in her right hand. The raised calash is carefully detailed with six shaded boned arches, and one can even make out the pinwheel of fanned pleats around the back, which is slightly cheated towards the viewer. Another trick of the satirist's pen is the scale and forced perspective of her servant, who stands slightly behind her on the path, carrying a huge closed umbrella that roughly measures the length of his body.[110] Like the calash, the umbrella was also a moving accessory, which opened on a spring system.[111] Worthy of further investigation, the umbrella appears to have been at a point of transition within the context of British fashion in the 1770s.[112] As an import from France (and originally further east), the umbrella and parasol for the majority of the century were strongly associated with the connotations of femininity, or rather effeminacy, and Francophilia.[113] Though T. S. Crawford and Jeremy Farrell both suggest that opinions were beginning to shift in favour of men using umbrellas, prints such as the Darlys' *This Is a Surprise*, published only a month after *The Ton at Greenwich*, denote that even when used by women, it was still an object of curiosity and satirical reproach.[114] Though in *The Ton at Greenwich*, it could be argued that the male servant merely carries the umbrella for his mistress, like Bigg's black serving boy in Figure 0.6, because he is carrying it entreats the viewer to question both characters' fashionability.[115] Likewise, bringing both an umbrella and a calash would have been sartorially repetitive. Much like Captain Calipash, who was armed with a sword and cane, the presence of both moving accessories casts doubt on whether or not the lady portrayed was actually a member of the ton, London's elite fashionable set.

Her geographical location hints that though she bears all the marks of fashionability, even a carrying a crook in her left hand, she too is an aspiring member of middling sort.[116] Like the range of clientele, pleasure gardens and green spaces also ranged in reputation. Warwick Wroth's 1896 survey of London pleasure gardens ranks only four of the seventy open in the eighteenth century within the upper tier: Cuper's, Marylebone, Vauxhall and Ranelagh.[117] The more exclusive gardens strove to earn and maintain the coveted stamp of politeness, scourging themselves of the vulgar by means of price increases, the destruction of Vauxhall's lover's lane, increased lighting and even foot patrols.[118] David Solkin has fittingly termed Vauxhall after its reopening in 1732, 'an Eden reborn without its lurking serpent'.[119] In contrast, Greenwich Park, identified by both the title and the recognizable architecture of the Royal Observatory in the right background of the print, did not compare to the reputation of its neighbours further west along the Thames. Generally, neighbourhoods south of the river were considered less fashionable, but Greenwich Park was also known for its annual fair, which like other fairs attracted more of the uncouth side of popular entertainments.[120] One visitor, identified only as 'a lady', described her displeasure at a visit to Greenwich Park in a letter to her aunt. Shocked by the throng of 'middling Objects' she beheld, she concluded that Greenwich Park 'is a Diversion you would not expect so near the polite City of London', and that 'the Park, tho' most beautiful in itself, is no way entertaining to' her.[121] While perhaps not as low as other green spaces, such as Bagnigge Wells, known for attracting the middling classes and a popular site of prostitution, that Greenwich Park is distinguished as apart from 'the polite City of London' casts a more discerning light on the calash wearer in the Darlys' print, whom, in turn, is distinguished as apart from the ton in London.[122]

Sociable calashes

Both of these satirical representations portray the calash as an accessory for walking, but also suggest it as part of the paraphernalia of the socially mobile.[123] Urban and gender historians have long argued that the eighteenth century saw the transformation of street conditions and subsequently an increase in accessibility and use.[124] With the introduction of paving stones replacing cobbles and dirt, street lighting, and the greater attention to maintenance and aided transportation, streets became more usable to pedestrians and the mounting popularity in leisure activities, such as shopping, drew out more female walkers.[125] German traveller Sophie von La Roche remarked in 1786, 'What number of people, too! How happy the pedestrian on these roads, which alongside the houses are paved with large, clean paving-stones some feet wide, where many thousands of neatly clad people, eminent men, dressy women, pursue their way safe from the carriages, horses and dirt.'[126] While women's presence on the streets had, the century before, primarily denoted poverty or prostitution, by the end of the eighteenth century, women's personal mobility was often a mark of a leisured, consuming member of society.[127] In an extensive study of London, published by W. Nicoll in 1768, the author observed:

> The women here have the most engaging charms, the most wit and the most beauty of any women in the world; yet the greatest latitude of freedom and behaviour is indulged to them. They frequent all public places of entertainment; make parties of pleasure; pay and received visits to and from those of either sex without restraint: and a lady will sometimes converse with a lover for years, before they are thoroughly satisfied with the disposition and circumstances of each other; and all this with perfect innocence and an irreproachable character. But this is what the sex in Italy, Spain, and Southern France will judge incredible, and seems chiefly owing to the liberty which they here enjoy, and the true esteem with which they are generally regarded.[128]

Nicoll's testimony of women's ambulatory liberty demonstrates a contemporary perception and awareness that women traversed the city beyond the designated promenades, for reasons beyond leisured ambulation and display. As Nicoll suggests, the increase in women's spatial movement aligned with and advanced their social mobility.[129]

While, as seen in the satires of promenading, the calash was associated with attempts of class ascension, it can likewise be considered as being used laterally to navigate and maintain a woman's footing within her social environment. Whereas promenading carried the potential of increasing a woman's standing through visibility, visiting was the key to expanding her reach and securing social relationships.[130] As Nicoll observes, London women 'pay and received visits to and from those of either sex without restraint'.[131] Travelling 'to and from' required visitors to traverse both their own neighbourhoods and those farther afield. Along these socially-motivated journeys, the calash can be seen to provide an essential conveyance. In *The Old Maids Morning Visit or the Calash Lady's*, published by Matthew and Mary Darly on 11 March 1777, two older women, once again bearing the accessory as a modifier, converse together in a parlour (Figure 1.23).[132] Typical of the Darlys' sparse interiors, the space is devoid of furnishings apart from the two chairs in which the ladies sit, four framed pictures and an oil lamp hanging on the back wall. Following satiric convention, the two women's physiques are severely contrasted. On the left, bulging from her stays, one woman reclines in a graciously sized armchair, resting her plump foot on a footstool. Her slightly upturned nose resembles a snout, contributing to her porcine likeness.[133] Her bony companion perches on a folding stool. The pointed and angular features of her nose, knees and chin accentuate her withered figure, unaided by the deflated rump resting on the back of the stool. Despite the fact that a calash would be lowered or removed while indoors, both women retain their raised calashes, each mimicking their contrasting physiques. The paintings on the wall of a lioness and two birds also echo the relationship between the seated women. The swell of the calash on the left is mirrored in the curling tail of the lioness on the left, whereas the angular points of the calash to the right are repeated in the pointed feathers and beak of the bird on the far right.[134] The attention drawn to the calash is furthered within the print in the

Figure 1.23 The Old Maids Morning Visit, or, The Calash Lady's, *1777, publ. by Mathew and Mary Darly, etching, 23 × 31.6 cm, Courtesy of the Lewis Walpole Library, Yale University.*

depiction of two discarded hats on the floor flanking the sitters. On the left, a wide-brimmed bonnet is infested with a litter of kittens, a biting commentary on the woman's post-menopausal infertility. The kitten in the left foreground mirrors the position of the lioness. On the right, a flat straw hat is being sprayed with a spaniel's urine. These cast-off and redundant styles of headwear, in conjunction with the title, 'Calash Lady's', and the prominently raised calashes, assert the calash as the preferred hat worn for visiting.[135]

At first this portrayal of two 'old maids' conforms to the satirical conventions surrounding the representation of older women. As Cindy McCreery has emphasized, such harsh depictions of 'old maids' were customary for satirists, whose work often flourished in producing images of female aging, which was seen as a declining demographic that fruitlessly clung to a decadent past.[136] In the Darlys' print, each woman is past her prime, one portrayed as gluttonous, the other as nearly emaciated, though both still attempting to appear fashionable. However, it is the social ritual that they are performing that is unusual within the genre of graphic satire, not their aging bodies. Despite its prevalence in practice, visiting was seldom visualized. The meeting and socializing of women are, instead, often depicted as a rouse for an affair or questionable behaviour.[137] Though not widely depicted, visiting was extensively illustrated discursively. For example, in Samuel Johnson's *The Rambler* magazine, he published a letter in 1752 in the voice of a fifteen-year-old young woman named Bellaria, who frets that having been confined to bed with a cold for four days, 'has already kept me from three plays, nine sales, five shows, and six card-tables, and put me seventeen visits behind-hand'.[138] Within a description of her daily routine, her mobility is evident and the time afforded to visiting prominent: 'I go to bed late, and therefore cannot rise early; as soon as I am up, I dress for the gardens; then walk in the park; then always go to some sale or show, or entertainment at the little theatre; then must be dressed for dinner; then must pay my visits; and from thence to the card-table,' later observing that she has 'so many visitants names to read over, so many invitations to accept or refuse, so many cards to write'.[139] The message cards left and received by visitors were a means of paying compliments, inviting visits of others and leaving one's respects when missed.[140] In *The Prater*, Edward Long and J. Holcombe under the pseudonym Nicholas Babble, wrote of the excessive use of message cards as a means of increasing visiting productivity, 'By assistance of these trusty Messengers, Visits are received and paid with the utmost Punctuality and – Ease; for a Lady can now-a-days receive four and twenty Visits in an Afternoon, without being fatigued with the sight of her Visitors, and pay as many without stepping out of her *Chair*.'[141] Likewise, William Alexander notes in his 1779 *History of Women, from the earliest Antiquity to the Present Time*, that:

> women of fashion … spend a great part of their time in receiving and returning visits; and in some of the politer nations [of Europe], modern visiting is not spending a social hour together; it consists only in her ladyship ordering her coachman to drive to the doors of so many of her

acquaintances, and her footman, at each of them, to give a card with her name, while the lady of the house, though, in the polite phrase, *not at home*, is looking through the window all the while to see what passes; and in some convenient time after returns the visit, and is sure to be received in the same manner.[142]

Alexander suggests that visiting has merely become a process of mobility, which may not even require the presence of the visitor. As Hannah Barker and Elaine Chalus have argued, 'prescriptive or satirical literature … provides insights … about the way that contemporaries conceptualized and talked about' a subject.[143] As published texts, which exaggerate and embellish for the purposes of instruction or humour, these published descriptions reveal the perception that visiting carried over the eighteenth century – that it was an ever-increasing ritual, which required and hinged upon personal mobility to and from.

Despite its prevalence, the practice of visiting has received relatively little scholarly attention.[144] Within her discussion of the busy social lives of the beau monde, Hannah Greig has accounted for this lapse in scholarship, observing that 'while references to social excursions were routinely made they were also typically brief, functional, and, to the modern reader, easily missed'.[145] When visiting has been addressed, it has been primarily acknowledged as a foundation of feminine politeness and sociability, specifically situated within and often eclipsed by the discussion of tea and the tea-table.[146] Bridging with Hellman's work, the relationship between the calash and the tea-table as the props of visiting is articulated in Carington Bowles's print *A Morning Visit – or the Fashionable Dresses for the Year 1777*, published on 1 January 1778 (Figures 1.24 and 1.25). Reissued on 24 June 1780 under the title *The Spruce Sportsman, or, Beauty the Best Shot*, the print portrays two women of fashion greeting one another in a well-appointed parlour.[147] Amanda Vickery's work on gender and the home has argued that 'the emergence of the urban culture of visiting revolutionised the uses of interior spaces', specifically that of the parlour, which became the setting for home-based sociability.[148] The scale of the space, whose high ceilings are elongated by the decorative panelling and denoted by the towering mirror above the fireplace, whose top is cut out of the frame of the picture, is echoed in the soaring heights of its female occupants. Once again conforming to the young fashionable figure of the late 1770s, with dainty feet and limbs, both women don large coiffeurs and headwear. On the left, layers of side curls and a chignon, which reaches down to her shoulder blades, is topped with a tilted straw hat, accentuated with ribbons, gauze and tinted ostrich feathers. Her companion on the right wears her hair in the typically high 1770s coiffeur, framed by sausage curls and topped with an elaborate cap, above which she wears a large black calash. The highly detailed calash is constructed of at least four boned arches, in between which, the black silk forms ruched valleys of light and shadow (Figure 1.26). A decorative trim surrounds the opening, which is tied with a ribbon bow under the neck, and an apron around the shoulders is finished in the same trim. In front of her hair, a thin black stroke of ink, which loops from the centre top of the calash to the side, represents the cord used

Figure 1.24 *John Collet,* A Morning Visit, or, the Fashionable Dresses for the Year 1777, *1 January 1778, publ. by Carington Bowles, mezzotint, 35.4 × 25.1 cm, Wellcome Collection, London.*

to raise and lower the calash's structure.¹⁴⁹ The calash's large size catches the attention of the seated 'sportsman', who stares up dumbfounded from his seat. The second title most likely gained inspiration from his presence in the print, and that his musket, cradled in his left arm, is compositionally pointed directly at the calash, further drawing the viewer's eye.

Brimmed Hats and Calashes 67

Figure 1.25 *John Collet,* The Spruce Sportsman, or, Beauty the Best Shot, *24 June 1780, publ. by Carington Bowles, hand-coloured mezzotint, 35.5 × 24.4 cm, Courtesy of the Lewis Walpole Library, Yale University.*

Figure 1.26 *Detail of John Collet,* The Spruce Sportsman, or, Beauty the Best Shot, *24 June 1780, publ. by Carington Bowles, hand-coloured mezzotint, 35.5 × 24.4 cm, Courtesy of the Lewis Walpole Library, Yale University.*

As the first title suggests, this print is yet another that mocks the extravagances of fashion and late eighteenth-century women's apparent unrestrainable indulgence in it.[150] Yet, it is specifically staged as a morning visit. With her calash raised, fur-trimmed cloak over her shoulders and muff in hand, it is evident that the young woman on the right has just entered the home of her welcoming friend, where the liquid rites of visiting are in preparation. In order to greet her guest, the hostess must manoeuvre past a small tea-table, the site around which female sociability and politeness were practiced and honed. Behind her, the boiling kettle in the fire place emits a trail of steam that mirror's the hostess's billowing plumage, and the maid, who enters the room carrying a tea-set, affirms the pending consumption of tea. As tea acted as a liquid catalyst and became synonymous with the practice of visiting itself, it is perhaps no wonder that tea drinking and the tea-table have eclipsed the ritual within which it was practiced.[151] Positioned as the feminine equivalent to the caffeinated spaces of the coffee house, the tea-table has been poured over and stewed upon as the cornerstone of polite feminine society.[152]

It is not the intention of this discussion to undermine tea or the tea-table's symbolic significance as one of the places around which women participated in eighteenth-century society; it is the intention of this chapter to look beyond it. Though tea is the underlying lubricant of conversation, framing the action of this print and symbolizing its occupant's sociability, when we return to the portrayal of the calash, whose prominence once again dominates the printed page, it signals not the polite conversation about to ensue, but the journey already undertaken and the one that will follow. It is this part of the visit, or rather these parts that flank the social custom, which have been so overlooked within the literature on eighteenth-century visiting and women's sociability that were, in fact, so prominent within eighteenth-century consciousness. By featuring the calash within graphic satires of visiting, Bowles and the Darlys' prints signify that in addition to coaches and chairs, women underwent these journeys on foot. Thereby, the travel involved in gaining and maintaining a wide social network is perhaps as significant a contribution to women's public visibility and participation outside the home as drinking tea may be within it. Whether walking with a calash or riding in a carriage or sedan chair, the journeys undertaken by women 'to and from visits' around the streets of London, the villages, towns and cities of Britain and her colonies increased their personal mobility. The calash, though not the catalyst of female sociability, was rather the facilitator, allowing her to manoeuvre the urban landscape, sheltered, protected and mobile beneath its collapsing arches of silk.

***

By the 1790s, the calash had burned through its ephemeral lifespan when classical and naturalistic aesthetics saturated style, and hair, for at least the time being, diminished in scale.[153] However, women's movement and visibility on the British streets continued to propel forward. In Francis Lathom's 1800 comedy, *The Dash of the Day*, Sir Gabriel, upon his return from walking, nostalgically reminisces:

> What an alteration has this city undergone, in the course of fifteen years! Ladies at the West end of the town, that used to think it an indulgence, if they were permitted to ride in a hackney-coach, now take the whip-hand of their husbands in phaetons and four; and citizens wives that now swing about in chairs, tricked out in their feathers, like a goose on her nest, used to walk a visiting in their pattens and calash, with a little errant-boy before them to carry the lanthorn![154]

His lament acts somewhat like the fulfilment of a satirical prophecy: the women of the bon ton have taken the reigns and the 'citizens wives', or those of the middling sort, have socially ascended the fashion ladder in both dress and means of transportation, causing Sir Gabriel to conclude, 'No wonder the bankrupt list is crouded[sic.]!'[155] While his monologue can be seen as the continued expression of these tropes and social anxieties, it also demonstrates the continued awareness of women's mobility. The increase in mobility, excessive in the author's opinion, is seen in an article in the 1818 magazine, *The Tickler*:

> Among the grievances of modern days, much complained of, but with little hope of redress, is the matter of receiving and paying *visits*, the number of which, it is generally agreed, "has been increasing, is increased, and ought to be diminished." You meet frequently with people who will tell you, they are worn to death by visiting: and that, what with morning visits, and afternoon visits, dining visits, and supping visits, tea-drinking visits, and card-playing visits, exclusive of balls and concerts, for their parts, they have not an hour to themselves in four-and-twenty. But they must go home and dress, or they shall be too late for their visit.[156]

Complaining of the exhaustion caused by increasingly frequent visiting, the anonymous author indicates a trajectory, that the demands of visiting were amassing exponentially, wherein the visit became an even more formalized 'institution' of nineteenth-century society, particularly for the female sex.[157]

Returning to the late eighteenth century, it is apparent that the calash and its fellow brimmed hats were key players in this crescendo of female mobility. The calash's functional mobility operated beyond its construction, facilitating and enabling the movements of its wearer. Examining the calash along this axis has allowed this discussion to rotate outward, from the minutia of the object to its social and geographical implications. Commencing with an interrogation of the calash's material construction initially positioned it as an accessory, a garment of headwear that was created by milliners to accommodate the expanding decorative edifice of the coiffeur. However, that its boned arches were not fused in an upright position, allowing for it to be raised and lowered like the carriage top for which it was named, draws the contemporary perception of its mechanical collapsibility. The calash's categorical permeation aligned it with the sails and rigging of a ship, and placed the accessory within a wider fascination for moving objects, such as mechanical and folding furniture. The calash's perceived mechanical mobility transformed it into a means by which to move its wearer. Visually personified in graphic satire, the calash and its wearer traversed the promenades of walks and pleasure gardens and socially ascended the within Britain's outdoor arenas of visibility and display. Yet, this social mobility was taken up most in the practice of visiting, whereas Sir Gabriel recalls, women 'used to walk a visiting in their pattens and calash'.¹⁵⁸ Though benched within the conventions of comedy, Sir Gabriel's remark affirms the calash's role within visiting, that it accompanied women walking on their travel amidst their social network. Echoing its structural mobility, the boned canopy of silk granted women a greater range of motion. Drawn up from the neck like a 'broad sail bulging in the wind', the calash enabled women to navigate their social and geographical landscape, sailing through the channels of society.¹⁵⁹

2

'Let us examine their tails':
The material and satirical lifecycles of cork rumps and bums

In John Lockington's adaptation of Matthew and Mary Darly's *The Preposterous Head Dress, or, The Feathered Lady,* the anonymous artist makes one significant alteration to the print's composition (Figures 2.1 and 2.2). Like other adaptations of prints where one design is lifted from another, the image is inverted and the figures have been reworked. Each print portrays a fashionable woman at her dressing table, attended by a maid holding a basket of vegetables and a stereotypically French-looking frisseur, who is placing ornaments and ostrich feathers in her tall coiffeur.[1] Both satires mock the rising heights of hair and the eccentric embellishments that adorn it. However, between the date of the Darlys' publication on 20 March 1776 and of Lockington's on 9 June 1777, a second fashionable appendage has emerged. In the earlier composition, the woman is seated and her frisseur stands on a footstool to reach her high coiffeur. In the latter, the woman is standing and her frisseur balances on large puffs of drapery that protrude from her lower back. The sight causes the painted figure in the upper left corner, a recognizable reference to Joshua Reynolds's 1776 portrait of Lady Seymour Worsley in her red riding habit, to gawk.[2] Lady Worsley's outstretched arms direct the viewer's eye not at the mountain of hair atop the woman's head, but at the mountainous protuberance projecting from her tail. The structure that enables the frisseur's precarious perch is identified to the viewer by the print's title: *The Utility of Cork Rumps 1777.*

Like bum-rolls of the late seventeenth and bustles of the late nineteenth centuries, the cork rump, also called a false rump and later a bum in the 1780s, was a stuffed, structural support, designed to lift the draped skirts of the polonaise, English and Italian gowns, which became fashionable in the

Figure 2.1 The Preposterous Head Dress, or, The Feathered Lady, *20 March 1776, publ. by Matthew and Mary Darly, etching, 38 × 27 cm, Courtesy of the Lewis Walpole Library, Yale University.*

late 1770s.³ These looped-style gowns signalled a dramatic shift in the female fashionable silhouette where emphasis moved from women's hips to women's posteriors. Throughout the century, hoops or panniers had provided the shape over which the wide-skirted mantuas and sacques were held.

Figure 2.2 The Utility of Cork Rumps 1777, 9 June 1777, publ. by J. Lockington, etching and engraving, 39 × 28 cm, Courtesy of the Lewis Walpole Library, Yale University.

However, in the 1770s, focus shifted to women's backsides, where the fabric of the outer skirt was gathered and arranged with ribbons, tapes, hooks and buttons (Figure 2.3). While numerous polonaise, looped-style, English and Italian gowns survive in museum collections, the item that facilitated

Figure 2.3 *Italian gowns, c. 1780–85, French and American, silk, Acc. Nos. 1976.146a, b and 1970.87a, b, Metropolitan Museum of Art, New York.*

their successful shape largely has not. Nor does it often survive on the pages contemporary diaries, correspondence, account books or inventories. Instead, it thrives like a weed on the satirical page: represented in graphic satire and fervently discussed in the diatribes and commentaries of magazines and newspapers. Between November 1776 and June 1777, at least eleven satirical prints featuring the cork rump were published by the London printsellers Matthew and Mary Darly, John Walker and John Lockington alone. This brief, yet saturated period of publication coincided with over forty textual discussions of rumps in published magazines, newspapers and books between 11 October 1776 and the end of the decade.[4]

Despite this concentrated representation in print culture, its absence in archives and museums has made the cork rump into something of an elusive, mythical object, resulting in its often scant treatment in previous scholarship.[5] Its quotidian nature, brief period of wear from 1776 to 1790s, and its composition of cork, horsehair and linen are all factors for its pointed absence from the historical record.[6] Aligning with the practices of sartorial recycling of the day, when the cork rump fell out of fashion, its materials would have been utilized for other purposes or degraded with time. This lack of material survival frames the cork rump as an example of what Viccy Coltman has termed 'immaterial culture', or 'artefacts that are lost in their material incarnation in its definitive state, but that survive through their representation as phantom objects'.[7] Although, unlike Coltman's work, which examines immaterial culture in the meticulously material portraits of John Singleton Copley, the cork rump's visual representation is nearly entirely satirical. Apart from two notable survivors, in the case of the cork rump, we contend with the challenge of how to approach an object that no longer exists materially when its representation is often anything but realistic.

The exaggerations and distortions of scale and subject matter that permeate satirical prints have previously made graphic satire a dress-history taboo.[8] However, here we once again chip away at that long-ingrained impediment, demonstrating that beneath and within the layers of satire we can uncover both a professed representation of an object and the inherent meanings that representation unveils. This chapter aims to re-examine the cork rump's visual representations to expose the contexts in which the cork rump was portrayed and the underlying tensions those representations reveal. Like Lockington's shift in focus, we follow the prescriptive direction of an anonymous columnist from the *St. James Chronicle* of 1 April 1780: 'But enough of their Heads, my dear Sir; and let us now candidly examine the Tails of the dear Creatures, where I hope to find something more relishing.'[9]

A material footprint

In 1954, Platt Hall, the Gallery of Costume of then Manchester City Galleries, received a donation of a trunk of clothes belonging to the house's former inhabitants, Thomas and Elizabeth Carill-Worsley (1739–1809, 1766–1833).[10] While the majority of the clothes belonged to her husband, dating from roughly 1760 to 1780, a few exceptions belonged to Elizabeth, including a rump or bum, one of two known full-sized extant examples in western collections (Figures 2.4 and 2.5).[11] Triangular in shape, the exterior is made of white linen and it has been stuffed with horsehair into ten compartments, each

Figure 2.4 *White linen and horsehair bum, c. 1780–1800, Acc. No. 1954.1010, Manchester Art Gallery, Manchester.*

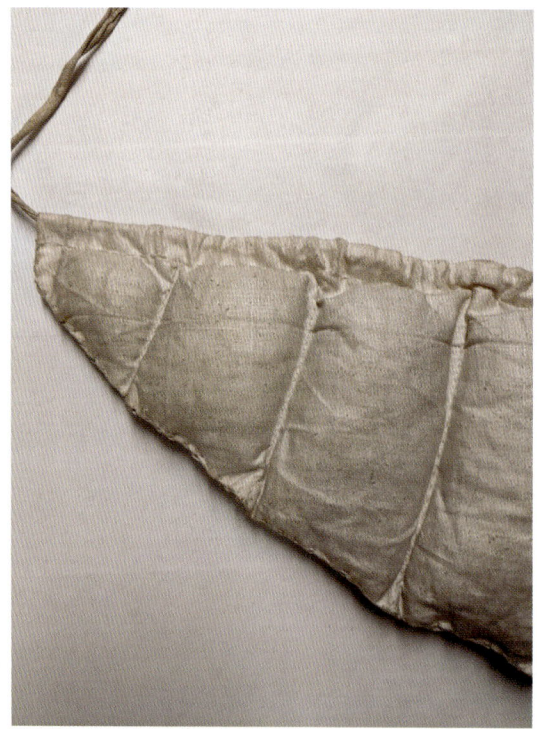

Figure 2.5 *Detail of white linen and horsehair bum, c. 1780–1800, Acc. No. 1954.1010, Manchester Art Gallery, Manchester.*

increasing in size towards a centre seam, ensuring an even distribution of stuffing.[12] A woven tape runs through a casing along the top, which could have easily been tied around the waist over her stays and beneath her outer gown, similar to how stay laces, petticoats and pockets were tied around the body.[13] Alternatively, the bum could have been attached directly to her stays. As will be addressed in Chapter 4, stays in the 1780s often featured two pairs of eyelets burrowed into the sides, just above each pelvic bone. The inclusion of these eyelets, which appear on numerous extant examples, would have allowed their wearer to tie a bum directly onto the stays, without adding any additional bulk around the waist.[14] That staymakers adapted their product to accommodate the attachment of a bum indicates not only its material existence, but also its prevalence.

Though originally made for the looped styles of the 1770s, rumps and bums were worn through the beginning of the 1790s, supporting the fabric of the gown and shaping the silhouette. An observer in the *St. James Chronicle* of 1780, notes that, 'One necessary Ingredient in a Lady's Apparel, is a very strong Cork Rump, so as to stick up pretty high above the Haunches.'[15] He elaborates on the method of obtaining the looped effect: 'Some Ladies of a peculiar Taste and Fansy have large Tassles to their Rumps, which are drawn up by small Brass or Steel Rings fastening to the Inside of the Gown; but these are chiefly Appendages to the Polonese Dress.'[16] Though the horsehair stuffing of the linen bum measures only about an inch (2.5 cm) high, it is accompanied by a pasteboard support covered in green and cream silk, which would have bolstered the rump from beneath. The petite size of the bum, even with the added pasteboard support, suggests it was most likely worn in the late 1780s or 1790s, when the prominence of the backside was diminishing towards what is now considered the neoclassical silhouette that marked turn of the century.[17] Though subtler in posterior prominence than the puffed drapery of the polonaise or looped gown, English, Italian, round, zone front and open gowns continued to be worn with bums or rumps, as evidenced by a second bum that survives with a zone front gown in Finland (Figure 2.6). Made of a blue ribbed silk that matches the gown, the bum forms a pointed crescent shape, stuffed with feathers that have been partially quilted down, shaping the volume of the stuffing. The Manchester bum also survives with a contemporaneous gown from the Carill-Worsley family, an open gown of cream silk embroidered with undulating floral sprigs. Not included with the original trunk of clothes, the gown from *c.* 1785–95, along with a matching embroidered silk muff, may have been worn by Elizabeth, the train of the dress supported by the linen bum.

Though shrouded in the conjectures of provenance, as we will never know with certainty if Elizabeth Carill-Worsley wore these garments or if she wore them simultaneously, these rare surviving examples ground our understanding of the bum in material reality. The contextual evidence, that of the adaptation of the stay's design and the very gowns themselves that now, if mounted, require padded support to correctly display their silhouettes, act as sartorial footprints left behind the rump's wake. These two examples bring this garment out of the realm of the mythical and into that of the material.

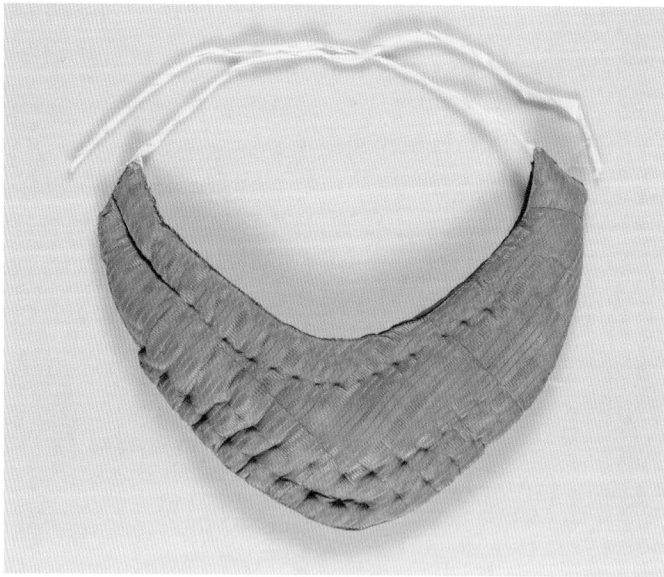

Figure 2.6 *Blue silk bum, c. 1785–1795, silk and feathers, Acc. No. TMM9002, The Museum Centre of Turku, Turku.*

Though they do not evidence the material composition of the rump's namesake, cork, neither do they exclude it as a plausible material component. It is with cork that we return to this garment's origin, turning to the medium in which it still survives in plentiful abundance, its visual and discursive representation within print culture.

Chloe's cushion: Fashionability, materiality and satirical discourse in the 1770s

The cork rump first appeared in graphic satire in 1776, worn by a young woman named Chloe. *The Cork Rump, or Chloe's Cushion* of 19 November 1776 and *Chloe's Cushion, or the Cork Rump* of 1 January 1777 both depict a female figure with a high coiffeur rising from her head and a prominent rump extending from her lower back (Figures 2.7 and 2.8). In her first printed appearance, published by John Walker, a London printmaker who specialized in stipples and mezzotints, she is depicted full length, standing in three-quarter profile against a plain background.[18] Only a line across the lower part of page denotes a sense of space or setting. Topped with a decorative mop cap and long dangling lappets, her elongated coiffeur features characteristic sausage curls, which rise like steps along the side, and a chignon, which has been twisted loose from the back of the head. From the top of her headdress, the eye travels down to

Figure 2.7 *The Cork Rump, or, Chloe's Cushion, 19 November 1776, publ. by J. Walker, etching & aquatint, 18 × 13 cm, Courtesy of the Lewis Walpole Library, Yale University.*

her lower back, which arcs out away from her body, creating a parallel protuberance. A curly haired toy dog balances on the extension of her gown. Acting like a shelf, the gown's rear support is identified by the title as a cork rump, which protrudes from the rather clumsily rendered gown.[19] The apron and rosebud in her hand project a rustic, country girl at odds with the devices of metropolitan fashionability.[20]

Figure 2.8 Chloe's Cushion, or, The Cork Rump, *1 January 1777, publ. by Matthew and Mary Darly, hand-coloured engraving, 35.2 × 24.9 cm, Courtesy of the Lewis Walpole Library, Yale University.*

Two months later, Matthew and Mary Darly's rendition sheds any doubt as to the cork rump's position as a necessity of fashion. The woman in the print conforms to the physique the Darlys' used to denote a woman of the 1770s bon ton: a small face, huge hair, elongated torso, tiny waist and minute feet. Again, standing in three-quarter profile, this Chloe is manipulated to show off the beacons of her fashionability. Dwarfed by her coiffeur and heart-shaped peak of overlapping gauze (the entire coiffeur measures the height of her body), she strides across a trim landscape. The placement of the large swell of fabric at her backside appears to bob above the waterline behind her. Her arms beckon the viewer to behold her appearance. The presence of her abundant sleeve ruffles, ribbons and flounces forecasts the April editorial in the *St. James Chronicle*, 1780, which observes that:

> each Side of which Rump is adorned with immense Bunches of Ribbands of various Colours, not in the least corresponding with the Complexion of the Gown. I do assure you, that the Quantities of Ribband are sometimes so large, most artificially done up in a Variety of Bows or Knots, that you would imagine one Female alone had unfurnished all the Shops in Spitalfields.[21]

In comparison to Walker's Chloe, the Darlys' is more precise in her appearance, which extends even to her lapdog: the indeterminate, frizzy-haired dog of Walker's print is replaced with a more exotic, Asian breed.[22] A dome-like structure of draped fabric, the volume of the rump is now entirely concentrated on the backside. Along with her high and overtly styled coiffeur, the cork rump has become part of the apparatus that conveys her fashionability to society.[23]

This visual recipe for what is fashionable in 1777 is delineated in *The LADIES HEAD-DRESS. A Receipt,* printed in June of that year:

> Give Chloe a bushel of horse-hair and wool,
>   Of paste and pomatum a pound,
> Ten yards of gay ribbon to deck her sweet skull
>   And Gauze to encompass it round.
>
> Of all the bright colours the rainbow displays
>   Be those ribbons which hang on her head,
> Be her flounces adapted to make the folks gaze,
>   And about the whole work be they spread.
>
> Let her flaps fly behind, for a yard at the least,
>   Let her curls meet just under her chin,
> Let those curls be supported, to keep up the jest,
>   With an hundred, instead of one pin.
>
> Let her gown be tuck'd up to the hip on each side,
>   Shoes too high for to walk or to jump;
> And, to deck the sweet creature complete for a bride,
>   Let the cork-cutter make her a rump.

> Thus finish'd in taste, while on Chloe you gaze,
>   You may take the dear charmer for life;
> But never undress her – for, out of her stays
>   You'll find you have lost half your wife.[24]

Published concurrently in three different magazines, the anonymous author picks apart each facet that constructs the current fashionable woman.[25] The poem lists the materials, amounts, proportions and exaggerations of women's dress like a formula. The poem crescendos as it moves down the body, observing the construction of her hair, accessories, gown and underwear. In the fourth stanza, the author looks below the waist, noting how the polonaise is looped up, 'her gown be tuck'd up to the hip on each side', and the height of her heeled shoes, 'too high for to walk or to jump', stressing a lack of pragmatism and sensibility. He concludes with the structural support that sits beneath the back of her gown, 'let the cork-cutter make her a rump'. Through this list of ingredients, the author draws back the veil of fashionable appearance, revealing each trick beneath the surface in rhyming verse.

Like the modern Venus, Chloe was a figurehead for the young fashionable female demographic of the late 1770s. The name Chloe, or Cloe, was one particularly associated with young women of marriageable age, upon whom the fleeting virtues of fashionability and beauty are granted. Used since antiquity, the name was re-popularized by Jonathan Swift's *Strephon and Chloe* of 1731, with editions published throughout the century.[26] Swift's poem revived interest in Chloe as a pastoral figure in numerous mezzotints.[27] Published songs, such as *Advice for Chloe*, recall the young woman's beauty as comparable to the gods, but are often laced with words of warning of beauty's inevitable fade.[28] Notably, Swift's character begins as a virgin, glorified as an nymph, who is void of mortal imperfections, yet on the night of her wedding to Strephon, her corporeal flaws are bluntly discovered.[29] Like Swift's Chloe, the theme of exposure persisted in the commentary surrounding the cork rump as a device of deception intended to enthral and capture the vows of duped husbands. In *The LADIES HEAD-DRESS,* the final stanza cautions its male readers:

> Thus finish'd in taste, while on Chloe you gaze,
>   You may take the dear charmer for life;
> But never undress her – for, out of her stays
>   You'll find you have lost half your wife.

The author warns that after marriage a husband will discover the structural supports that bolster and perfect a wife's silhouette and appearance.[30]

This anxiety of deception originated in the first published discussion of the cork rump: an editorial addressed to the printer of the *Public Advertiser*, Mr Woodhall, on 11 October 1776. The author, under the pseudonym, 'BUMFIDDLE', expressed concern that women:

have transferred their Attention from their Faces to their B – ms! … 'tis not the prettiest Face, but the largest A –, for which our Women now contend; and she who is not blessed in the Extreme, in this Particular, supplies herself with a Cork Round-about, made with a tempting Swell, which they conceal in the Folds of their upper Garment.[31]

He divulges the source of his recent knowledge as a dialogue that had occurred with his wife, whereupon observing a 'new Appearance BEHIND' he asks her, 'how you encrease! but it does not seem to me to be naturally placed! … Oh! Lord! my dear Harry, said she, shrinking from me, don't press me so hard, you will spoil my CORKS!'[32] He observes that in the ritual of courting, women 'no longer exercise the Language of the Eye, or Lip, but (oh! monstrous!) will turn her BACK upon her Admirer, as the more prevailing Charm'.[33] Bumfiddle incites the publisher, and by extension his fellow male readership:

> but what should we feel, in a Game of Romps, with any of these handsome Cork-rumped Devils? – I am afraid we should not (as we may, by means of your Paper) have a fair SLAP at them. – Then let me intreat you, Sir, to let the Severity of our Criticism be no longer pointed at their HEADS, let us attack their Tails.[34]

His condemnation resounded through subsequent discussions of the cork rump's appearance. On 22 October, the author of 'the Speculator' published a letter from a 'new-married man' who, after describing his love's goddess-like attributes, upon their wedding night 'stumbled over something', which his bride bashfully admitted, 'tis only my RUMP'.[35] Infuriated that his bride 'may be *made up* all over – a mere *artificial* woman', when he discovers a '*false bottom*, a whole set of teeth … a pair of delicate chestnut eye-brows … an entire head of hair, with curls, wool, pins, paste, &c …. and her *French* stays', he throws the lot out of the window (Figure 2.9).[36] The concern surrounding the disrobing of a bride's body, symbolic of the point of revelation and intimacy between spouses, was echoed in an editorial to the *Weekly Miscellany* in December 1776, which advocates, 'What with the enormous false head-dress – painting – and this new-fangled cork substitute – it would be almost impossible for a man to know his bride the morning after their nuptials.'[37] Some disgruntled commentators even suggested that the wearing of a cork rump was grounds for divorce or evidence of witchcraft.[38]

Though these published anecdotes are saturated in opinion, mockery and jest, they play on the underlying anxieties concerning the cork rump as a tool for deception, a theme that flourished in the literature surrounding women's bodies and fashion over the century. The cork rump, whose prominence made it as an easy target, particularly in that it emphasized a sexual zone of the body, became the latest male grievance linking fashion, deception and superficiality.[39] By associating the cork rump with Chloe, a female character whose mortal imperfections once hidden from her male companion are grotesquely revealed, satirists and commentators first grappling with

Figure 2.9 *False cosmetic supplements including cheek plumpers, eyebrows, patches and breast pads, 1701–1800, English, cork, feather, felt, lace, leather and paper, Acc. No. A158810,* © *The Board of Trustees of the Science Museum.*

this new fashion were able to capitalize on the unnerving alteration of the female form. Their fixation with this apparatus as deceitful quickly gave way to an obsession with the rump's material composition of cork.

An obsession with cork

An anonymous contributor to the *London Chronicle* in December 1776 attempted to describe the construction of the 'new article of female dress' that had 'lately sprung up': 'an addition to the hinder part of their dress, [made] by sewing several large pieces of Cork under the straps of their stays, in order that by the protuberance of this new additional Rump, their waists may seem the smaller and the more delicate'.[40] Though the author's constructional accuracy is dubious, his insistence on its material components is more noteworthy. While there is no surviving material evidence indicating that rumps and bums were made of cork, the fixation on their cork composition was pervasive.[41]

Sourced for its light, buoyant and impenetrable properties, and imported from the Continent, cork was used widely in eighteenth-century life: in the soles of shoes, life preservers, buoys, prosthetics and, most commonly, as stoppers for bottles.[42] Satirists were quick to draw comparisons, transforming the appendage into a variety of cork-composed objects. For example, Matthew and Mary Darly published two prints on 11 April 1777, *The Siege of Cork* and *Long Corks, or the Bottle Companions*, where the cork rump literally takes the form of a cork stopper (Figures 2.10 and 2.11).[43] In the first, a woman highly reminiscent of Chloe is under siege by a collection of open bottles attempting to take back their cork stoppers.[44] Fleeing across the page from an anthropomorphic flock of winged bottles, the woman's gown flaps up to reveal their target, a spherical orb of cork. The pursuit of the bottles is echoed a few months later in a print by John Collet, where plucked ostriches attempt to retrieve their feathers from the dressed coiffeurs of two women's heads.[45] Both types of 'birds' attempt to regain what fashion has appropriated. In the second print published on the same day, *Long Corks, or the Bottle Companions*, the Darlys portray two older women of contrasting physiques, the festoons of their skirts supported by giant, swelling cork stoppers, ballooning up from the necks of two brown bottles. Sitting across from each other, a rotund woman on the left with bulging breasts, an expansive double chin and plump hands gazes down at her emaciated companion, who's pointed and withered features are dwarfed in comparison. In contrast to Chloe, these old women are cast as indulging in the extremes and frivolities of fashions reserved for the young.[46] Similar to their treatment of *The Old Maids Morning Visit or the Calash Lady's*, Figure 1.23, published one month prior, the Darlys not only lampoon the older women's attempts at fashionability, and what is currently deemed fashionable itself by this metaphorical comparison, but also suggest a sartorial naivete, that like the women they portray on the page, the artist is unaware of the cork rump's actual construction.

Despite the obscurity surrounding the cork rump, cork's role in tailoring had fully developed by the mid-1770s in the development and production of cork jackets.[47] From the 1760s, a flood of interest for a new life preserver made of canvas and cork appeared in London newspapers. As described in Dr Wilkinson's *Tutamen Nauticum: or, The Seaman's Preservation from Shipwreck, Diseases, and other Calamities indicent to Mariners* in 1766 (first published in 1757), the latest design of the cork jacket was:

> composed of two pieces of thin light canvas (for fine ones indeed silk may be used) sewed together in a proper form; betwixt these, duly inserted and well secured, are put a sufficient number of oval-formed pieces of select sound compact cork, cut into particular sizes, and disposed in so convenient a manner as to be perfectly conformable to the insertions of the muscles, according to the external anatomy of the human trunk ....[48]

Wilkinson's detailed, illustrated treatise was published and republished amidst an escalating rivalry contesting the inventor and best purveyor of the cork jacket, publicized in the press from the mid-1760s to the early 1790s (Figures 2.12 and 2.13). John Ward, 'Cork-Cutter, at the Sign of

Figure 2.10 The Siege of Cork, *11 April 1777, publ. by Matthew and Mary Darly, etching and engraving, Courtesy of the Lewis Walpole Library, Yale University.*

the Cork Jacket, the Foot of London-Bridge, Southwark', challenged Wilkinson in a competition of advertising.[49] Ward claimed that though Wilkinson had introduced the design for approval to the Society of Arts, he presented jackets made by Ward, which were subsequently never paid for. Between 28 March 1764 and Ward's death on 11 December 1778, over forty advertisements, declarations of

Figure 2.11 Long Corks or the Bottle Companions, *11 April 1777, publ. by Matthew and Mary Darly, hand-coloured etching and engraving, 44 × 30 cm, Courtesy of the Lewis Walpole Library, Yale University.*

patents, attacks of authenticity and promotions of the cork jacket appeared in five London newspapers. In addition to the hype generated in print, public exhibitions and displays were also held to test and encourage the use of the cork jacket.[50] Ward's estate auction discloses valuable insights on the London cork trade. In addition to 'three thousand gross of CORKS and BUNGS' which were corks already cut

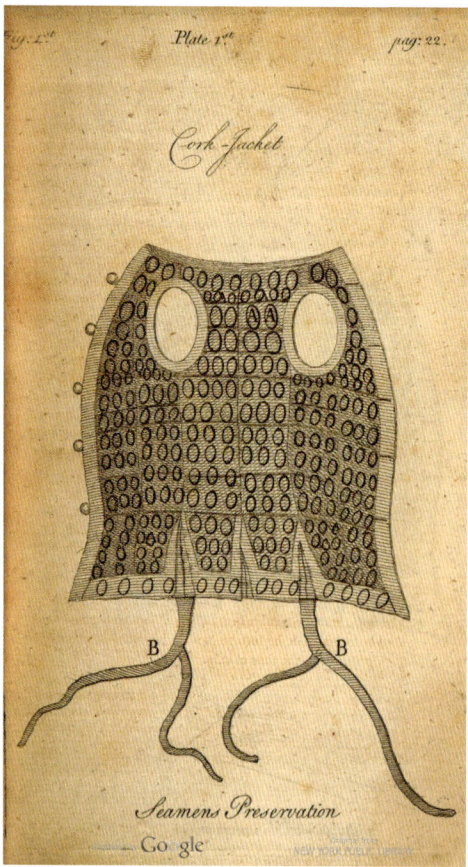

Figure 2.12 *John Wilkinson, 'Seamens Preservation', 1766,* Tutamen Nauticum: or, The Seaman's Preservation from Shipwreck, Diseases, and other Calamities incident to Mariners, *From the New York Public Library, New York.*

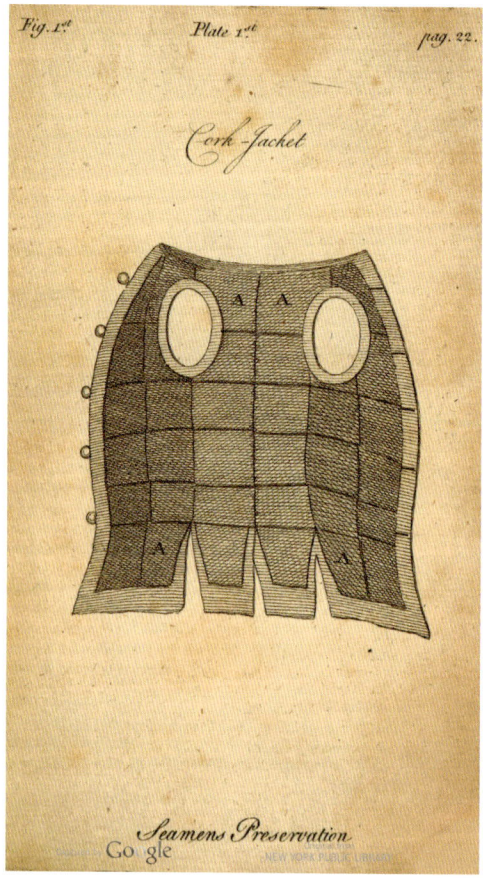

Figure 2.13 *John Wilkinson, 'Seamens Preservation', 1766,* Tutamen Nauticum: or, The Seaman's Preservation from Shipwreck, Diseases, and other Calamities incident to Mariners, *From the New York Public Library, New York.*

and shaped, Ward's stock at the time of his death included 'two hundred bundles of long ALICANT CORK'.[51] Cork was designated by its place of origin, as can be seen in advertisements for 'Port Cork' and 'Faro Cork'.[52] Once bought from importers, cork, like other raw materials, travelled through specific channels of London trade in order to be finished by cork-cutters to form the desired effect.

Ward's business as a cork-cutter aligned with the sartorial trades through his focus on cork jackets. His reach into practicing the garment-making trades is demonstrated in an advertisement on 18 May 1775, which notes that he 'had been favoured (since the approach of the Water Regatta) with considerable orders for fancy dresses in cork ….'[53] While no other description of these 'fancy dresses' survive, we can only presume that Ward was adding cork into other items of clothing beyond a cork jacket, or waistcoat, prior to the appearance of the cork rump in 1776. While no documentation suggests that Ward, nor his fellow cork-cutters, ever sold cork rumps, their prolific advertising campaigns and publicity potentially indicate why, when the cork rump appeared, satirists and commentators alike fixated on its ability to float. As Susan Vincent observes, 'notwithstanding any erotic appeal that the rump may or may not have held, in the pages of the press at least, the male imagination was almost exclusively exercised around the propensity of cork to float', casting women into a literal river of fashion.[54]

The most graphic visualization of a floating cork rump can be seen in *The Cork Rump: the Support of Life*, c. 1776, in which a fashionable young woman bobs serenely in the immediate aftermath of a boating accident (Figure 2.14).[55] Two young men, their wigs falling off, cling to the bottom of capsized boat, while two people in the foreground struggle to keep afloat. The feet of a fully submerged woman surface next to them. Amidst her drowning comrades, the young woman in the centre maintains her composure and appearance, with all her necessities of fashion intact – including her feathered coiffeur on her head and toy dog on her lap. The means of her buoyancy echoes a suggestion published in 'The Speculator' on 22 October 1776, in which the author asks 'Why should there not be *cork rumps*, as well as *cork jackets*? With such *rumps*, our women will no longer feel the smallest aversion to a *water party*.'[56] Contrasted with her drowning companions, she is saved by her cork rump.

This print illustrates a contemporary series of newspaper publications, some satiric and some sincere. The first, 'A Lass with a Cork Rump' was penned on 18 November 1776, by an anonymous author under the pseudonym 'Pushpin', who related 'a true narrative of an unfortunate accident (if it may be called so)'.[57] Pushpin's satirical tale describes how a woman fell into the Thames, but survived due to the buoyancy of her cork rump. Like the author of 'The Speculator', he suggests that it is 'as reasonable for [women] to wear Cork Rumps as [men] to wear Cork Jackets'.[58] It sparked a series of comic stories, playing on the cork rump as a floating saviour to waterborne women. One account on 4 October 1785 cites that a woman, who fell into the Thames, was so violently pulled downstream that it was by a miracle, or occult interference that she survived. The author recalled:

> for as she was stricken in years, and her dip in the Thames having restored her shrivelled countenance to its native sallow, the ladies of Billingsgate, with one united voice, pronounced her a *witch* – nor could she have escaped their fury, if she had not *proved*, that it was not to the *Devil*, but to a *cork rump* she owed her safety.[59]

In 1777, *A Panegyric on Cork Rumps, or, A May Morning's Excursion on the Water* was published, exulting the cork rump in verse as the device that 'sav'd our females from sinking' in a great storm.[60] On 27 June 1778, the *General Evening Post* reported 'a very ludicrous accident [that] happened at Henley upon Thames', where:

Figure 2.14 The Cork-Rump the Support of Life, c. 1776, etching, 21.3 × 29.6 cm, British Museum, London.

A large party from town went after tea to enjoy the coolness of the evening on the banks of the river. Youth and spirits hurried them into such fallies of vivacity, that in running with too much precipitation, a lady's foot tripped, and she fell into the Thames. The consternation was general; but how much was every body surprized, to see her swim like a fishing-float, half immersed, and half above water! It seems, this unfortunate lady had been furnished with an immoderate sized cork rump, which buoyed her up so completely, that, in the golden age of fiction, she might have been passed for a Naiade, or even Venus herself first rising from the water. She was towed to shore by a gentleman's cane, without the least injury but wet petticoats.[61]

Though not an unembellished report, with classical references to water nymphs and the birth of Venus, its publication in the society news, rather than as an editorial or fictional narrative, indicates the possibility that an event of such nature may have indeed taken place, spurring both the imagination and production of such satires and commentaries, as *The Cork Rump, the Support of Life*.

Satirical and sartorial dialogues

Dialogues between prints and viewers, prints and newspapers, and prints and customers were fundamental to the dissemination and consumption of graphic satire in the second half of the century. In a 'Dialogue in the SHADES between Mrs. Woffington and Kitty Fisher', a fictional conversation between the by then deceased actress and courtesan, printed in the September 1778 *Town and Country*, Kitty Fisher and Margaret Woffington remark on current fashions:

> Mrs. W. What an uncomfortable fashion! I wonder they are not ridiculed in print.
> Kitty. Fanny M. from whom I had my intelligence, tells me, that they brave ridicule, and that in proportion as the print shops exhibit their caricatures, and the News Papers satirize their extravagance, they heighten their heads, and enlarge their rumps.[62]

The dialogue emphasizes the cyclical relationship between dress and print culture, that fashion inspires prints and prints in turn inspire fashion.[63] Likewise, satirists were quick to depict the socio-cultural and political news of day, and *vice versa*. It is clear that viewers and consumers of prints were aware not only of this correlation, but also actively aligned both media through their deliberate practices of assemblage. For example, a newspaper clipping is pasted on the back of the Sarah Sophia Banks's copy of *Monsieur Le Que*, which depicts a cork cutter cutting and fitting women's rumps. The source of the clipping, 'Morning Post Feb: 24. 1777', has been written in an eighteenth-century hand. Cut from the society news, the text describes an incident of a lost rump at an assembly:

> One evening last week a master of the ceremonies of an assembly not many miles north west of the metropolis, saw a plump pair of *Cork-rumps* lying in the middle of the room, after the conclusion of a *cotillion* by a buck-some city party: As many enquiries as decency would permit were made after the owner, but all in vain, though the losing party was guessed at, by a visible decrease of bulk from a certain lady's *entrè* to her *exit*. – No one owning the well-turned *expletives*, they were hung over the fire-place at the head of the room, by order of the master of ceremonies, that the real owner may know where to apply for them, when she gets the better of her present *embarrassment*.[64]

Banks's annotation demonstrates how both forms of social commentary were collected and collated, each enhancing the other.[65] Banks is not an exception, as numerous annotated prints and bound scrapbooks survive, such as those owned by Horace Walpole, Anne Seymour Damer and even Anne Scafe, a maidservant of Georgiana Spencer Cavendish, Duchess of Devonshire.[66]

The relationship between prints and texts coincides with the dialogues that occurred within graphic satires themselves. As seen in Figures 2.1 and 2.2, designs could be adapted and modified. They could also directly address and respond to previous publications. For example, the subtitle of *The Cork Rump, the Support of Life*, references an earlier published print, which underscores the cork rump's revenge.⁶⁷ The first line of the subtitle reads: '*You smil'd when like a* Shuttle-cock *I flew*,' referring to a print published on 6 December 1776 by Matthew and Mary Darly, titled *Miss Shuttle-cock*, dating *The Support of Life* to after 6 December 1776 (Figure 2.15). Stylistically, *The Support of Life* also adopts the arrangement of five feathers at the top of the coiffeur featured in *Miss Shuttle-cock*. The inclusion of the lapdog and gauze lappets indicates that the artist was also aware of *The Cork Rump, or Chloe's Cushion* or *Chloe's Cushion, or, the Cork Rump*. The treatment of figures and stylization suggests that the print was most likely published in 1777 by John Lockington, who published other adaptations of the Darlys' work, as seen at the beginning of the chapter.⁶⁸

The interplay between prints was not limited to the adaptation of designs. *Miss Shuttle-Cock* (6 December 1776), *The Back-Side of a Front Row* (1 January 1777), *The New Rigatta* (20 February 1777) and *Dolefull Dicky Sneer in the Dumps, or the Lady's Revenge* (1 April 1777) form a sequence following three 'Cork'd & feather'd' ladies, a round bellied clergyman, and a thin, long-queued fop in a visual game

Figure 2.15 *R. S. [Richard Sheridan], Miss Shuttle-cock, 6 December 1776, publ. by Matthew and Mary Darly, etching, 29 × 43 cm, Courtesy of the Lewis Walpole Library, Yale University.*

tug of war over the fashion for cork rumps (Figures 2.16–2.18).[69] The prints are attributed to playwright and social commentator, Richard Brinsley Sheridan under the pseudonym Richard Sneer, and were published by Matthew and Mary Darly roughly a month apart.[70] Sheridan's signature, an interlinked 'RS', appears along the bottom edge of each print.[71] In *Miss Shuttle-cock*, Sheridan transforms the fashionable feathered coiffeur and cork rump into a shuttlecock's components, the subtitle of the print explaining the substitution of parts: 'Ladie[s] likes Shuttle-Cocks are now array'd, The tail is Cork'd & feather'd is the head'.[72] Like fashion's metaphorical volley in the press, in the print, the cork'd and feather'd woman is batted back and forth. The print employs the game of badminton as a visualization of the rivalling commentaries on women's fashion. The moralizing clergyman and society's fop thwack the fashionable woman back and forth through the air. In this visual exchange, each vies for influence over the fashionable, envisioning the constructions of sartorial dialogues and diatribes.[73] As demonstrated throughout this book, printed diatribes, ridicules and satires of women's dress, and thereby women themselves, were ever present in the public interpretation and reception of the fashionable world.[74] Here, the metaphorical tug of war between opposing parties enables Sheridan to simultaneously criticize fashion's latest protuberance, while also reflecting, like Kitty Fisher and Margaret Woffington, on the role of satirical prints in the construction of sartorial dialogues and diatribes.

The subject of sport is brought into full view in the second print of the series, where five plump and padded bottoms are on display. Joined again by the cleric and fop, this group of seated women each wears a cork rump beneath her gown. Each 'backside' is portrayed slightly differently: on the left, the rump is divided into two spheres by a sharp point; her neighbour's gown has a deep v-shaped back with bows on either side; next, the back of the gown is rounder, creating a large egg-shaped rump; the fourth's gown forms a diamond-like point, with a smaller rump; the final rump can be seen to swell beneath the drape of the sacque. The variety of bums, heads and bodies that are presented in the 'front row' of society are drawn deep into the picture space, far away from the imagined seat of the viewer positioned to cast judgement. Of the elite figures depicted, three of the women, those whose faces are slightly turned to the viewer, reappear in the next print in the sequence.

In *The New Rigatta,* three women float downstream, their feathers shaped like sails, and their spherical cork rumps bobbing like boats on the river. Their formation echoes that of the flock of ducks paddling beside them. Like *Miss Shuttle-cock*, Sheridan again adapts a sporting event to suit the satire of fashion. Though published nearly six months later, the print may in part commemorate, or at least recall, the Richmond Regatta of 22 August 1776, celebrating the Prince of Wales's birthday.[75] Horace Walpole, who attended the event and later owned a copy of Sheridan's print described the regatta as 'the prettiest and the foolishest sight in the world', where 'nobody [was] more in masquerade than they are every day'.[76] Walpole's comment on the theatrical absurdity of day's appearance is visualized in Sheridan's satire.[77] The three women are propelled downstream by three male bodiless heads in the clouds on the left of the print, their cork rumps acting as their 'keels in the tide of fashion'.[78] Unlike the

Figure 2.16 R. S. [Richard Sheridan], *The Back-side of a Front Row*, 1 January 1777, publ. by Matthew and Mary Darly, etching and drypoint, 29 × 37 cm, Courtesy of the Lewis Walpole Library, Yale University.

sculling rowers in the distance, these women are portrayed as passive participants, on display for the riverbank crowd. The prizes favour the latest trends in this apparent race of fashion:

1. Prize. An entire new WIG, compleatly furnished with curls, cushion, feathers. &c &c. and free admittance to all public amusements.
2. Prize. A new pair of CORKS – with Patent machine invented by Mess–rs Pulley & Lever for tight Lacing.
3. Prize. A privelege of appearing in public either sans Fichue or without Petty-coats as the Lady shall judge most decent.

First place wins a fully constructed coiffeur and admittance to 'public amusements', like the theatre, much to the pleasure of those sitting behind them.[79] Second place receives both a 'pair of CORKS', which adopts the same sartorial language used to refer to a pair of stays, which is the second prize, which Sheridan dubs a 'Patent machine'. The third-place prize allows the bestowed to go without an article of clothing, either without her petticoats, thus exposing her legs, or without her handkerchief, exposing her breasts. Like the coiffeurs above that catch the prevailing winds of fashion, the cork

Figure 2.17 R. S. [Richard Sheridan], *The New Rigatta, 20 February 1777, publ. by Matthew and Mary Darly, etching, 27 × 38 cm, Courtesy of the Lewis Walpole Library, Yale University.*

rumps beneath allow these women to follow the current. Here cork's buoyancy has become a part of the wider drift of fashion, no longer singled out for its material, but acting as a vessel, transporting those who wear it to the next fashionable trend in front of all to see.

In the final print of the series, the three women and the cleric finally take up arms against the producer of their derision. In *Dolefull Dicky Sneer in the Dumps, or, the Lady's Revenge*, our victims intend to bring justice against the architect of their mockery. The three women and the cleric are portrayed sneaking up on Sheridan as he sits drawing an inverted sketch of *Miss Shuttle-cock*. His large initials 'RS' on the bottom corner of the sketch and that he has the pen in his hand, confirm the fop's identity as the artist. In response to the print he is drawing and a framed copy of *The Back-side of a Front Row* that hangs on the wall, the group seeks an eye for an eye, as the middle woman raises her left fist in the air. The manner of this revenge is foretold in a second framed print at the far right, where four female figures with feathered headdresses and plump rumps throw a petite man up in the air using a blanket. The title confirms the artist's fate, where 'Dicky Sneer', or Richard Sheridan, will be thrown 'in the Dumps'.[80] 'Lex talio', abbreviated from *lex talionis*, or the law of retaliation, is inscribed beneath the blanket toss. At the bottom right of the print, an inscription reads: 'Heus bone tu palles', or 'hey good man, you look pale' – reflecting the fear in Sheridan's face.[81] 'Sukey spightful fect', an

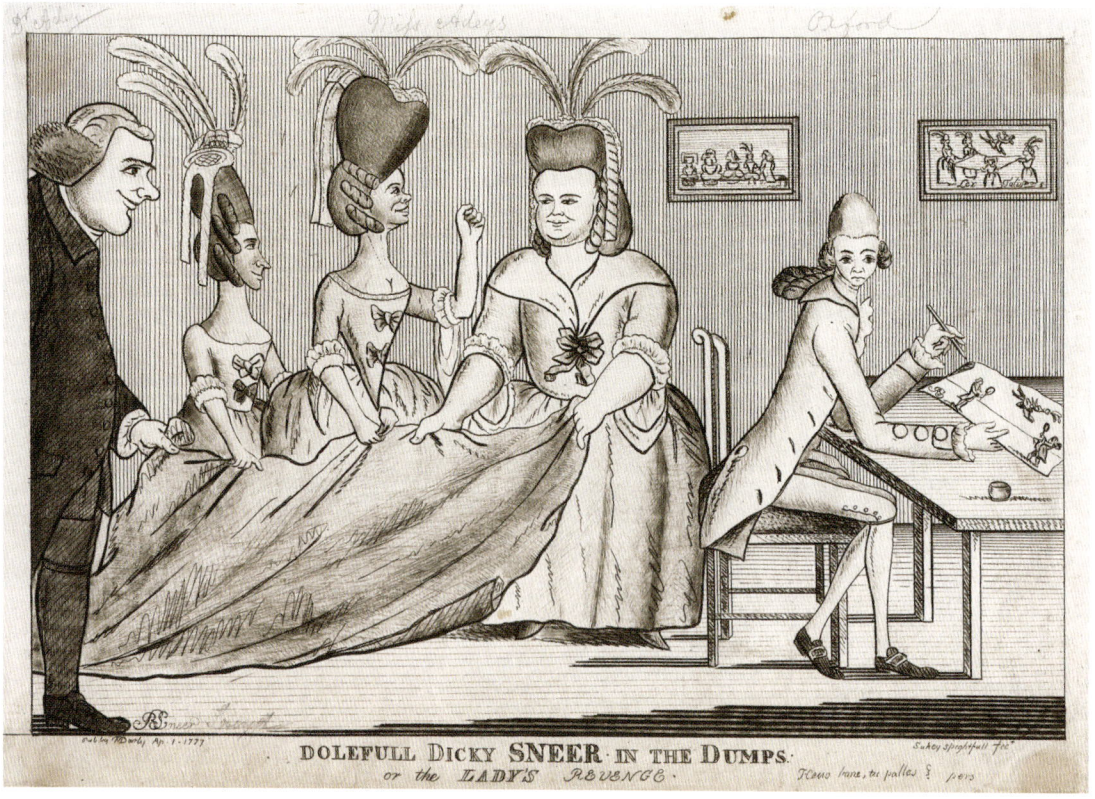

Figure 2.18 *R. S. [Richard Sheridan], Dolefull Dicky Sneer in the Dumps, or, The Lady's Revenge, 1 April 1777, publ. by Matthew and Mary Darly, etching and drypoint, 25 × 36 cm, Courtesy of the Lewis Walpole Library, Yale University.*

abbreviation of *fecit*, implies that the designer of the print was one of the women portrayed above, identified by the name Sukey Spightfull.[82] However, the print is signed on the left with the traditional 'RS', to which has been added 'neer', forming 'RSneer', referring to Sheridan's abbreviated surname in the title. The print acknowledges the role of the satirist as an instigator of sartorial debates within a medium that fostered an active engagement between artist and viewer, and by extension, social critic and the socially criticized.

Though playfully self-reflective, Sheridan's prints participate in the satirization of fashion. While the figures within them appear to retaliate against the perpetrators of sartorial criticism, they do so within the paradigm.[83] Sheridan's prolific production of prints, as well as his roles as playwright and politician, would further disseminate the dialogues surrounding feminine fashionability. Within the mostly male-dominated visual and textual discourses, which, like the badminton players, volleyed the benefits and flaws of the latest fashion back and forth, a female defender is rarely heard.[84] Echoing the indignation of the three women who intend to throw off their satirist, a female authoress stands against her male counterparts, the authors of printed sartorial diatribes.[85] In a January 1778 editorial addressed 'To the OBSERVER', a column of *Town and Country,* 'Cordelia', asserted on behalf of the female sex, 'Our poor cork rumps must be severely flaggelated, after you (or your correspondents) have done all you can to tear off our caps, and pull down our heads.'[86] But against the printed onslaught, she wrote, 'we rise superior to censure, and the more you rail at our heads, we will rear our crests higher, and let you be of what party you may, you shall not down with our rumps'.[87] In an aggressive closure to the editorial, she penned, 'A truce with your sarcasms upon us and our dress, or we shall declare open war, and you will find the Amazons, as of old are no cowards.'[88] Her threat of war echoed the current conflict with the American colonies, and references one of the earliest jests, that the cork rump was intended to be a taxable product to help the war effort.[89] Like the fictional 'dialogue in the Shade', a woman is again portrayed as railing against fashionable criticism.

Though this editorial is only one of many printed, just as graphic satires about cork rumps are only a fraction of the fashion satires produced, by tracing these dialogues we can unpack the active discussions surrounding dress. Print culture put forth a dynamic debate, in which members of the public participated through collecting and as contributors both in text and image. In the case of the cork rump, the prolific output surrounding its appearance, materiality and wear enables us to situate it as a widely acknowledged article of dress of the late 1770s. However, in the first years of its wear, it is clear that the understandings of its construction, function and practicality were vague. This ambiguity, informed by contemporary perceptions of the uses for cork, allowed satirists to exploit its materiality, as an unknown device of potential deception and folly. This naivety of its physical construction has contributed to its modern treatment in scholarship as a thing of myth, a purely satirical entity. However, in the following decade, we witness the development of the cork rump within dress, and within public awareness, as a tangible garment.

Bums and bum-makers: The cork rump in the 1780s

Throughout the final years of the 1770s, the cork rump was handled with uncertainty as to its construction, apart from its composition of cork. However, by the mid-1780s, representations and understandings had shifted. Between the cluster of prints produced between 1776 and 1778, and the cork rump's reappearance in graphic satire in 1785, a lapse of fashion satires occurred as publishers focused on the political climate, as exacerbated by the war with colonial America.[90] While personal and social satires, to borrow Dorothy George's classifications, were still produced in the interim, they primarily portrayed individual members of society, rather than the generic beau monde or socially climbing figures that populated fashion prints. Yet, with the end of the war in 1784, fashion satires once again flourished as satirists sharpened their pens to portray the new female figure, with over thirty prints produced between 1785 and 1789 that focused directly on the pouter pigeon silhouette.[91] Unlike earlier depictions, the rump, now nearly ubiquitously called a bum, was re-envisaged in the

1780s as a structural undergarment, demonstrating a wider understanding of its construction, and its maker. No longer reliant on material associations, satirists directly addressed the rump as a product firmly of the millinery trade, fostering a more mature interpretation of the garment they satirized.

In July 1785, *The Westminster Magazine* published a column subtitled 'About the Ladies BOTTOMS'.[92] After relaying the supplements of fashion to the face, neck, waist and feet, it observed:

> And after all this being done, a Lady was supposed to be quite finished–
>
> No such thing –
>
> What was wanting?
>
> What was wanting? Blockhead! Don't thee know?
>
> A BUM was wanting!!!
>
> A BUM!
>
> Mercy on us! Who would have thought Nature could have made such a mistake as to create ladies without *bums*.
>
> Nothing is more certain. –
>
> *Bum* shops are opened in many parts of Westminster for the sale of *cork* bums, and report says they go *swimmingly* on.
>
> Tall ladies, and short ladies – fat ladies and lean ladies, must have *bums* ....[93]

The anonymous author, after referencing the cork rump's earlier aquatic associations, concludes the dialogue by stating: 'Let it be recorded, that in the auspicious year 1785, BUMS FOR LADIES, were *made*, *cleaned*, and *repaired*, so as far to exceed *nature* in *size*, or *convenience*.'[94] This progression in terminology is again seen in the, 'Levities of Fashion', on 20 August 1785 in the *General Advertiser*, whose prolific observer of fashion noted:

> There is something, it is alleged by connisseurs in female proportion, in the hindmost movements of a fine Woman, peculiarly elegant and beautiful. The Cork Rump originated in this lascivious idea; and it gave apparent elasticity to those parts, about which the imagination of most men are often busily employed:
>
> But now this posterior embellishment is actually converted in to, what is called a *Bum*. How this operates, or what may be its specific dimensions, is not yet clearly ascertained among the learned. It has of late however been as common for Ladies to call for a new bottom, as to call for new shoes. And whenever a petticoat is ordered, the most essential point to be settled is, whether it shall be with or without a *Bum*.[95]

The enlarged derriere that characterized the silhouette of 1780s was first visualized in S. W. Fores's *The Bum Shop* of 11 July 1785, signalling the re-emergence of the conspicuously enlarged rump in graphic satire (Figure 2.19).[96] Samuel William Fores, who was established at No. 3 Picadilly in 1783

Figure 2.19 The Bum Shop, *11 July 1785, publ. by S. W. Fores, hand-coloured etching, 33 × 45.8 cm, British Museum, London.*

amidst the heyday of West End printshops, became one of the principle publishers of fashion prints during the late 1780s.[97] His publication of amateur designs, such as *The Bum Shop* by R. Rushworth, contributed to a substantial set of fashion-focused satires that continued the iconographic traditions set forth by amateur designs published by Matthew and Mary Darly in the 1770s.[98] While his output was varied in subject matter, including an extensive breadth of political and social subjects, the subset of prints that highlight the ballooning female silhouette of the second half of the 1780s suggests a concentrated expertise and interest in this fashion from both his artists who were producing them and his clientele who were buying them.[99] Unlike the depictions of the cork rump in the 1770s, in Rushworth's print of *The Bum Shop*, he does not shy away from portraying the rump's construction. In the print, five women wait in a shop, identified by the title as a bum shop. They are attended by two men, one of whom helps a client position the rump around her body, while the other attends the woman in the centre. He gestures with his right arm to the rumps hanging on the back wall. His client's breasts pop out from her stays, as she stands choosing her next enhancement. To the right of this pair, a rounder woman perches on a stool, examining a rump in her hand. Beside her, to the far right of the print, a woman, wearing a rump, uses a hand mirror to inspect the added protuberance in the mirror hanging on the wall. Just in front of her, a small poodle-like dog stands on its back legs. Its fur has been cut to mimic the women's swelling bosom, while its bushy extended tail imitates their new bums. On the far left of the shop, next to the window, the viewer can see the finished silhouette of a woman standing in profile. She wears a ruffled handkerchief around her neck and chest, while her rump extends out behind her like 'a *camel* with a *hunch* in the middle of the back', as *The Westminster Magazine* identified.[100]

Like *The Westminster Magazine's* account, the print visualizes the interior of a shop in which women could purchase a new bum. The male staff echoes the magazine's fictional exchange between patron and client:

> "*Mr. Rumpus*, I want a new *bum*." –
> "Very well, Ma'am, happy to serve you – proud to say my *bums* have been very much approved" –
> "But how long do they last?"
> "O! Ma'am – you may have your *bum* cleaned by me at any time – I repair *bums* by the year." …[101]

The suggestive behaviour also exists in the print, where the kneeling male attendant stares directly at one patron's backside while fitting a new bum. In the centre of the print, the shopkeeper, identified by the name 'Derriere', 'measures' the area of his client's body requiring improvement. Beneath, the subtitle reads like a newspaper advertisement:

> DERRIERE begs leave to submit to the attention of that most indulgent part of the Public the Ladies in general, and more especially those to whom Nature in a slovenly moment has been niggardly in her distribution of certain lovely Endowments, his much improved (aridae nates) or DRIED BUMS so justly admired for their happy resemblance to nature. DERRIERE flatters himself that he stands unrivalled in this fashionable article of female In-vention, he having spared neither pains nor expence in procuring every possible information on the subject, to render himself competent to the artfully supplying this necessary appendage of female excellence.[102]

The conclusion of the advertisement plays upon the sexual double entendre of his familiarity with women's corporeal rumps; however, it is also indicative of satirists' greater familiarity of false rumps and their makers. Though both accounts draw on the potentially sordid relationship between a woman and her bum supplier, the actual makers of bums can be confirmed in three articles, published in 1781, 1785 and 1787. In the *Morning Herald,* an editorial 'On Female RUMPS' conveys that 'the *woman of fashion*, who is so fortunate as not to have outlived the good opinion of her milliner, is elegantly *padded* all round with *swelling collops* of most delicious satin', implying that the best cork rumps were covered in expensive fabric.[103] The *Morning Post and Daily Advertiser* reports that a theft occurred at 'a milliner's shop, when the thieves got clear off with a lady's cork-rump', and in an editorial in the *St. James Chronicle or British Evening Post,* a celebrating bachelor rejoices that he has 'no cringing Milliners, nor 'Mantua-Makers', with their Boxes of Caps, Cork Rumps and Cushions' to pay because he has no wife.[104]

That milliners sold rumps is also evident in satirical representations. In *A Milliner's Shop*, published by S. W. Fores on 24 March 1787, which mocks the royal family's reputation for frugality by depicting them shopping at a milliner's, three rumps hang on the wall behind the counter (Figure 2.20). Two are portrayed as stuffed orbs, beneath which, a petticoat has been sewn, and one is depicted as a sharp crescent, whose volume increases from the sides to the centre. One of the princesses tries this type of rump on over her gown at the far end of the counter. It curves up, creating the necessary volume and height for the silhouette. A month earlier, both of these types of rumps were portrayed in *A Man Millener*, published by S. W. Fores on 16 February 1787 (Figure 2.21).[105] Supporting the effeminacy associated with men in the millinery trade, the figure is presented with delicate, androgynous facial

Figure 2.20 A Milliner's Shop, *24 March 1787, publ. by S. W. Fores, hand-coloured etching, 38.7 × 51.1 cm, Courtesy of Yale Center for British Art, Yale University.*

features.[106] He wears a puffed handkerchief poking out of his jacket and waistcoat as he carries a large hat and characteristic blue hatbox in his hands. A pointed, crescent rump, reminiscent of the extant Finnish bum in Figure 2.6, is looped on the crook of his arm, and he wears, like a woman, a large petticoat style rump around his backside. The handkerchief and rump give him the feminine pouter

Figure 2.21 *Detail of* A Man Millener: The Muff, *16 February 1787, publ. by S. W. Fores, hand-coloured etching with stipple, 26.2 × 39.3 cm, Courtesy of the Lewis Walpole Library, Yale University.*

pigeon silhouette. Both prints were designed by Henry Kingsbury and published by Fores over a year after *The Bum Shop*. Kingsbury's depictions of the rumps echo those produced by Rushworth, whose print portrays a variety of rumps hung, worn and piled throughout the shop. Eight rumps hang on display, of which the three largest are divided in two orb-like sections, which appear to be directly sewn to the petticoat beneath. Their volume is managed through seams, indicated by vertical lines on the rumps that further divide the two sections indicating channelled indentations in the rump. The smaller rumps are divided more clearly into padded sections, forming circular, triangular, rounded or winged shapes. On the floor, a pile of three rumps lies discarded, similar in shape to the rounded rump between the heads of the two attended clients. While it is possible that the consistency in the cork rump's portrayal is due to Kingsbury's access and adaptation of previous designs, the proliferation of visible bums peripherally across graphic satires suggests a wider familiarity rather than merely copying.[107] In addition, the extant rump at Manchester in Figure 2.4 strongly resembles the small, triangular construction of the rump hung lowest on the wall, suggesting a better understanding of the rump's construction and ability to portray the rump as a garment, rather than alternative manifestation.

This arguably more mature handling of the cork rump's depiction, not as a cork stopper or shuttlecock, but as it may have been constructed, speaks to the advanced awareness of the cork rump as a material garment. The close similarities in design between the bums portrayed in *The Bum Shop* and *A Milliner's Shop* and the surviving bums in Manchester and Turku echo the portrayal of other garments in graphic satire, that despite being potentially exaggerated, often strongly resembled the material artefacts they represent. The cork rump's pervasiveness in graphic satire, as both a depicted garment and as implied by the prominent silhouette of the pouter pigeon, suggests an understanding of those satirists portraying it. Like the material adaptation of stays to include eyelets, the satirical adaptation to portray the rump's construction indicates its common existence by the mid-1780s. The rump was visually conveyed as a product of fashionable consumption, made by milliners, who produced the accessories and addendums that supplemented women's gowns. Though still comically and sexually charged, retaining its close connection to the area of the body which it enhanced, the rump's widespread appearance across satires in a sartorial form speaks to its quotidian ubiquity.

✻✻✻

Of the garments examined in this book, the cork rump has the shortest lifespan, ranging only from 1776 into the 1790s.[108] Though structural underwear worn on the posterior would reappear as small crescent bum pads in the 1810s–30s, and later as the wire-framed bustle of the late nineteenth century, in the late eighteenth century the ephemeral prominence of the backside waned almost as quickly as it appeared. A print published by S. W. Fores in January 1788 proclaims the rump's fall from fashion (Figure 2.22).[109] In *The Bumless Beauties*, two women stand facing each other in a sparsely denoted landscape. Both wear expansive hats, overstated handkerchiefs and long hair hanging down their

106   *The Modern Venus*

backs.¹¹⁰ The shorter woman on the right wears an exaggeratedly large fur muff.¹¹¹ Their inflated heads and torsos bear all the hallmarks of the amplified 1780s silhouette, but, as the title indicates, what is noticeably missing from the familiar pouter pigeon silhouette is their bums. The subtitle beneath the print reads:

Figure 2.22 The Bumless Beauties, *January 1788, publ. by S. W. Fores, etching with stipple, 27.4 × 20.2 cm, Courtesy of the Lewis Walpole Library, Yale University.*

Both Bums and Rumps are now no more,
With merry Thoughts the Fair are blest,
Their Beauties now you may explore,
All bare and therefore all expresst.

Without their artificial bums, the contours of the women's legs, and even pelvis, are visible beneath their tightly clinging skirts. While we cannot treat this isolated print as a bookend of the cork rump's appearance on the body, as the pigeon silhouette would continue to be depicted throughout 1788 and 1789, and the rounder, though less pronounced figure would continue into the 1790s, it does foreshadow the rump's decline and fashion's progression.[112]

The rump's depletion was noted two years earlier by Betsy LeFanu, Richard Sheridan's sister, in a letter to their sister Alicia, describing the fashions: 'However you may tell her as a friend gradually to reduce her Stuffing as Rumps are quite out in France and are decreasing here but can not be quite given up 'till the weather grows warmer.'[113] LeFanu's advice to their friend, Maria Walker, constitutes a rare reference to rumps and bums outwith the satirical sphere. Like the extant bums, her remark both affirms the cork rump's existence off the printed page, but also highlights the discrepancies between the fluctuation of fashion on the corporeal body and that on the satirical body. Her letter dates to the beginning of the most prolific period of production of prints depicting the rump as an integral part of the female silhouette. Like Figure 2.22, her observations of the change of fashion are a solitary observation, to be viewed as a contributing facet rather than a concrete certainty. Despite the disparity in date, both demonstrate a contemporary awareness of the cork rump's ephemerality, and the fluidity of fashion as dictated by minute variations, like a reduction of stuffing.

The cork rump's brief, yet prominent period of wear enables us to approach its complete lifecycle, from its infancy to its demise. Despite its scarce material and archival survival, its pervasion throughout graphic satires and published newspapers and magazines renders a view of public understanding and interpretation of the cork rump and offers an opportunity to address an immaterial artefact of dress. Through its initial associations with Chloe, we can trace the speed at which the cork rump became a requisite of fashionability, but also the uncertainty shrouding it, casting the cork rump as a device to deceive husbands and grounds for divorce. Its portrayal as cork stoppers and shuttlecocks affirms this ambiguity, particularly surrounding its physical construction. With the influence of recent publicity surrounding the cork jacket, print culture fostered a fixation with its supposed material composition of cork. While no material evidence survives affirming its cork interior, as the correlation with cork was so prevalent, it is probable that at least early versions were constructed using cork, then later to be stuffed with horsehair, wool or feathers. Aside from indications of its materiality, the cork rump's treatment in graphic satire exhibits the interplay between prints and newspapers, collectors and prints themselves. Within graphic satires, as well as publications, we witness the acknowledgement of satirists and authors in the debate and discussion of the cork rump, reflecting their engagement as agitators in dress's public perception.

With the representations produced in the 1780s of the cork rump as a garment, the depictions mature, echoing its progression from ambiguous novelty to quotidian necessity of fashionable dress. The variations, and more significantly, consistencies of the rump's representation indicate an awareness of construction, which can be correlated across numerous depictions in graphic satire, as well as with the surviving artefacts. The extant bums and the surrounding material footprint enables us not only to demonstrate the cork rump's material existence, but also to establish the interlaced relationship between dress and its portrayal in graphic satires. Rather than distinct entities revolving around separate axes of the satirical and the material, the close proximity and exchanges between these spheres highlight the influence and perception of dress and satire. The cork rump is particularly pertinent as a case study of immaterial culture, due to its nearly sole satirical representation, enabling us to re-evaluate the boundaries, limitations and ultimately benefits of examining dress in graphic satire. On and off the printed page, the cork rump was an integral ingredient in fashioning a woman's silhouette, one, which despite its ephemerality, left a sizable wake behind it.

3

By hand: Silk and fur muffs

In March 1786, *Walker's Hibernian Magazine, or, Compendium of Entertaining Knowledge* (1771–1812) published the 'Modern Venus', a one-and-a-half page editorial describing the attributes of the contemporary goddess of love. Drawing comparisons between the classical goddess of Greece and Rome and that of the present beauties of Britain and Ireland, the anonymous author 'present[s] the public with a view of a *Modern Venus* [sic.], as much excelling the Goddess of Antiquity, as the Modern Hercules did the Demi-god of Greece and Rome'.[1] 'The Modern Venus' was printed as a pendant to the 'The Modern Hercules', published three months earlier in December 1785, featuring the current modes of modern men as compared with Hercules. Each text was accompanied by an illustrative engraving (Figures 3.1 and 3.2). In the witty juxtaposition of classical mythology and contemporary customs, both editorials satirically compare the ancient demi-god and goddess to the modern man and woman of fashion, in actions and manners, but particularly in dress and appearance. The modern Hercules 'wears the spoils of a Taylor, whom he hath never paid', citing his high 'coller', long flowing 'side-locks [that] hang just like the ears of a Bologna lap-dog', and 'his hat (equal in size to the seven-fold shield of Ajax)'.[2] Likewise, the 'The Modern Venus' sports all the hallmarks of mid-1780s fashionability, like Figures 0.1 and 0.2 of the same name. Her hair is 'frizzled, and creped, and rumpled, till [it resembles] the stuffing of a saddle, or the curled horse-hair crammed into a chair-bottom'.[3] Atop her hedgehog hairstyle, she wears an 'enormous *parachute hat*', which is 'wantonly cocked on one side to invite the eye'.[4] The ruffles of her exaggerated handkerchief give way to the bulk of her skirts behind her, elevated by a bum, making the width of her backside as wide as her hat. Framed by the undulating curves of her bouffant breast, the raised skirts of her looped gown and the wide-brimmed hat, the final feature that completes this modern Venus's ensemble is a large fur muff. The magazine relays to its readers that while 'the Venus of Antiquity had her hands bare, and shewed her rosy fingers; that of modern times, thrusts her arms into a muff'.[5]

The muff was first introduced in Britain in the sixteenth century.[6] Originally subject to sumptuary legislation, muffs warmed the hands and fingers of British royalty and the aristocracy over the bitter

Figure 3.1 *'The Modern Venus'*, Walker's Hibernian Magazine, or, Compendium of Entertaining Knowledge, *March 1786, This image is reproduced courtesy of the National Library of Ireland [J 05].*

Figure 3.2 *'The Modern Hercules'*, Walker's Hibernian Magazine, or, Compendium of Entertaining Knowledge, *December 1785, This image is reproduced courtesy of the National Library of Ireland [J 05].*

months of winter. When sumptuary legislation surrounding fur and dress was eased at the opening of the seventeenth century, the muff remained an elite accessory, prohibitive due to its cost and worn only by men and women whose hands were unoccupied by labour.[7] Muffs in the eighteenth century were fashioned from fur, feathers or silk and were commonly featured in painted portraiture of the gentry and nobility throughout the second half of the century. Both men and women wore muffs; however, men's muffs were largely limited to fur and by the turn of the century the fashion had shifted entirely to women's hands.[8] The 1760s saw a taste for feather muffs, and in the 1770s and 1780s, fur muffs ballooned in size along with other features of the modern Venus's silhouette.[9] Fur remained the most popular material throughout the period and fur muffs maintained their oversized scale throughout the 1790s. On the other hand, silk muffs presented women with a medium on which to invest their haptic creativity, sentimental engagement and visual expression. Though often dwarfed by their fur counterparts in both size and historiographical attention, silk muffs reveal women's networks of making and sartorial expression. As silk muffs were often products of their wearers' hands, they acted as sites of haptic, social and emotional engagement that spanned the muff's lifecycle, from its inception and design, to its embroidered and pictorial ornamentation, to its wear. Delving deeper into the representation, reputation and reality of fur and silk muffs allows us to move beyond the fur muff's carnal fashionability and understand both types of muffs as contrasting mediums of self-fashioning and display.

Venus in furs

On 17 November 1786, an anonymous commentator in the *Morning Chronicle and London Advertiser* penned that:

> The ladies now a-days were [sic] such enormous fox-muffs, that there is no approaching them within three feet at least, and if we were not apprized of the reality, viz. its being really but the skin of the animal, we should be induced to shrink like Shakespeare's Thane, and cry out, "Taken any shape but that."[10]

One of countless quips ridiculing the current mode that peppered the columns of British newspapers, the author cleverly satirizes the latest women's fashion for fur muffs. Not a new fashion, fur muffs had been worn by men and women in Britain since the 1570s.[11] The naturally insulating and the luxuriously tactile quality of fur lent it exclusivity throughout the early modern period.[12] By the late eighteenth century, fur, like other luxuries, found wider ownership than the wardrobes of royalty and the nobility to which it had originally been ordained.[13] Britain had first secured a foothold in the Eurasian fur trade in the mid sixteenth century with the foundation of the English Muscovy Company, and later in the North American fur trade with the formation of the Hudson Bay Company under Charles II.[14] Following victory over the French in the Seven Years' War, which had secured for Britain control of the Canadian fur trade, newspapers of the early 1760s scolded women as unpatriotic for not wearing enough muffs made of fur, preferring those of feathers instead.[15] Twenty years later, the features that this particular commentator draws attention to are the muff's 'enormous' size and its perceived innate transformability. Not only are muffs so large that a person cannot walk 'within three feet' of a woman carrying a muff, but, like Shakespeare's Macbeth crying out in fear upon seeing Banquo's ghost, contemporaries too will 'shrink' back and cry 'Taken any shape but that', suggesting that if we had not known the muff was made of animal fur, one would be sure to think that women had become some type of monstrous beast.

Satirical fur muffs

Satirists were quick to visualize these concerns for public consumption, both of the fur muff's size as well as its mutability. Some prints playfully suggested women's metamorphosis into their muffs, like *A Stage Box Scene; Mrs Bruin, Miss Chienne, Miss Renard*, published 1 January 1787 by J. Wicksteed (Figure 3.3). In the print, three women sit in their box at the theatre, each identified by the fur of their muff in their French surnames, translating to: Mrs Bear, Miss Bitch and Miss Fox. Each muff matches the colour of its wearer's hair and is held hanging over the side of the balcony, blocking the woman's bodies from view and suggestively implying that these three women are their muffs. This suggestion is made more overtly in S. W. Fores's *The Muff*, published 16 February 1787, in which a woman is literally engulfed by her fur muff that reaches from her shoulders to her ankles (Figure 3.4). The print forms half of a diptych with *A Man Millener,* whom we met in Chapter 2 carrying his wares, including two bums, a signature blue milliner's box, and large hat. He not only carries these articles in his arms, but also wears them about his body. A large blue bum protrudes from his backside and a puffed white handkerchief juts out from his breast, giving him the all contours of the present female silhouette. Millinery was traditionally a female profession and the man milliner became a popular literary and visual trope in the late eighteenth century.[16] Dubbed 'the HE-SHE shopkeepers of the metropolis', man milliners, like the one portrayed in Fores's print, culturally embodied late eighteenth-century anxieties surrounding gender and national identity.[17] In the diptych, the man milliner sartorially adopts the underwear and accessories that signify the female form, those that should be worn by his female clientele to his left. Instead, the man milliner's feminized body is displayed, while the woman's figure is hidden, eclipsed by the enormity of her fur muff.

Though the scale of the 1780s fur muff made for easy sport for satirists, muffs had held metonymic significance throughout the century. Aside from their traditional associations with the cold, frosty

Figure 3.3 A Stage Box Scene: Mrs Bruin, Miss Chienne, Miss Renard, *1 January 1787, publ. by J. Wicksteed, hand-coloured aquatint, 18.5 × 20.7 cm, Courtesy of the Lewis Walpole Library, Yale University.*

months of the year, often featured in seasonal personifications of winter, muffs held a more explicit corporeal connotation. Scholarship has often highlighted the concerns surrounding the fur muff's association with women's sexuality. In mid-century novels, including Henry Fielding's *Tom Jones* (1749) and Samuel Richardson's *Clarissa* (1748), the fur muff features as a device signalling the female heroine's sexuality, and is used to channel the male protagonist's erotic desires.[18] On the painted canvas, fur muffs became increasingly popular in portraits of actresses of the London stage, further muddying their ambiguous and sexually charged reputation.[19] As early as 1699, the term 'muff' was recognized as slang for female genitalia, defined as 'a Woman's Secrets', and later, in Francis Grose's 1785

Figure 3.4 *A Man Millener: The Muff, 16 February 1787, publ. by S. W. Fores, etching with stipple, 26.2 × 39.3 cm, Courtesy of the Lewis Walpole Library, Yale University.*

A Classical Dictionary of the Vulgar Tongue, as 'the private parts of a woman'.[20] This metonymical substitution was underlined by the muff's cylindrical construction and fur exterior, as fur itself was fetishized.[21] Notably, John Cleland played upon the visual and material similarity between fur and women's pubic hair in his salacious 1748 *Memoirs of A Woman of Pleasure*. Through a crack in a wall, Cleland's protagonist, Fanny Hill, gazes on a fellow sex worker, Polly, as her client 'stole … the shift off the girl', leaving her 'standing stark-naked'.[22] As Fanny eyes Polly's naked body, she describes Polly's *mons pubis*: 'the curling hair that overspread its delightful front, cloathed [sic.] it with the richest sable fur in the universe'.[23] Cleland's use of fur as a metaphor within the sexualized and voyeuristic scene translates to the fur muff's portrayal in graphic satires, the most explicit being *The Virgin Unmasked*.

The Virgin Unmasked, published after 16 June 1786, presents a half-dressed and half-naked woman (Figure 3.5).[24] The left side of her body is fully clothed in all the puffery of the pouter silhouette; her right side is naked, revealing her emaciated and grotesque body usually hidden beneath the artifices of fashion. In addition to her teased and feathered hair, a large handkerchief and protruding bum, she holds a fur muff over her hips, the fur muff covering her *muff* beneath. On closer inspection of the

Figure 3.5 The Virgin Unmasked, c. *1768, publ. by S. W. Fores, etching and engraving, 22 × 15 cm, Courtesy of the Lewis Walpole Library, Yale University.*

print, the outline of her inner thigh, hipbone and pubic hair become visible. An un-censored earlier version, once owned by the royal family and never discussed in previous scholarship, survives in the Library of Congress and retains its publisher's line in full, identifying S. W. Fores as the publisher and 16 June 1786 as the date of publication (Figure 3.6).[25] In this version, the woman's genitalia are, like the rest of the right side of her body, laid bare for the viewer. The unclothed half of the woman's body

Figure 3.6 The Virgin Unmasked, *16 June 1786, publ. by S. W. Fores, hand-coloured etching, 24 × 17 cm, Courtesy of the Library of Congress, Washington, D.C.*

reveals her torso, leg and pelvis, including her pubic hair, which is only partially covered by her right hand for modesty. Her hand was seemingly deemed not enough, and the plate was re-etched to extend the muff, the texture of the fur attempting to conceal the original design. This explicit depiction, in which the satirist portrays the outline of the woman's *mons pubis* just beneath her fingers, is perhaps the most overt visual articulation connecting the fur muff with a woman's genitalia produced in the late eighteenth century, leaving no doubt of the muff's loaded connotations.

Satirical prints, like *The Virgin Unmasked* and *The Muff and the Man Millener*, were printed, displayed and sold amidst the bustle of commerce, fashion and politics of London's West End. The fashionable location of Fores's printshop at 3 Piccadilly, near Hay Market, which later moved to 55 Piccadilly in 1795, was only surpassed by fellow printseller Hannah Humphrey, who in 1797 relocated her printshop from New Bond Street to St. James's Street itself.[26] Producers of fashion satires, like Fores, were not isolated from the people or garments they satirized, but amongst them. Eager onlookers scouted for their delineations on the printed pages of satirical prints that hung in printshop windows, where their display was part of a symbiotic relationship between print and fashion (Figure 3.7). Printshops were simultaneously sources of fashionable knowledge and fashionable commentary.[27]

Figure 3.7 *J. Elwood, 1790, drawing on paper, 37.4 × 53.1 cm, British Museum, London.*

Prints and fashion were each rapidly produced: mantuamakers could make a gown in a day and publishers could transform a drawing into an engraved print ready to be sold overnight.[28] This rapid turnaround enabled quick responses and adaptations of dress and prints alike within the streets of the West End, where printshop, maker and customer were housed side by side. The proximity of the fashionable to the satirical is especially close in the case of the fur muff and man milliner.

The fur muff business

The fur muff's metonymic associations did little to impede its fashionability, reaching a socially and geographically broader demographic than previous centuries.[29] Fur muffs were advertised in newspapers as far as the *Calcutta Gazette* and a steady supply of fur, feather and silk muffs were readily imported to and made up by colonial milliners.[30] In London, the centre of the sartorial trades for luxury accessories, and in the capital's West End, milliners and furriers offered their clients an extensive range of fur muffs.[31] Just a few streets away from Fores's printshop, we find the man milliner not an object of cultural apprehensions and ridicule personified in the literary and satirical tropes, but firmly rooted within the sartorial trades, whose commercial history would feature all the highs and lows of eighteenth-century business. Two firms, the first at 44 Wigmore Street, Cavendish Square and the second at 89 Pall Mall, share an entwined saga of formed and dissolved partnerships, shoplifting, bankruptcies, seizure of goods, royal warrants of appointment and even convictions of treason. The first, James Harshorn, milliner and haberdasher, began his business in June 1778, selling 'a new and genteel assortment of every thing that is fashionable in millinery' at 44 Wigmore St, a premise he would occupy until he sold his business in 1790.[32] In March 1779, he partnered with Robert Dyde and the pair sold millinery by the season, including 'all sorts of fur trimmings, muffs, &c'.[33] Over the course of their six-year partnership, their business expanded to include numerous locations including at the assembly rooms at Southampton, Brighthelmstone, the Circus at Bath, and 89 Pall Mall. Though they continued to sell an assortment of millinery over the spring and summer months, their business became increasingly focused on fur and fur muffs. When their partnership dissolved on 5 November 1785, each tradesman was identified as a fur merchant, rather than a milliner. While Harshorn remained at 44 Wigmore Street, Robert Dyde continued to sell at 89 Pall Mall, joining up with a new partner Achilles Scribe in 1787, and later a third partner John Playter in 1788. After a tumultuous end of their business, Dyde and Scribe was sold and the premise and stock were bought by Harding and Co., taking over 89 Pall Mall in 1797. Harding and Co. would continue trading in a wide variety of millinery and fancies until 1820, their shop interior captured for the ages in *Ackermann's Repository* in 1809 (Figure 3.8).

Both outfitters increased their footholds in the fur muff business over the course of the 1780s. New fur muffs were advertised in October and were offered alongside services for last season's muffs to be cleaned, repaired and 'enlarged, agreeable to the present fashion', with clients urged 'to get them

Figure 3.8 *'Inside view of Messrs. Harding, Howell & Co. 89 Pall Mall'* in Rudolph Ackermann's The Repository of Arts, Literature, Commerce, Manufactures, Fashions, and Politics, *1809, British Library, London, UK © British Library Board. All Rights Reserved/Bridgeman Images.*

done before the season commences'.³⁴ Customers were able to purchase muffs through an agent, by correspondence or in person. Hartshorn and Dyde enticed potential clientele through assurances of their effective sales practices and comfortable retail spaces, their retail tactics reflecting the increased prioritization of the activity of shopping.³⁵ They noted their quick 'punctuality and dispatch' of ordered stock and described their shop interior at 89 Pall Mall as 'particularly warm, and in detached rooms, and … stocked with the very best manufactured goods of every kind they deal in, and are in every respect calculated to accommodate Ladies of the first distinction'.³⁶ Both firms sold fur muffs from an extensive range of furs from around the globe. In an advertisement for 'the Curious in Furrs', Hartshorn informed the ladies that 'he has imported a quantity of rare and valuable Furrs, among which are some real Silver, Bear, and natural spotted Lynx', as well as 'an extensive assortment of black, brown, and grey Bear; Siberia and Canada Foxes, Hares, &c. from eight shillings to Three Guineas, made large and handsome, but in style of lightness and elegance, not equalled by any other Furrier in the kingdom', assuring his clients that 'every article in the Furr branch is manufactured in [his] own House'.³⁷ In the adjacent column of the newspaper, his competitor Dyde and Scribe offered their clients a similarly exhaustive variety. Their customers ranged from a Mrs Turner, who bought a 'Fine Fox Muff' for two pounds, twelve shillings and six pence from Hartshorn & Dyde on 25 January 1783, to the Prince of Wales and the Duke and Duchess of York.[38] On 8 March 1786, Dyde, Scribe & Playter sent a bill to the Prince of Wales, the future George IV, for 'a fine Ourson Muff', or bear cub muff, for eight pounds and eight shillings and 'an Elegant extra size neck Fox Muff stuff'd with Eider Down' for thirty-five pounds.[39] The enormous cost of the fox fur muff was due to its plentiful size and type of fur; for comparison, a Wedgewood Portland vase cost thirty guineas, or thirty-one and a half pounds. Selling muffs to the top of society, Dyde and Scribe was one of the most successful millinery and fur merchants in London, their name outshining and outliving Harthorn's.[40] Even after the dramatic end to their business in 1796 when they were accused of treason for exporting goods to France in the midst of the War of the First Coalition (1792–7), customers still referred to the occupants of 89 Pall Mall as Dyde and Scribe long after the shop had changed hands.[41]

The fur muff business was booming in the 1780s. Fur muffs were not only popular, but an essential element of the fashionable wardrobe and milliners shaped their businesses to accommodate and feature them. However, despite the extensive record of fur muff businesses both in the printed press as well as in surviving business accounts, and the fur muff's prolific presence in painted portraiture and graphic satire, nearly no material examples of these garments survive.[42] Extant examples of fur muffs dating before 1800 are incredibly rare.[43] In the age of sartorial recycling, along with their material susceptibility, it is of little surprise so few fur muffs survive. Fur is especially vulnerable to pests and decay, and due to its value, was likely to be reused, re-worn or sold by relatives and descendants. It is perhaps ironic that the muffs that survive so plentifully in the visual and written record survive so poorly in museum collections whereas those that survive fairly abundantly in material form are often absent from the cannon of eighteenth-century dress history: the silk muff.

Mediums of expression: Embroidered and satin print muffs

Silk muffs had been in circulation since the seventeenth century.[44] Unlike fur's three-dimensional, movable texture, the flat surface of silk allowed for ornamentation and muffs from the seventeenth and early eighteenth century are heavily adorned. By the late eighteenth century, silk muffs were decorated with embroidery or satin prints, printed images on silk often in an oval or medallion shape. Working silk muffs with embroidered floral patterns or satin prints made them a more personalized accessory than one made of feathers or fur. Silk muffs could be made more easily at home, and were often sewn by the hands of the wearer. Since Rosika Parker's intervention in the study of embroidery sparked a reconsideration and revaluation of needlework and other 'domestic arts', scholarship has positioned embroidery as both a gendered practice as well as a means of self-expression and a material embodiment of selfhood.[45] In the embroidered silk muff, we find a space of haptic, social and emotional engagement that encompassed the muff's lifecycle, spanning its inception, making and wear. Silk muffs offered women both a repository for emotional connections and a creative medium of display, a position reinforced through the practice of satin prints, where the silk muff transformed into a portable canvas.

'Quick in Love with it': Embroidering muffs

On 7 February 1781, Frances Mabel Sparrow wrote a letter from her aunt and uncle's farmhouse in Spath, a small hamlet in Staffordshire, to her cousin, Henrietta Whitmore (later Pennington), affectionately addressed Henny for short, in Kensington Gravel Pits at the edge of the gardens of Kensington Palace. She employed her cousin:

> Pray are you a great Workwoman & what is your favorite employment? I have just learnt Embroidery & am quick in Love with it; but to my great Mortification I cannot get any patterns in [this] country properly … shaded so as [to] give me any instructions in that particular; If any such things sho'd fall in your way, either small natural sprigs fit for a Gown, or the pattern of a Muff &c &c I sho'd esteem it as a favor if you procure them for me; as any thing of that kind is now become valuable to me; & I will thankfully remit to you what ever they cost; but would not wish to go to any great expence.[46]

This brief letter, written during a period of youth and learning in Sparrow's life, highlights the significance attached to the practice of needlework. It demonstrates the relationship Sparrow and her cousin shared through their common 'employment' of embroidery, specifically embroidering muffs. The relationship fostered through their correspondence functioned on numerous levels. Practically, it offered Sparrow a means of procurement of supplies and patterns from the metropolis. Didactically, it acted as a channel of communication, learning and news, where Sparrow could seek her older cousin's advice and opinions. And personally, it presented a commonality and token of connection, the produced muff acting as a physical reminder of their friendship symbolically bridging the distance between London and Spath, 120 miles north of the capital.

Acquiring patterns

Having 'just learnt Embroidery', Sparrow's request for patterns from her cousin, whom she esteemed 'a great Workwoman', or embroiderer, is emblematic of her aspiring didactic progression. She seeks her cousin's guidance and procurement of embroidery patterns to improve her needlework skills with increasingly difficult designs, specifically asking for a pattern where she can improve her shading. Needlework on samplers and small garments formed an elemental part of feminine education.[47] The muff's manageable size lent it to be a stepping-stone in a girl's development of learning embroidery, easily worked on in company and more manageable and less valuable than handling yards of fabric for a gown.[48] Unlike pockets, whose placement beneath the gown and petticoat enabled them to act as more forgiving epistemological spaces for practice and mistakes, hidden away from scrupulous eyes, muffs were carried about the hands.[49] Sparrow's specific request for a pattern for a muff suggests that when she wrote to her cousin she had reached a level of confidence in her skills that she wanted to incorporate her work into her visible wardrobe.

Sparrow and Whitmore had already established an epistolary conduit of shared sartorial knowledge.[50] Sparrow's wish for her cousin to send patterns from London to her in rural Spath is one of a number of requests for fashionable news from the capital, and her new skill forms a common topic of conversation between the cousins.[51] Sparrow mentions previously sent patterns before expressing her new fondness for embroidery, writing to her cousin, 'Be so good when you write next as to let me know what I am endebted to you for the two patterns you were so good as to procure for me & I will take care to remit you the money.'[52] By intrusting the selection of patterns to her cousin, Sparrow positioned her cousin in the role of instructor, who would guide her progression regarding the level of difficulty and complexity in the patterns she selected. Whitmore's greater experience as an embroider was coupled with her access to embroidery patterns in London shops, as well as her perceived access to the source of fashion itself: the beau monde. On 7 October 1777, Sparrow writes '[I] expect when you are once again got amongst the beau monde [to hear] something of the fashions'.[53] Whitmore's alleged access to the 'people of fashion' gave her credibility in her cousin's eyes as a font of fashionable knowledge, insuring that the patterns she selected were both technically challenging, but also in the latest mode.[54]

Various channels facilitated the dissemination and acquisition of embroidery patterns, which connected Whitmore to her cousin in the country, and London to its rural and colonial outposts.[55] In the capital, hand-drawn embroidery patterns could be purchased from professional embroiders, such as William Roome, 'Embroider to the Royal Family', at 68 Pall Mall. On 4 December 1786, he advertised in the *Daily Universal Register*: 'Ladies supplied with all sorts of materials, &c. for embroidery, and all sorts of patterns drawn,' in addition to finished embroidered muffs, 'Ladies Muffs, in great variety, richly embroidered in shneels, gold, &c.'.[56] However, over the course of the eighteenth century, embroidery patterns were increasingly printed. As this book argues, print culture formed an active source of fashionable knowledge. Unlike fashion plates, which offered their viewers visual suggestions of fashionability, patterns were a form of fashion that could be held in the hand, interpreted and transcribed into dress. Printed patterns had been circulated through pattern books since the sixteenth century and could be acquired from circulating libraries and bookshops.[57] Botanical pattern books, like Augustin Heckle's *Bowles's Drawing Book for Ladies; or Complete Florist: Being An Extensive and Curious Collection of the most Beautiful Flowers, All Drawn after Nature by A. Heckle. With A short*

Introduction to Drawing, and Directions for Mixing and Using of Colours. Also Several Proper and Easy Examples. The Whole adapted for the Improvement of Ladies in Needle-work (1785), specifically promoted their designs' suitability for needlework. By the late eighteenth century, printed patterns, which could be used for a variety of applications, became progressively more specialized.[58] While early modern pattern books were passed generation to generation, in the 1770s and 1780s, individual patterns for embroidery became one of the first iterations of 'fast fashion', produced, printed and distributed monthly in magazines.[59]

For those without a cousin in Kensington to provide them with the latest fashions, monthly serials, in particular *The Lady's Magazine, or Entertaining Companion for the Fair Sex* (1770–1832), offered their readers serialized novels, news, entertainment and most importantly, fashionable intelligence. In addition to the illustrated plates, songs, broadsides and sporadic fashion plates, *The Lady's Magazine* included 'the most elegant patterns for the Tambour, Embroidery, or every kind of Needlework' each month for an expansive range of dress and home accessories.[60] *The Lady's Magazine* published roughly 650 embroidery patterns over the course of its publication.[61] Though *The Lady's Magazine* was the most consistent in its monthly inclusion of embroidery patterns, patterns were also published in the *New Lady's Magazine; or, Polite and Entertaining Companion for the Fair Sex* (1786–95), *Walker's Hibernian Magazine,* and even in newspapers like the *London Evening Post*.[62] London printsellers, like Robert Sayer and Carrington Bowles, also sold patterns in catalogues or sets of individual sheets, offering women an array of published options.[63] As Davida Tenenbaum Deutsch has demonstrated, the consumption of these patterns was not geographically limited to Great Britain, but like other forms of fashion dissemination, extended to colonial American markets.[64] Women on both sides of the Atlantic increasingly purchased and used published embroidery patterns to update their apparel with an element of the current fashion, as it was easier and more cost-effective to make up an accessory than a new gown.[65] As Jennie Batchelor and Chloe Wigston Smith have argued, embroidery patterns transcended from the printed page into the wardrobes of the magazine's readers, forming a tactile bridge over which women could touch, transfer and make fashion.[66] Printed seasonally in October, November, December or January, *The Lady's Magazine* published twelve patterns for muffs between 1770 and 1800: the earliest in 1775 and the latest in 1794. Between 1783 and 1786, patterns for muffs were printed each winter, reflecting the pervasiveness of silk muffs in the 1780s. Yet despite the plethora of published patterns available to the eighteenth-century maker, relatively few survive today.[67]

Surviving patterns demonstrate a range of designs, motifs and levels of intricacy that when viewed with surviving artefacts highlight the personal relationship between an embroiderer, her pattern and her finished muff. A pattern for an 'Elegant Pattern for a Fashionable Muff or Work Bag', published in the July 1786 edition of *Walker's Hibernian Magazine, or Compendium of Entertaining Knowledge*, depicts a densely populated cluster of roses, buds and leaves, surrounded by a scalloped border of peacock feathers (Figure 3.9).[68] A spray of flowers within an oval or circular border became one of the most popular designs the 1780s.[69] Like Sparrow's request, the pattern offers its maker complex shading and intricately, delicate motifs of both the central arrangement and the detailing of the feathers. In comparison, an earlier pattern in *The Lady's Magazine, or Entertaining Companion for the Fair Sex*, published in December 1779, offers more simplistic motifs of singular undulating stems with small leaves and buds with complexity in the design's delineation (Figure 3.10).[70] The disparities in these patterns allow for varying levels of skill and technique of the maker, as well as her taste and desired level of ornamentation. While neither the patterns Sparrow received nor the muff she may have produced survives, numerous extant silk muffs demonstrate the breadth of decorative production of maker's hands.

Figure 3.9 *'Elegant Pattern for a Fashionable Muff or Work Bag,'* Walker's Hibernian Magazine, or Compendium of Entertaining Knowledge, *July 1786, From the New York Public Library, New York.*

Figure 3.10 *'A Pattern for a Lady's Muff,'* The Lady's Magazine, or Entertaining Companion for the Fair Sex, *December 1779, Bavarian State Library, Munich.*

Sprigs, spangles and silk

Unlike fur muffs, several silk muffs survive in museum collections. The construction of silk muffs is fairly consistent. The cylindrical silk exterior formed from a rectangular piece of silk was padded with wool batting or down, and could be either closed with a drawstring casing or finished squarely.[71] Sometimes a small pocket was included within the lining, enabling women to store and conceal small objects in their muffs.[72] Variation of silk muffs occurs in their exterior decoration. Though, like fur muffs, a silk muff could be enlarged, for a change in fashion, the exterior of the muff would be changed and a new muff made.[73] The silk could be embroidered with silk thread, chenille or ribbon. Floral motifs were the most common, including sprigs, flowers, buds and chains of leaves. Designs were accented with spangles, beads or seed pearls. Oversized bows often flank the openings along with added trim work in fur, pleated ribbon or lace, like Figure 3.11. The exterior silk of a muff from the 1770s is a pink plain weave with weft patterning, giving the surface of the silk a ribbed texture (Figure 3.11).[74] The openings of the muff are gathered, accented with long, dangling pink taffeta bows, and edged with linen lace trim. Undulating chains of buds, leaves and flowers entwined with ribbon garlands diagonally cross the surface of the muff. The pattern alternates between chains of buds and chains

Figure 3.11 *Silk plain weave muff with silk embroidery, 1770s, silk plain weave embroidery, silk taffeta ribbon and linen lace trim, Acc. No. M.2007.211.136, Los Angeles County Museum of Art, Los Angeles, photo © Museum Associates/LACMA.*

of blooming flowers overlapping with alternating green, brown and pink ribbons and bows. Minute silk thread chain stitches form the green vines, while the ribbon garlands, flower petals and leaves are formed using ribbonwork.[75] Ribbonwork was less demanding than threadwork; using an ombré-woven ribbon provided shading and depth of colour in each stitch. Beneath the ribbonwork, pencil marks peek through where the placement of the needle did not align with the transfer (Figure 3.12). The angular pencil marks behind the petals suggest that the pattern selected was most likely intended for threadwork, which could form more intricate designs and accurate shapes, and demonstrates the choice, individualism and skill of the muff's maker.

By considering the material detail of her stitches, we can begin to place the needle back in the maker's hand. The praxis of needlework is founded in a kinetic relationship between the fingers, needle, thread and fabric, where 'bodily knowledge is as important, if not more so, than vision and cognitive knowledge in embroidery – the feel of the fabric, thread, and needle, as well as the movement of the hand, require a kinetic familiarity'.[76] In the execution of each stitch, we witness the maker's haptic familiarity with her materials and the means of executing her designs, what Serena Dyer and Chloe Wigston Smith have coined her 'material literacy'.[77] The ability of a maker's hands along with her material choices results in innumerable potential variations. As Jennifer Wearden has aptly described:

> Given technical ability, the effects that can be created through embroidery are almost limitless. While each stitch or group of stitches have their own qualities and characteristics, it is the embroiderer's ability to select and exploit them that will transform a plain piece of fabric into a pleasing and unique work of art. The power to perform magic with a needle comes through the embroiderer's familiarity with stitches: with their structure, with hand movements required to make them and with their seemingly infinite variation.[78]

Figure 3.12 *Detail of silk plain weave muff with silk embroidery, 1770s, silk plain weave embroidery, silk taffeta ribbon and linen lace trim, Acc. No. M.2007.211.136, Los Angeles County Museum of Art, Los Angeles, photo © Museum Associates/LACMA.*

Though the undulating diagonal floral design of this muff was most likely traced or adapted from a pattern similar to the 1779 *Lady's Magazine* design, no two muffs would have been exactly alike, even from the same maker's hands.[79]

A second worked muff made in the 1780s bares many of the same material signatures of the first, including its ribbon-work embroidery, pink taffeta bows and linen lace trim (Figure 3.13).[80] The face of plain silk features a central wreath of ribbon-work laurel leaves around a posy of rose buds. The circle of laurel leaves is hung like a medallion from a purple and yellow-stripped, ribbon-work bow at the top of the muff and is encircled with small sprays of rosebuds and bluebells. The advancement of the maker's technical ability is seen both in her attention to detail as well as the intricacy of her execution. For example, the maker employs an ombré ribbon for the exterior leaves of the laurel wreath, but a solid green ribbon for the interior leaves. The brown and green leaves of the roses also vary in colour, giving a more naturalistic impression. Her technical improvement and advanced level of difficulty are also seen in the execution of the rosebuds and stems. The stems of the rosebuds include thread-work thorns and the flowers of her rosebuds overlay and incorporate both threadwork and ribbonwork to create more complex, if somewhat prickly, flowers. Her pencil marks are still discernible beneath some of the laurel leaves and under one of sprays of flowers, the drawn outline of a bluebell is entirely visible, where, upon sewing, she has ignored the drawn design and shifted the position and orientation of the overlapping bluebell (Figure 3.14). A figurative inversion to Sparrow's

Figure 3.13 *Silk plain weave muff with silk plain weave ribbon embroidery, 1780s, silk embroidery, silk satin ribbon, and linen lace, Acc. No. M.2007.211.137, Los Angeles County Museum of Art, Los Angeles, photo © Museum Associates/LACMA.*

Figure 3.14 *Detail of silk plain weave muff with silk plain weave ribbon embroidery, 1780s, silk embroidery, silk satin ribbon, and linen lace, Acc. No. M.2007.211.137, Los Angeles County Museum of Art, Los Angeles, photo © Museum Associates/LACMA.*

letters, here the identity of the maker has been lost, but her material output survives. Her material identity endures in her distinct choice of fabrics, colour, technique and alterations of the designs.[81]

Stitching meaning

The selection of colour and stitch executed could far surpass the technical ability of the maker. Instead, these aesthetic choices signified a creative and artistic expression, which allowed the maker to imbue and assign meaning and sentiment to the piece they produced. These weighted practices, in which needlework provided its maker 'a space in which to stitch not only a seam but also a self', are particularly evident when the pattern was also of the maker's own design.[82] This symbolic and artistic investment is evident in the correspondence of Sparrow's aunt's aunt, Mary Delany (1700–88, née Granville). Though best known for her shellwork and paper flowers, Delany's embroidery practice foreshadows the bond shared between Sparrow and Pennington.[83] Her surviving correspondence illustrates both the significance she placed on designing her own work as well as the symbolic meaning she imbued into her pieces.[84] Nearly fifty years before Sparrow sought instruction from her cousin, Delany wrote to her younger sister, Anne Granville (1707–61, later D'Ewes), 'The work I design sending you is some I have ready drawn, but it must not be traced – traced work is very ugly, and quite out of fashion.'[85] Instead, she urges her sister to take artistic risks and experiment rather than copy, 'You that have a knowledge of shading cannot be at a loss, and if you should spoil a bit of canvass, what does it signify.'[86] Like Pennington, Delany took on a didactic role with her sister, who was seven years younger, and embroidery formed a common thread in their correspondence.

This shared interest and sororal bond was manifested through the production of an embroidered muff. In a letter to Granville in 1733, Delany writes 'I have made up my green muff, and it looks very pretty; Lady W. [Lady Weymouth] liked it prodigiously, but I could not make her a compliment of it because it is a counterpart of yours, and sort of emblem of you and me, and so I must cherish it.'[87] These brief lines illuminate the personal sentiment that could be physically worked into an embroidered muff.[88] Her fleeting consideration of gifting it to Lady Weymouth illustrates 'the frequency with which female handicrafts were given as gifts [and] suggests both the prestige put upon them and the power they had to connect women'.[89] Yet, Delany implies that the muff is one of a pair, 'a counterpart of yours', making it unsuitable to be given to another friend. Her identification of the muff as 'a sort of emblem of you and me' highlights the personal significance that clothing which was shared between friends or sisters could assume and embody. The embroidered muff had become 'a mediator' between Delany and her sister, a material bond figuratively stitched with meaning and memory.[90] While neither the muff nor designs for its embroidery survive, the haptic process was emblematic of a kindred relationship embedded into the embroidered surface of the muff, one which Delany would 'cherish' in her hands long after the last stitch was sewn.[91]

Delany's remarks about self-designing patterns and the social connections those patterns could symbolize situate the embroidered silk muff as both a receptacle for haptic meaning and a silk canvas for artistic display. While Sparrow and Delany's correspondence demonstrates the personal and sentimental motivations intertwined in embroidering muffs, a rare portrayal of an embroidered silk muff survives in the hands of Mary Huddesford (1743–1819, née Edwards), wife of satirical poet and amateur artist George Huddesford (1749–1809), in her portrait by the circle of Sir Joshua Reynolds (Figure 3.15). Huddesford is depicted in half-length, her head turned slightly outward as she gazes pensively into a middle distance. Around her shoulders, she wears a hooded cape made of cream silk

Figure 3.15 *Circle of Sir Joshua Reynolds,* Mrs. Huddesford, *c. 1778, oil on canvas, 75.3 × 65.5 cm, Private Collection Photo © Christie's Images/Bridgeman Images.*

and trimmed in brown fur. Beneath the soft folds of silk of her cape, her hands are encased within a cream silk muff, embroidered with a serpentine line of green vines and six pink rosebuds. While fur and feather muffs frequently appeared in women's portraiture, this portrait is a singular example of an embroidered silk muff. Though no records survive detailing Huddesford's wardrobe, the muff she wears in her portrait aligns with the linear order and spacing characteristic of 1770s patterns, like the December 1779 *Lady's Magazine* pattern. When worn in a portrait, the surface of the silk muff transitions from a space of inward employment to outward projection. Transforming into a canvas within a canvas, the silk muff becomes a vehicle for display of the artistic expression of the maker's hands. This promotion of artistic representation was realized in a second type of decoration, the satin print, which transformed the silk muff into a portable frame.

Wearing satin prints

The silk muff was a medium on which to display the haptic talents of its maker and wearer. However, the muff's role as a canvas for visual display becomes deliberate with the production and application of satin prints in the early 1780s. Echoing the style of embroidered neoclassical medallion motifs, satin prints were copperplate printed silk pictures, engraved in stipple. They were cut to size and sewn onto articles of dress or home accessories.[92] Within the history and development of printed textiles they play a minor, and often overlooked, role. Overshadowed by the inventions and mechanization of calico-printing that transformed the textile industry and the structure of late eighteenth-century society, stipple prints on silk are a drop in the ocean of industrialization.[93] As Mary Schoeser has demonstrated, the origin of copperplate printed cottons lay in copperplate printed silks from the seventeenth century, invented by commercially astute London mapmakers whose access to copperplates allowed for experimentation and the production of colour-fast printed silk maps, handkerchiefs and small accessories, like gloves.[94] By the early 1780s, when the race for printed calicos was well underway, a second set of intrepid printmakers again began to experiment, not chasing industrialization, but producing a more specialized adornment that directly intersected fashion and print.[95]

Returning to the engraving of 'The Modern Venus', at the centre of her fur muff is an atypical amalgamation of materials: a satin print has been sewn onto the fur, the stitches visibly delineated in the etching (Figure 3.16).[96] The author notes that the modern Venus's muff often 'bares on its front some pretty picture or device, not infrequently the portrait of her Hercules in waiting'.[97] However, the satin print does not depict her Herculean love, but a seated woman wearing loose drapery with long hair hanging down over her shoulders.[98] Though the depiction at first appears to be illustrating for the reader the idealized woman to whom the modern Venus is compared, classicized women are frequently the subjects of satin print muffs. While the combination of a satin print on a fur muff survives only in printed representation, on extant silk muffs, the fashion for satin prints can be marked as short-lived, yet pervasive, transforming the muff into a portable frame.[99]

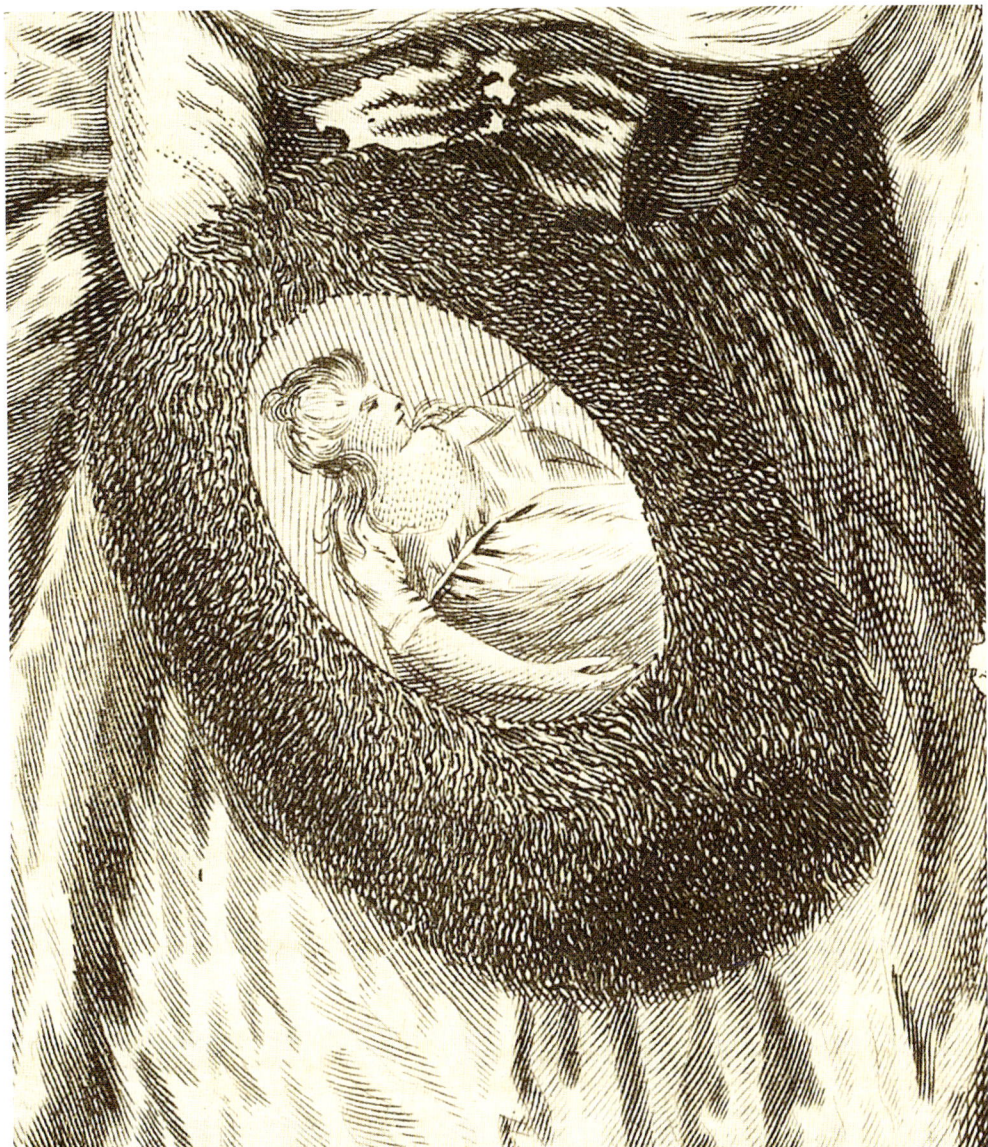

Figure 3.16 *Detail of 'The Modern Venus',* Walker's Hibernian Magazine, or, Compendium of Entertaining Knowledge, *March 1786, This image is reproduced courtesy of the National Library of Ireland [J 05].*

Satin print muffs

Three silk muffs survive in the Museum of Fine Arts, Boston, each featuring a satin print as their central decorative element. The first muff is made of a cream satin exterior with drawstring casings closing each opening and lined with plain silk, similar in construction to a green silk muff (Figure 3.17 and 3.18).[100] The third muff of cream silk satin also features gathered openings and is lined with silk (Figure 3.19).[101] However, it is the most stylistically complex of the three, with pleated silk ribbons

Figure 3.17 *Silk satin muff with silk mezzotint, silk embroidery, pearls, gauze appliques and silk plain-weave lining, 1782–1800, Acc. No. 43.1820, Photograph © [2023] Museum of Fine Arts, Boston.*

Figure 3.18 *Silk satin muff with mezzotint medallion, spangles, foil embroidery and silk plain-weave lining, 1781–1800, Acc. No. 43.1823, Photograph © [2023] Museum of Fine Arts, Boston.*

Figure 3.19 *Silk satin muff with mezzotint medallion, silk embroidery, beads, and silk, plain-weave lining, 1781–1800, Acc. No. 43.1820, Photograph © [2023] Museum of Fine Arts, Boston.*

forming a decorative edging next to the gathered openings. Apart from Figure 3.20, on which an oval floral chain of pink and white gauze flowers, buds and ribbon bows has been worked, these muffs have little to no silk thread embroidery (Figure 3.20). Instead, they feature beading, spangles and foil trim. The wreathed chains form concentric frames around the satin prints at the centre of each muff. The decorative borders of beads, spangles and pearls provide a functional as well as aesthetic purpose, hiding the raw edges of the print from view. However, beneath the spangled border of Figure 3.21, two segments of text peak out (Figure 3.21). On the left reads 'Ang. Kauffman inv.' and on the right, 'F. Bartolozzi Sculp.,' revealing that the print was designed by Angelica Kauffman and engraved by Francesco Bartolozzi.

While these printed inscriptions identify the artist and engraver, they do not identify the publisher or title of the print.[102] The figure on the green muff is a young woman in profile, holding a piece of fabric to her breast. Her dress is a combination of classicized drapery and pastoral costume – a loosely draped shift beneath a pair of stays, with a blue shawl over her left arm. The palette of the print is a muted range of blues, greens, pinks and browns – a subdued contrast to bright fuchsia foil leaves and yellow-green satin of the muff. The colour palette is mirrored by the silk medallion on the beaded cream muff, which depicts a young woman, whose curled hair is crowned with a light pink turban (Figure 3.22). In three-quarter view, she points with her left arm out of the frame of the picture, the bend of her elbow meeting the edge of the oval medallion. She is attired in Turkish dress. The long-sleeved, white silk gown, or *gömlek*, is worn beneath a brown, embellished *yeleks*, or waistcoat, and

Figure 3.20 *Detail of silk satin muff with silk mezzotint, silk embroidery, pearls, gauze appliques and silk plain-weave lining, 1782–1800, 23.2 × 41.9 × 1.9 cm, Acc. No. 43.1820, Photograph © [2023] Museum of Fine Arts, Boston.*

belted beneath her breasts with a jewel.[103] The similarities in colour and execution suggest that they are both drawn by Kauffman, engraved by Bartolozzi, and printed by the same publisher.

Corresponding paper engravings confirm these conclusions. William Palmer published *Felicity* and *Sincerity* as a pair on 1 October 1781 (Figures 3.23 and 3.24).[104] Emblematic of Bartolozzi's mastery of stipple engraving, these allegorical prints personify the virtues of felicity and sincerity.[105] Beneath each title are poetic inscriptions from *The Fireside* by Nathanial Cotton and *An Essay on Conversation* by

Figure 3.21 *Detail of silk satin muff with mezzotint medallion, spangles, foil embroidery and silk plain-weave lining, 1781–1800, Acc. No. 43.1823, Photograph © [2023] Museum of Fine Arts, Boston.*

Benjamin Stillingfleet. *Felicity* reads 'If true Felicity we prize, Within our breast this jewel lies.' By the print's publication in 1781, Cotton's poem had been published frequently since its inclusion in Robert Dodsley's 1755 *A Collection of Poems in Four Volumes*, which preached the joys and merits of marriage and motherhood over fashionable life, and had been adapted into sermons and songs.[106] The aptly chosen couplet compliments Kauffman's figure, adding significance to the jewel on her belt. Likewise, the inscription beneath *Sincerity* also illustrates its subject: 'No art she knows, in native whiteness dress'd, Her thoughts all pure, & therefore all express'd.' Taken from Benjamin Stillingfleet's *An Essay on Conversation* (1737), the couplet in the poem describes the 'resistless charms' of Sincerity, which

Figure 3.22 *Detail of silk satin muff with mezzotint medallion, silk embroidery, beads, and silk, plain-weave lining, 1781–1800, Acc. No. 43.1820, Photograph © [2023] Museum of Fine Arts, Boston.*

when read within the context of Kauffman's figure who holds her hand covering her heart, expresses Stillingfleet's desire for Serenity to 'Watch o'er my heart, and all my words attend'.[107] While these inscriptions do not accompany the satin prints on the muffs, their textual, printed popularity and the earlier publication of the paper stipple prints allow for the possibility that an eighteenth-century

Figure 3.23 *Angelica Kauffman,* Felicity, *1 October 1781, publ. by W. Palmer, stipple engraving, 15.3 × 11.3 cm, National Galleries of Scotland, Kenneth Sanderson Bequest 1943.*

audience may have recognized the figures in association with their poetic inscriptions and titles. The publication of the satin engravings was advertised in the *Morning Herald and Daily Advertiser* on 2 December 1782: 'Prints in Colours on Sattin. Just Published, FELICITY and SINCERITY, from Angelica Kauffman. LOVE and HARMONY, LIBERALITY and ADMIRATION, from Cipriani; and

Figure 3.24 *Angelica Kauffman,* Sincerity, *1 October 1781, publ. by W. Palmer, stipple engraving, 27.8 × 19.8 cm, Courtesy of Yale Centre for British Art, Yale University.*

engraved by Mr. Bartolozzi. Price 8s. Published by W. Palmer, No. 159, Strand, London.'[108] William Palmer published both sets of paper and satin prints.

In the third satin print, the young woman is portrayed within a pastoral landscape, almost full-length in semi-classicized dress, with loose drapery attached at the shoulder and a turban draped over her curled hair. Unlike *Felicity* and *Sincerity*, the virtue she personifies is immediately apparent from the lamb on her knee. The corresponding paper print, *Innocence* was published by John Walker on 1 February 1782 (Figure 3.25). The stipple engraving was designed by Kauffman and engraved by Robert Samuel Marcuard. John Walker, 'Carver, Gilder, and Printseller, No. 148 in the Strand', first

Figure 3.25 *Angelica Kauffman,* Innocence, *1 February 1782, publ. by J. Walker, stipple engraving, 23.8 × 17.7 cm, British Museum, London.*

advertised his 'Sattin Prints' in the *Morning Harold and Daily Advertiser* on 14 February 1783: Walker 'respectfully acquaints the Nobility, Gentry and others that he has a large and curious assortment of Prints on Sattin, from Angelica Kauffman, and others; engraved by the best makers, beautifully printed in colours, for lady's muffs, work baskets, watch pieces, screens &', indicating that even though he printed the paper version in February of 1782, he did not begin printing on satin until 1783.[109] Walker's satin prints are regularly advertised, even when his wife Eliza took over the business due to her husband's illness in July 1792.[110] Walker in particular specialized in satin prints after Kauffman, capitalizing on the benefits and appeal of stipple engraving and Kauffman's subject matter to create a new type of printed adornment.[111] Stipple created a soft appearance that imitated chalk drawings through densities of dots on the ground, and, innovatively, could be printed either in a single colour, or coloured prior to printing, as Walker advertises.[112] Like the success of the seventeenth-century London mapmakers, Walker's access to Kauffman's original works and their stipple copperplate counterparts, which could produce more impressions than the more dominant tonal style of engraving, mezzotint, enabled Walker to print interchangeably on paper and silk using the same press.[113] Though prior to 1783, Walker had produced engravings in other styles, including mezzotint, by 1784, he refers to his business as a 'sattin print manufactury', which were produced exclusively in stipple, and offered clients both loose prints to attach, as well as 'a variety of muffs compleat', and 'a large assortment of muffs, completely made up'.[114]

John Walker and William Palmer were not alone in publishing satin prints, nor were they specifically limited to Kauffman's output or for adorning muffs.[115] Two silk screens at the Museum of London feature satin prints engraved by Thomas Burke, Irish stipple specialist and a favourite engraver of Kauffman, and published by James Birchall, whose printshop was located at 473 Strand, near St Martin's Church (Figures 3.26 and 3.27). The pair of screens depicts Lady Una with her protective lion from Edmund Spencer's 1590 epic poem *The Faerie Queene* and the pastoral shepherdess Abra from William Collin's 1742 *Persian Eclogues*. The corresponding paper versions were published on 2 February and 15 July 1783, each accompanied by lines of verse extolling their heroine's innocence and virtue.[116] Around the satin prints, the screens are both embroidered with intricately shaded thread-work flowers, accented with chenille bows, pearls and spangles, blending the use of virtuous, pastoral subjects with floral, stylistic embroidery. Satin prints, however, did not always feature idyllic women. Echoing the observations of the author of 'The Modern Venus', Holland and Peacock advertised a satin print of 'A VERY beautiful Likeness of the Prince of Wales', which the 'Ladies may be desirous of embellishing their muffs with this elegant Portrait'.[117] Other surviving unattached silk prints include pastoral genre scenes, contemporary and classical lovers, and portraits of fashionable women.[118]

In satin prints, we find the printseller not only publishing fashionable commentaries, news or patterns, but fashion itself. However, the fashion for satin prints was relatively brief. We can mark their ephemerality in two adaptations of a calendar mezzotint, *Winter*, published by Sayer and Bennett on 12 May 1785 (Figure 3.28). Typical of calendar mezzotints, the print features a fashionable woman

Figure 3.26 *Silk satin print embroidered screen, 1780s, Acc. No. NN8146, © Museum of London.*

Figure 3.27 *Silk satin print embroidered screen, 1780s, Acc. No. NN8145, © Museum of London.*

Figure 3.28 Winter, *12 May 1785, publ. by R. Sayer and J. Bennett, mezzotint, 35.3 × 25.4 cm, British Museum, London.*

Figure 3.29 Winter, *12 May 1794, publ. by Laurie & Whittle, hand-coloured mezzotint, 35.3 × 25.4 cm, Courtesy of the Lewis Walpole Library, Yale University.*

dressed in a fur trimmed cape and muff, appropriate for the season. Though women with fur muffs often appear as personifications of winter, her muff is made of silk trimmed with fur.[119] On its face is a satin print medallion of a young woman, wearing a matching hat with a coronet and feather as the wearer.[120] The appearance of the satin print muff in the scene attests to its current fashionability as calendars characteristically portray contemporary styles. When the print was republished in 1794, the dress was changed to reflect the current mode, including the muff, which is now portrayed as oversized black fur (Figure 3.29). By the mid-1790s, satin prints were no longer being advertised, and as the alteration of the muff in *Winter* suggests, fashion had moved on and the brief lifespan of the satin print's popularity had begun to wane.[121]

A portable canvas

Satin prints have primarily been associated Angelica Kauffman's artistic output in relation to needlework paintings.[122] While needlework paintings after Kauffman could use satin prints as the underlying pattern, these prints were intended not to be hidden beneath embroidery, but displayed directly on accessories like muffs.[123] For example, in her advertisements of satin prints, Jane White of 39 Tavistock Street, Covent Garden, offers 'a large assortment of new medallions, plain and coloured for screens, muffs, and boxes', as well as satin prints of the seasons specifically 'designed for fans and muff'.[124] The prominence of Kauffman's allegories on satin prints, both in extant artefacts and in published advertisements, suggests not only the preference for Kauffman's work, but also its specific applicability for muffs.[125] Kauffman's allegorical, mythological and pastoral works were particularly suited for textiles, ceramics, decoration and furniture due to their decorative and feminine qualities.[126] The stipple technique, which created soft, tonal images, was considered especially attractive to the female consumer, befitting the depiction of sentiment and emotion.[127] However, the prevalence of allegories in satin prints, particularly the personification of virtues, carries a more direct significance to its wearer beyond simply the call of fashion or feminine consumption.[128] Scholarship surrounding Kauffman's allegorical work has focused primarily on allegorical self-portraiture and the personification of the artistic muses as an expression of feminine creativity within the male-dominated art world; the allegorical personifications of virtues have been largely left untouched.[129] When attached and worn on a muff, Kauffman's personified virtues, like those of Felicity, Sincerity and Innocence, enable the wearer to project a self-selected virtue and transform the muff into a portable medium of display.

When late eighteenth-century women purchased, affixed and wore these idealized representations of the virtues, they were not only participating in a wider trend of classicized motifs in dress that appeared in the early 1780s, but self-fashioning themselves to emit the virtue displayed.[130] An autobiographical depiction of this self-representation is visualized in a watercolour painted by Ann Frankland Lewis (1757–1842) in her *The Dress of the Year 1784* (Figure 3.30 and 3.31).[131] Lewis

Figure 3.30 *Ann Frankland Lewis,* The Dress of the Year 1784, *1784, watercolour on paper, AC1999.154.1-.32, Los Angeles County Museum of Art, Los Angeles.*

Figure 3.31 *Detail of Ann Frankland Lewis,* The Dress of the Year 1784, *1784, watercolour on paper, AC1999.154.1-.32, Los Angeles County Museum of Art, Los Angeles.*

painted thirty-two watercolours between 1774 and 1807, each 'a sartorial self-representation' that chronicles Lewis's life through her relationship with dress and fashion. Each full-length portrayal is a 'microcosmic social, cultural and fashionable time capsule'.[132] Like the 'Modern Venus', a seated woman is depicted in a salmon pink gown and petticoat, high-collared handkerchief and transparent, feathered brimmed hat. Her hands are hidden inside a white silk muff, which displays all the hallmarks of the satin print medallion fashion.[133] Green and purple floral chains flank an oval medallion of a seated classicized figure holding her left hand over her breast and her right arm extended. Though the detail of the watercolour blurs the representation of the satin print, the figure echoes the position and style of Kauffman's personified virtues.[134] The deep blue violets budding on the serpentine garlands suggest that the figure could be a personification of modesty.[135] To the eyes of eighteenth-century viewers, 'a society nurtured in the Classics and accustomed to the conventions of allegory and symbolism', the identification could easily be made.[136] The watercolour is the last phase of the satin print's life cycle. Lewis has selected the print, purchased it, sewn it to the silk, made the muff, worn it and portrayed it. At each stage, her kinetic connection to the print was reinforced, from shopping to sewing to wearing to painting. Not only did Lewis presumably wear her satin print muff, projecting her selected virtue, but she also recorded it for posterity.

Significantly, the medallion is exhibited on the surface of the muff, hung from an embroidered purple bow above. The green garlands act like cords hanging a framed picture on the wall, reinforcing that silk muffs were sites of exhibition. In particular, this medium of wearable dissemination patronized the artwork of Angelica Kauffman. With the choice of satin print, the wearer concurrently voiced her choice of artist, participating in a broader network of female patronage. Angela Rosenthal has demonstrated the mutual channels of patronage between Kauffman and her female sitters, both of particular patrons and groups of creative individuals, arguing that Kauffman's success lay in the cultivation of her female clientele.[137] However, when we consider the incorporation of the wearable, portable and significantly less expensive medium of the satin print, a much wider scope of female patrons becomes visible. While satin prints can be viewed as another facet of the decorative craze for Kauffman's designs, on silk muffs they function as miniature commissions in support of Kauffman's work, distinguished by the haptic and symbolic relationships formed between print, muff, maker and wearer. Worn in public, the muff acted as a portable frame to display Kauffman's work that simultaneously aligned its wearer as a supporter, or even connoisseur of Kauffman's oeuvre. Distinguishing the satin print as an exhibited, wearable work challenges the traditionally gendered attributions of connoisseurship.[138] Though satin prints play a role in the history of women's fashionable consumption, the wearer can be elevated from consumer to public patron. As these muffs were worn throughout the social landscape, their viewing space was not geographically limited to within the interiors of the home, gallery or studio. Instead, due to their portability, reaching as far as the muff was carried, silk muffs acted as one of the most visible manifestations of Kauffman's output, acting as a platform of self-fashioning and patronage.

***

Throughout the eighteenth century, the muff remained a constant feature encircled around, worked on and touched by women's hands. Originally designed to warm the hands of the elite from the winter cold, like other garments discussed in this book, the muff surpassed its intended function. Fur would remain the most popular material for the construction of muffs and the development and expansion of the fur muff business would continue through the end of the century. Fur provided warmth and tactile luxury as well as ample material for playful double entendre for the satirist's pen. However, silk muffs offered women a varied, complex and symbolic medium through which to express artistic creativity, personal sentiment and artistic patronage through embroidery and satin prints.

In the coming century, the silk muff, both embroidered and adorned with satin prints, would be overtaken by the fashion for fur and feathers, like exotic birds of paradise imported from the ever-expanding reaches of the empire.[139] Yet, during the late eighteenth century, silk muffs flourished. Operating beyond the shadow of the satirical gaze, they offered a canvas for women to artistically express and self-fashion themselves, while appreciating and supporting the art of fellow women. The silk muff acted beyond the sartorial expectations of dress and accessories. Instead, it was a means of propelling women into the position of women connoisseurs under the veil of the 'meretricious artificial beauties of a modern Venus'.[140] Sharing an intimate relationship with maker and wearer, the muff embodied one of the most expressive and symbolic agents in a woman's oeuvre.

4

Tight lacing: The motifs and materiality of stays

In an editorial for the *Whitehall Evening Post*, titled the 'The Mutability of Female Fashion' and penned under the pseudonym 'Antique', the author playfully reflected on past and present fashions. Written in May 1796, the author wrote:

> To take the argument *a posteriori* – The Cork Rump was most becoming to a "lathy consistency," and tight lacing also to such; for however nature was oppressed *below*, she found ample amends *above*, by bringing her lovely hemispheres, gently swelling, over the horizon of the tucker, which would otherwise have remained in oblivion beneath it.[1]

Pondering the silhouette of the decades prior, the witty author praises the addition of a cork rump to a woman's posterior, but in particular lauds the effects of tight lacing for its role in displaying and heightening the breast, crediting that the oppression of the waist and torso below enabled the bust to rise above. Nearly twenty years earlier, this push and pull of the body had been visualized in a print published by William Humphrey on 17 January 1778 (Figure 4.1). In *Titus Shapes Figure Frames*, a complex apparatus of pullies, ropes and dowels push, pull and prod the two female subjects' bodies into the burgeoning fashionable figure, their proportions carefully calibrated by a Mr Titus Shapes at the side. Beneath the print, the text jokingly advertises that after only one month of treatment, the subject will no longer require the use of 'Pads, Plumpers, Corks, Tight Stays and Roller'.[2] While posterior effects of rumps and bums have already been addressed in Chapter 2, this final chapter centres on the middle of the body, on the garment around which women's dress in the eighteenth century pivots: stays.

Women's torsos had been supported, shaped and sculpted by structural undergarments since the sixteenth century.[3] Originally termed a pair of bodies and called a pair of stays by the late seventeenth

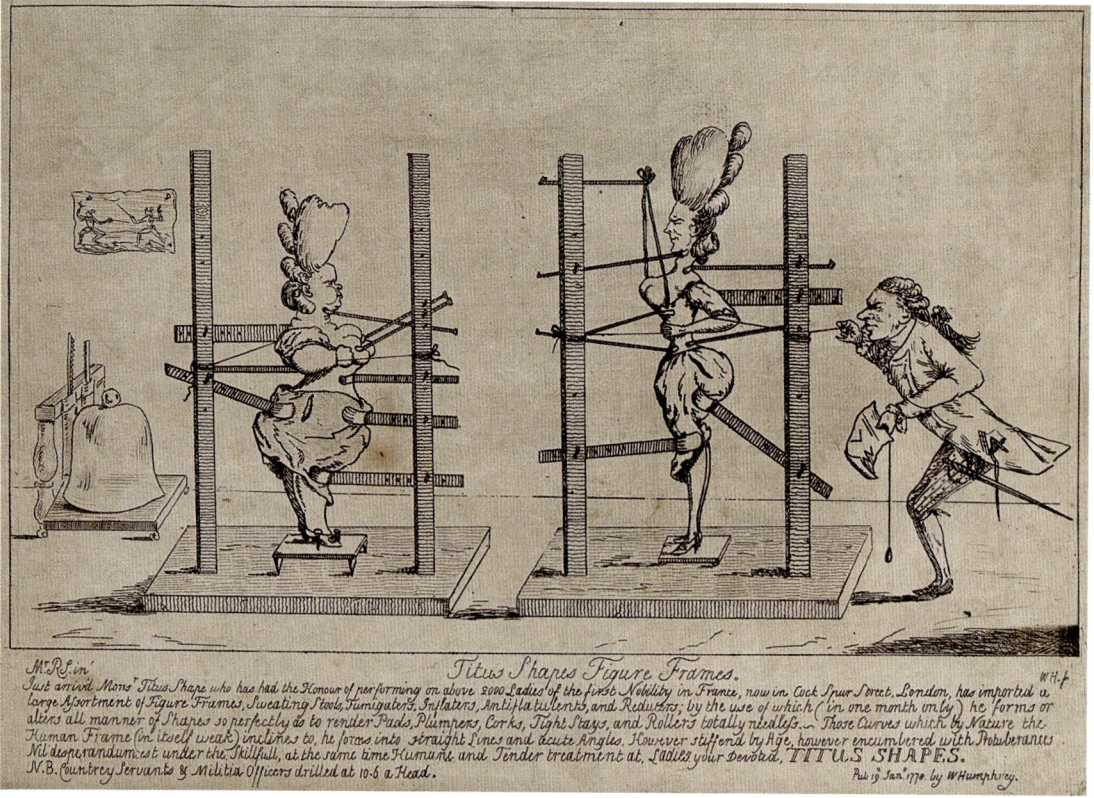

Figure 4.1 Titus Shapes Figure Frames, *19 January 1778, publ. by W. Humphrey, etching, 19.9 × 33.6 cm, Wellcome Collection, London.*

century, and evolving into the better-known term corset in the nineteenth century, stays provided the fundamental framework over which a woman's outer garments were fit, draped and pinned, and were an elementary necessity in women's wardrobes across the strata society.[4] Worn over a linen shift, which formed a launderable barrier between the skin and clothes, stays compressed and lifted the bust and supported the lower back, creating the visible shape of the gown above. Unlike the other garments of this book, which can be designated as fashionable, and thus largely prohibitive to the lower ranks of society, stays were ubiquitous, worn by every woman of every rank from infancy till death, and in some cases, even in effigy.[5]

As John Styles has argued, the lower classes of society were not distinguished by wearing different types of garments, but rather by the quality and quantity of garments they owned, a particularly pertinent sentiment regarding women's stays.[6] While women of the upper ranks had bespoke stays made of silk, linen or wool damask and boned with baleen, spending upwards of two pounds a pair, like Lady Anne Spencer, Countess of Sunderland, those of the lower orders wore stays of twilled canvas or leather.[7] By replacing expensive baleen with reeds, cane or straw stiffened with paste, or using wool or cotton instead of glazed linen or silk, or even forgoing the construction process entirely and using scored leather, stays were accessible for every class of society.[8] One maker of leather stays advertised that 'for Beauty equal, and in Strength and Ease, excel any made of Bone; as they better support the body', selling pairs for only twelve shillings.[9] Poorer women purchased stays second-hand or ready-made and mended, altered and repaired stays to extend their lifespan, like an extensively mended and altered pair of twilled-cotton stays in Manchester (Figure 4.2).[10] The theft of stays was also common, for without the structured support around them, women were classed as sex workers, destitute, criminals or mentally insane.[11] For example, in William Hogarth's *The Rake at Rose Tavern*, the woman in the foreground is identified to the viewer as a fallen woman through her cast off stays, which lie on the floor, the whalebone still retaining shape (Figure 4.3 and 4.4).[12] Throughout the century and across society, stays were the defining garment of the female sex.[13] Yet despite this ubiquitous past, the stay has garnered a narrow reputation, one that is dominated by the practice of tight lacing. This chapter seeks to explore and expose the origins of this iconographic motif.

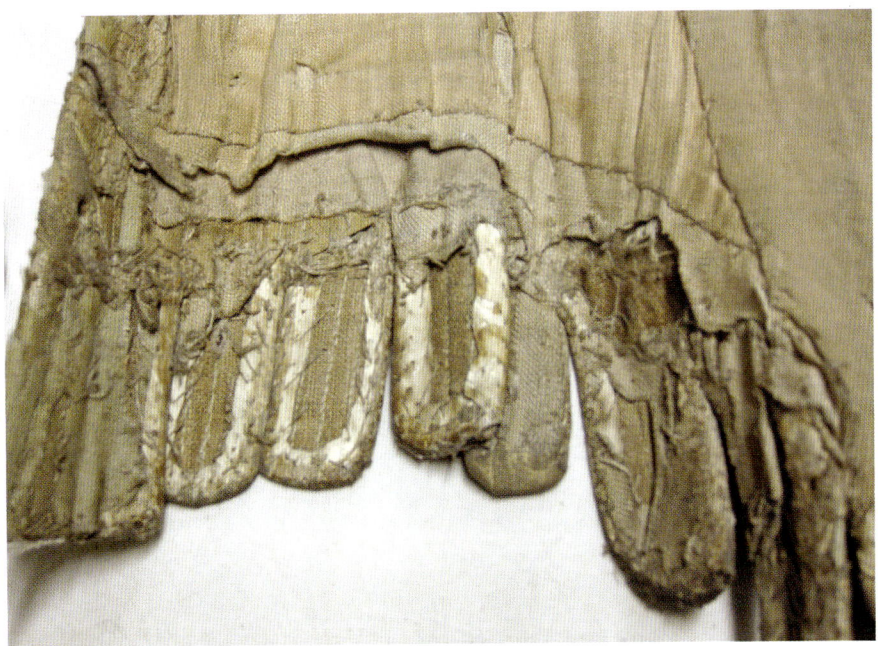

Figure 4.2 *Interior detail of twilled canvas stays, mid-eighteenth century, Acc. No. CAG.1940.598, Manchester Art Gallery, Manchester, Photograph in the Collection of the Author.*

Figure 4.3 *William Hogarth,* The Rake's Progress: 3, The Rake at Rose-Tavern, The Orgy, *1732, oil on canvas, 62.5 × 75.2 cm, © Sir John Soane's Museum/Bridgeman.*

Figure 4.4 *Detail of William Hogarth,* The Rake's Progress: 3, The Rake at Rose-Tavern, The Orgy, *1732, oil on canvas, 62.5 × 75.2 cm, © Sir John Soane's Museum/Bridgeman.*

Eyelets and tapes: A shift in construction

Resonating with the transformations elsewhere on the body that occurred during this period of change, the 1770s saw a fundamental shift in the construction of women's stays. Stylistically, stays had remained fairly consistent in construction and shape for the first six decades of the eighteenth century. Though fairly formal due to an additional layer of pasteboard across the front panels, which acts in place of a busk, a pair of duck egg blue, glazed wool damask stays presents a typical example of fashionable stays from the middle of the century (Figure 4.5).[14] Eight panels form the characteristic upright, conical shape. Shoulder straps, which have been sewn to the back panels, tie with ribbons to the top of the front panels, which taper into a soft point above the lower abdomen. Each panel ends in a tab, allowing the stays to smoothly extend over the hips without digging into the body.[15] They are laced behind with fourteen hand-sewn eyelets, which are representative of back-laced stays: eyelets spaced about an inch apart and slightly alternating, with top left and bottom right pairs closer together to allow for the single lace to be knotted (Figure 4.6).[16] Consistent with the formulaic composition of eighteenth-century stays, an inner layer of buckram, which adds extra stiffness, sits in between the wool damask and a natural linen lining, which could be easily changed and replaced once worn through.[17]

Through these layers, a multitude of meticulous seams are sewn side by side to form the boning channels, through which thin strips of baleen, or whalebone have been inserted, creating the stay's upright structure. Baleen formed an ideal material because its fibres run parallel, not coiled, making it easier to cut into the thin strips needed while maintaining its strength.[18] Whalebone provides support and structure, while becoming more supple with the absorption of heat and moisture from the body, thus allowing stays to further mould to the contours of their wearer's torso over time.[19] In addition to these vertical bones, a heavier curved bone has been inserted horizontally across the bust, rounded by the application of heat prior to construction.[20] This curved bone, which became a staple from the middle of the century, gave a permanent roundness to the bust and emphasizes the conical shape of the lengthened torso.[21]

The 1770s witnessed an evolution in boning technique, as the continuous channels of fully-boned stays were replaced with a more advanced understanding of the directionality of boning. A second pair of stays from Manchester Art Gallery exhibits the significant constructional advancements which occurred in the 1770s and 1780s (Figures 4.7 and 4.8).[22] Again, composed of eight panels and from the typical three-layer composition of cream statin, buckram and linen, this pair differs in that the two front panels are separated by a gusset, that is closed with a small lace that loops over the bones. Behind it, a thick horizontal piece of whalebone that has been permanently curved prior to insertion lies across the top of the stays. The curved shape of the bust is made all more prominent by

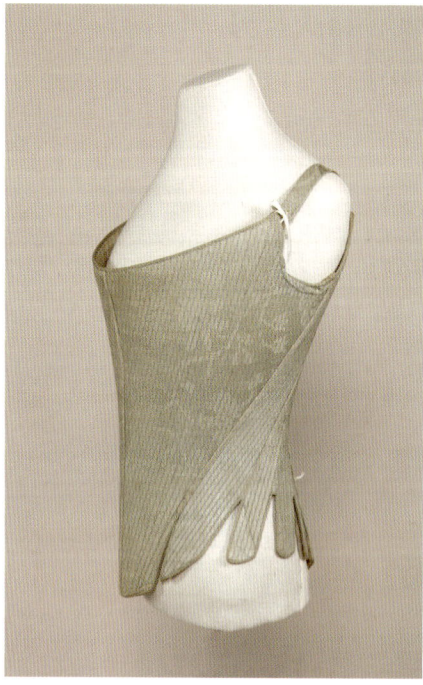

Figure 4.5 *Wool damask and linen stays, 1740–1760, Acc. No. 1947.1622, Manchester Art Gallery, Manchester.*

Figure 4.6 *Wool damask and linen stays, 1740–1760, Acc. No. 1947.1622, Manchester Art Gallery, Manchester.*

Figure 4.7 *White silk satin stays, 1780–1800, Acc. No. 1947.1624, Manchester Art Gallery, Manchester.*

the shaping of the panels and varied directionality of the boning. The boning channels are placed at varying distances and angles, achieving the same effect as if the stays were fully boned. This pattern of boning, in combination with the sharp curving of the side panels, creates a shape on the body that is very rounded in front, which then dramatically draws inward to create a narrow circumference around the waist – forming the characteristic serpentine shape of the pouter pigeon silhouette of the early 1780s.[23]

This change in boning pattern is exemplary of the constructional advancement in the stay's shape during the 1770s and 1780s; however, two further anomalies are perhaps more intriguing.[24] As seen Figure 4.8, a cream silk ribbon has been tied in a bow through two eyelets, which have been pierced on each side of the back of the stays. The eyelets, which would have aligned just above each pelvic bone on the lower back of the wearer, would have facilitated the attachment of a rump or bum, which were addressed in Chapter 2. The eyelets would have allowed the wearer to attach a bum directly to the stays without having to tie an additional band around the waist, eliminating extra bulk.[25] Not a new practice, fixtures, including hooks and eyelets, to the backs

Figure 4.8 *White silk satin stays, 1780–1800, Acc. No. 1947.1624, Manchester Art Gallery, Manchester.*

of stays span their design from the seventeenth century and into the nineteenth.[26] However, that the design of stays was altered to include these eyelets affirms both that the mythical cork rump's existence was not only real, but also common enough that the design of stays was altered to accommodate it.

A second adaptation on the satin stays is the straps. Strap design until the late eighteenth century consisted of short finished straps that were sewn to the back of the stays, coming over the shoulders and tying at the front, like those on the glazed wool damask pair. Alternatively, strapless stays were also common from the middle of century. However, the straps of this pair are made of wide pieces of woven tape, which do not originate from the back shoulders, but instead are attached at the lowest point of the underarm and have been sewn forward, extending to the top front of the underarm curve. Significantly longer than traditional shoulder straps, these straps were passed through two small twill, ribbon or linen loops, one on either side of the back above the shoulder blades. This is particularly clear on a second, almost identical pair of satin stays, also in the Manchester collection (Figures 4.9 and 4.10). Through the loops, the straps were crossed across the back, similar to a modern racer-back style sports bra, and hooked in front of the hip bones or tied under the point of the stays, using the point as ballast. While no hooks are visible on the first satin pair, one hook remains attached to the second pair, which would have had a mirrored twin above the other hip.[27]

The combination of light, or half-boning and tape straps has previously been identified as the material markers of riding stays, including one pair of beige cotton stays in the McCord Museum (Figure 4.11 and 4.12).[28] The pair retains its tape straps, which are fed through the directional loops on the back to create a crossing pattern and hooked to the front. The McCord stays have a long gusset and are lightly boned, alternating between tightly boned sections and single and even serpentine boning patterns. Advertisements for riding stays began to appear in the late 1770s and continue through the end of the century. For example, John Burchett advertised on 11 February 1778, that he made riding stays, amongst many other styles, for 'ladies in the country', who instead of being fitted in person, 'may be supplied without taking any measure of them, by only sending the old lining of their stays with their particular directions how they would have them made'.[29] The overlap between staymakers and riding habit-makers originated in the mid-eighteenth century. Carruthers, a staymaker and habit-maker in New Palace-yard, advertised 'Ladies riding habits made in the completest Manner', on 8 March 1755.[30] Though there is an abundance of advertisements mentioning the sale of both habits and riding stays, like most advertisements, they do not provide specific descriptions of the material qualities that qualify a pair of riding stays, as contemporary readership would have been materially familiar with the distinctions. This material knowledge, or material literacy, eliminated the need for lengthy description, no doubt a benefit to the makers, paying for advertising space by the line.[31] Over the latter part of the eighteenth century as boning styles evolved and new lighter styles were imported from France, types of stays abounded. For example, one staymaker, Jaquin Laglasse, advertised 'Stays, Riding Stays, and Stays en Travor; Corset a la Duchesse, a la Circassien, in the newest and most fashionable taste', with no indication of their material construction or design.[32] Nor does the style of stays purchased typically appear in the often meticulous of personal accounts of eighteenth-

160   *The Modern Venus*

Figure 4.9 *White silk satin stays, 1780 1800, Acc. No. 1949.130, Manchester Art Gallery, Manchester.*

Figure 4.10 *Detail of white silk satin stays, 1780–1800, Acc. No. 1949.130, Manchester Art Gallery, Manchester.*

Figure 4.11 *Beige cotton stays, 1785–1790, Acc. No. M969X.26, McCord Stewart Museum, Montreal.*

Figure 4.12 *Beige cotton stays, 1785–1790, Acc. No. M969X.26, McCord Stewart Museum, Montreal.*

women, which note even the smallest of sartorial purchases down to buttons and pins. In Elizabeth Motley Austen's diligently kept personal accounts dating from 1772 and 1782, she notes her regular bills from Saltzman, her staymaker, but rarely specifies what the bill is for.[33] Exceptions include a pair of white tabbey stays for two pounds and two shillings purchased on 1 May 1775, a pair of jumps on 26 January 1776 for two pounds, five shillings and six pence, as well as the alterations on pairs already owned on 22 February 1777, 1 June 1779 and 16 June 1780.[34] In January 1778, Lady Mary De La Warr bought a pair of stays for her daughters Charlotte and Georgina for four pounds.[35] Not unique to stays, the language employed for clothing and dress is indiscriminate and ambiguous; definitively matching a name and a material object is often beyond the dress historian's reach.

However, the material record suggestions that tape straps do not exclusively signal riding stays, but were rather the latest fashionable innovation. Stays with tape straps and the thrustier boning pattern, often accompanied by eyelets for bums and a gusset allowing the breast to expand, are plentiful in museum collections (Figure 4.13). Made of satin, linen, glazed cotton and silk, these stays are too numerous and too varied to all be one niche style, suggesting not a narrow constraining of

Figure 4.13 *Pair of stays with tape straps in store, c. 1770s–1780s, Acc. No. 1947.1623, Manchester Art Gallery, Manchester, Photograph in the Collection of the Author.*

these material characteristics, but rather evidence of innovation.³⁶ The fashionability of tape straps is even evidenced in a diminutive pair, belonging to the 1780s doll in the DeWitt Wallace Museum of Decorative Arts, seen in Chapter 1. As the foundation of her fashionable wardrobe, she wears a miniature pair of stays (Figure 4.14).³⁷ The cream stays are carefully boned with bright blue seams to mimic the new boning patterns of the 1780s. Like their full-size counterparts, linen tapes have been

Figure 4.14 *Stays for doll, 1780–1790, Acc. No. 2005-102, 8, DeWitt Wallace Museum of Decorative Arts, Williamsburg, The Colonial Williamsburg Foundation. Museum Purchase.*

sewn to each front corner between the top edge and the curved underarm (Figures 4.15 and 4.16). On the back panels, two blue twill threads have been sewn to create the loops over the shoulder blades. Within this miniature fashionable wardrobe, the new boning patterns and tape straps are fashionable, though unnecessary for a doll's body. However, on a human body the need for tape straps is more apparent as the shape of stays shifts from the conical to the serpentine, creating a silhouette much

Figure 4.15 *Stays for doll, 1780–1790, Acc. No. 2005-102, 8, DeWitt Wallace Museum of Decorative Arts, Williamsburg, The Colonial Williamsburg Foundation. Museum Purchase.*

Figure 4.16 *Stays for doll, 1780–1790, Acc. No. 2005-102, 8, DeWitt Wallace Museum of Decorative Arts, Williamsburg, The Colonial Williamsburg Foundation. Museum Purchase.*

wider across the bust, yet quite dramatically narrow at the waist, with the front panels brought into a curved point at the lower abdomen.[38] This far curvier shape in conjunction with the lighter methods of boning may have required more support, particularly for a larger bust, which the straps, crossed over the back, would have been able to provide.[39] This may have held true for both pairs of satin stays, which have quite a wide bust to waist ratio. However, when we consider the fashionable silhouette of the time, one that was more top heavy than previous decades, perhaps it is the very proportions of the silhouette that necessitated an alternative method for supporting the bust, requiring the extra support from above as well as below. These minor alterations signal much larger changes in the stay's design and subsequently major changes to the shape of female body as articulated through the contours of stays. It is with these physical effects in mind that we turn to how the stay was portrayed and the first visualization of tight lacing.

Tight laced: Stays on the satirical body

The modification in the design of stays that widened at the bust and drew in more sharply at the sides created a more prominent bust and the visual illusion of a smaller waist. This material change coincided with the exponential growth of the satirical print and resulted in the sudden abundance of stays represented in graphic satire.[40] The stay became a fulcrum around which late eighteenth-century social, gendered and political apprehensions were transmitted and deliberated. By the mid-1770s, stays became protagonists within the medium of social satires, becoming one of the most adaptable and damning symbols within a satirist's sartorial arsenal, manifesting in the iconography of tight lacing.

The origins of a motif: The iconography of tight lacing

In the visualization of tight lacing, satirists altered the female figure through stays to achieve minute physical proportions – creating a visual iconography that expanded beyond the fashionability of the beau monde and a visual legacy whose reverberations still resound today. As Valerie Steele has argued, tight lacing was less a common practice and more a social perception, which was widely debated and made an ideal scapegoat, embodying the dangers of fashion.[41] Diatribes against the method of lacing a pair of stays too tightly, also termed straight lacing, echoed across the pages of printed texts and graphic images. More than any other topic associated with stays, the outcry against straight or tight-laced stays was printed in article after article, newspaper after newspaper. Vitriolic, and often misogynistic medical testaments, such as 'On the Inconveniences and Disorders Arising from Strait-Lacing in Stays. By a Physician', argued that 'there are no evils the world is less aware of, than those which are owing to fashionable customs', that of straight lacing.[42] One author claimed that 'tight lacing in general occasions pains of the stomach; suppression of the menses, hysterical affection, fainting fits, low spirits, difficult labours, and a variety of other complaints'.[43] Primarily these published editorials highlighted moralizing medical opinions, arguing that stays, particularly when worn by a growing child, actually caused rather than aided distortion.[44] On the pages of satirical prints, satirists manipulated the concerns of physicians and moralists by visualizing the newly shaped figure of women to the extreme. First as a depiction of female vanity of the fashionable elite, the iconography of tight lacing expounded, broadening out to encompass the concerns surrounding the social female other, and later the political anxieties of society.

Chronologically, *Tight Lacing or Hold Fast Behind* was the first print and forerunner of the iconographic tradition, published on 1 March 1777 by Matthew and Mary Darly (Figure 4.17). Standing on a decorative carpet, a woman holds a bedpost with both hands while a man leans backward, pulling the lace of her stays with his left foot pushing against her backside.[45] Peripheral elements reappear from previous Darly prints, such as the dressing table and man's wig, which is nearly identical to the frisseur's wig in Figure 2.1, situating this print within the Darlys' series of prints that highlights the extremes of women's fashion. Like the attributes within the room, the woman herself is emblematic of the Darlys' depiction of the fashionable woman of the mid-1770s. She balances on tiny feet and her towering hair, dressed with eight sausage curls and an enormous crown of gauze and lace lappets, reaches as high as the finial.[46] The central action of the print revolves around the dramatic pulling in of her stays, which creates an anatomically miniscule waist that emphasizes her other out-of-proportion features. The shadows cast from the gown draped on the chair in the foreground and beneath the bed, along with its skewed perspective, all aid in pulling the viewer's eye across the page with the motion of the lacing. The gesture of tightening is so exaggerated that the servant requires a bodkin to aid him, further emphasizing her skeletal proportions.

Like big hair and tiny feet, the print identifies tightly laced stays as the latest vehicle for feminine vanity in the pursuit of fashion. Previously neglected in the literature around stays, this print can be identified as the catalyst for the motif of tight lacing.[47] This is the earliest published representation depicting the lacing of stays as a physical tug of war, where tightening of the waist was exaggerated by a second person physically leaning back and pushing away from the wearer's body. Four subsequent prints of women being tight laced in this manner were published. Only a few months after the Darlys' publication, a second print, and perhaps the most familiar, was published. John Collet's *Tight Lacing, or Fashion before Ease* was first published by Carington Bowles (later Bowles & Carver upon his death in 1793) (Figure 4.18).[48] Collet's version presents a far more complex depiction of the subject of tight lacing, which arguably extends the meaning of the print beyond fashionable frivolity and feminine vanity, and requires more extensive investigation.[49] Mirroring the Darlys' composition, Collet's print frames an ensemble of figures with a canopy bed on the left, and an almost identical chair in the lower right foreground. Unlike the Darlys, who often place their figures within sparse settings with little more than a horizon line denoting space, Collet uses the wall panelling and the angled door to create a sense of depth in which the action of his figures becomes more tangible for the viewer. In the centre of the print, a fashionable woman, with conventional tiny feet and big hair, is being laced by three members of her household. She is portrayed wearing a salmon pink shift, fully-boned stays, pockets and petticoat lifted by a large cork rump behind.[50] She uses the bedpost as an anchor, as behind her,

The Motifs and Materiality of Stays 169

Figure 4.17 Tight Lacing, or, Hold Fast Behind, *1 March 1777, publ. by Matthew and Mary Darly, etching and engraving, 35.1 × 24.7 cm, Courtesy of the Lewis Walpole Library, Yale University.*

Figure 4.18 John Collet, Tight Lacing, or Fashion Before Ease, c. 1770–1775, publ. by Bowles and Carver, hand-coloured mezzotint, 34.9 × 25 cm, DeWitt Wallace Museum of Decorative Arts, Williamsburg, The Colonial Williamsburg Foundation. Museum Purchase.

a man in a red coat and powdered wig pulls her laces, aided by a maid and a non-white serving boy, indistinguishably Black or from the sub-continent.[51] The position of the figures visually pulls the eye across the print, the angle amplified by the bent position of their bodies. At first, the satire seems to mock the need for three people to lace a woman's stays; however, when we consider the identities and actions of each figure, further anxieties become apparent. Rather than aid in the lacing, the maid and servant boy appear more interested in their corporeal proximity, each embracing the waist of the figure in front of them. Flirtatious sparks fly with each cheeky grin and wandering hand.

With a fashionably tied cravat at his neck and toys jangling at his hip, the man in a red coat holds a lace in each hand, parallel to the floor, pulling with the weight of his body. Too smartly dressed to be a servant, we may identify him as her husband or another member of the family. Arguably throughout his oeuvre, Collet showed a particular eye for clothes and this print is no exception. At the centre of the composition, he carefully delineated the woman's stays, including the panelled sections lined with stay-tape, tabs around the hips and eyelet holes down her back. So it is with pause that we look at the position of the parallel laces held in the gloved hands of the man in the red coat. Though a minor detail to the modern eye, whose perception of laced undergarments is seen through the lens of twentieth-century cinematic representations of corsets, to an eighteenth-century viewer a pair of laces pulled from centre back is a glaring blunder. Until the end of the second decade of the nineteenth century, stays were laced in a spiral fashion, with one lace tied at the bottom, zigzagged up the alternating eyelet position, and tied at the top, which can be seen in Figure 4.12. Yet, rather than a mistake, this sartorial misstep is the foil of the print, transforming the scene in an equine fashion, where the laces are more the reins of a horse than the laces of a pair of stays.[52] Look again at the man's coat, gloves and hat, which he has left discarded on the chair; he is dressed for riding. Holding the reins of his mare in his hands, the man's action of tight lacing is transformed into an articulation of gendered dominance, where the pair of stays becomes a bridle. Collet's subtle manipulation of sartorial detail in combination with the evocative positioning of his figures aligns a woman's pursuit of fashionability as something needing to be kerbed and reined in, and demoting her position within the hegemonic structures of her household, and in turn, society.

Echoing the devices of his mentor William Hogarth, a monkey points to an open book on the floor, identifying the woman as 'Fashions Victim of Satire'.[53] The term victim is a loaded choice. While at first resonating with the published diatribes criticizing tight lacing, identifying this young woman as just another victim of fashion, elsewhere in his work the word is charged with specifically sexual implications. A later print from 1790, *The Victim*, for example, depicts a young sex worker recently cajoled into serving a decrepit old man by her controlling madam.[54] Victims of fashion also carried more literal connotations within contemporary society. Mary Delany expressed concern for the habits of her niece's niece, Frances Mabel Sparrow. On 1 October 1775, she wrote to her sister's daughter, Mary Port (previously Dewes, and addressed as Mrs Port, of Ilam):

I hope Miss Sparrow will not fall into the absurd fashion of ye *wasp-waisted* ladies. Dr. Pringle declares he has had four of his patients *martyrs* to that folly (indeed *wickedness*), and when they were open'd it was evident that their *deaths* were occasioned by *strait lacing* …[55]

As Steele has noted, the deaths of the four victims on Dr Pringle's autopsy table cannot be definitively linked to the results of tight lacing, but that they were included as examples in Delany's letter demonstrates a public awareness and perception of the possible bodily effects warned of in the press.[56] However, the relationship between Delany and Sparrow has never before been addressed. Delany's affection for Sparrow can be seen throughout her surviving correspondence with her great-niece, one of her prime confidants in her later life after her sister Anne's death in 1761, as has been established in Chapter 3. Sparrow often spent time with Delany, who showed great interest in her growth and well-being.[57] While Delany's comment has previously been viewed as a satiric remark generated by gossip and the distancing of one party from the implied immorality of another, that the subject was her close acquaintance and someone for whom she cared a great deal, genuine concern overtakes ironic sarcasm, fearing more for Sparrow's welfare than her reputation.[58]

The antithesis of Venus

The first two prints of tight lacing conform with the eighteenth-century social norms of beauty – depicting young, white and attractive women. However, the iconographic trope also features two body types of the social 'other' of female society, the emaciated old and the masculinized corpulent, as was articulated in satirical prints like *The Three Graces* from 1 July 1778 (Figure 4.19).[59] *Tight Lacing* was published by William Humphrey on 5 March 1777 – five days after the Darlys', the RS signature again attributes the designer of the print to Richard Brinsley Sheridan (Figure 4.20).[60] Unlike the previous prints, the woman being laced into her stays has wrinkled arms, a bony neck and chest, and a comely face on which a wig covers her balding scalp. Still dressed in fashionable regalia, she sartorially clings to the follies of youth as she physically clings to the bedpost. The maid, whose stretched skin and pointed face gives her a rat-like appearance, pulls the lace of the lady's stays with a bodkin.[61] The cruel depiction of mistress and maid, striving for the figures of youth, echoes the harsh treatment of women in the public light after child-bearing age. As Cindy McCreedy has established, while young women were mocked and objectified in satire, older women were scorned, portrayed as wasting their time, efforts and money on fruitless pursuits.[62] Similar devices were employed to comment on women's age, particularly through cosmetics. Perhaps most cutting is the portrayal of republican historian Catherine Macaulay, *A Speedy and Effectual Preparation for the Next World*, published on 1 May 1777 by the Darlys (Figure 4.21).[63] Here, the satirist depicts the then forty-six-year-old with a hearse as her headpiece applying paint and rouge to her face as a skeleton beckons behind, foreshadowing her timely death.[64] The fruitless use of cosmetics to alter her appearance despite death being at her doorstep echoes Sheridan's depiction of the

Figure 4.19 *The Three Graces, 1 July 1778*, hand-coloured etching, 38.2 × 27.9 cm, Staatliche Museen zu Berlin, Berlin, bpk / Kunstbibliothek, SMB.

fruitlessness of tight lacing stays to attempt to contain an elderly woman's malleable flesh.⁶⁵ The pursuit of beauty by means of cosmetics or baleen becomes a sign of decrepit vanity, demonstrating the belief that post-menopausal women were parasitic, non-contributing members of society.

A second type of woman that lay outwith the inner circle of the graces, but whom the trope of tight lacing reached, was those whose proportions out-girthed normative ideals of beauty. In Thomas Rowlandson's pendant prints *A Little Tighter* and *A Little Bigger*, published by S. W. Fores on 18 May 1791, a couple's abundant girth is attempted to be sartorially controlled (Figures 4.22 and 4.23). The prints portray a corpulent women and her equally corpulent husband being fitted and dressed. In *A Little Bigger*, the man's breeches and shirt are being measured to accommodate his waistline. In the preliminary watercolour sketch for the print, the tailor's roll of fabric swatches and scissors lie on the floor (Figure 4.24). In *A Little Tighter*, a skinny staymaker, whose scissors are poking out from his back pocket, pulls the lace of the woman's stays tightly across her back.⁶⁶ Unlike the previous

Figure 4.20 Tight Lacing, *5 March 1777, publ. by William Holland, hand-coloured etching, 27 × 27 cm, Courtesy of the Lewis Walpole Library, Yale University.*

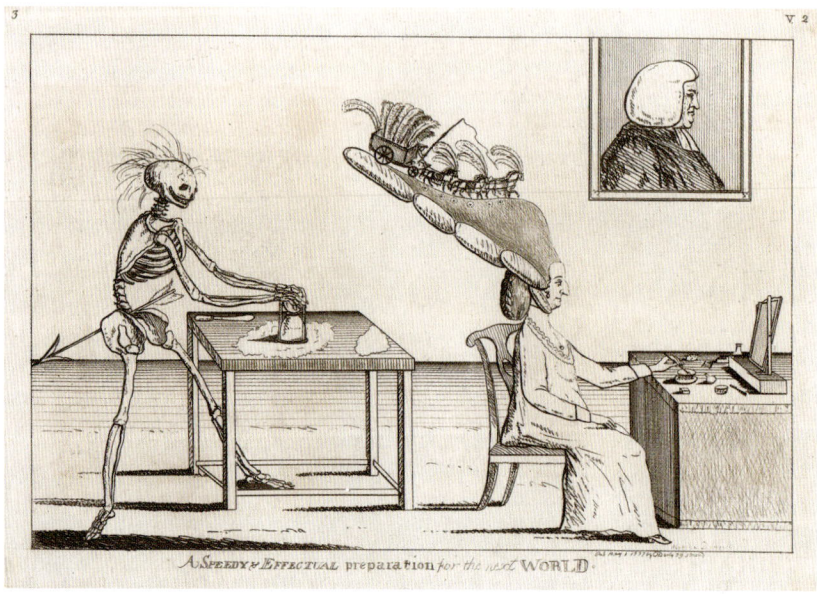

Figure 4.21 A Speedy and Effectual Preparation for the Next World, *1 May 1777, publ. by Matthew and Mary Darly, etching and drypoint, 24.5 × 35.1 cm, Courtesy of the Lewis Walpole Library, Yale University.*

The Motifs and Materiality of Stays 175

Figure 4.22 Thomas Rowlandson, A Little Tighter, *18 May 1791, publ. by S. W. Fores, hand-coloured etching, 39 × 31.2 cm, Courtesy of the National Gallery of Art, Washington, D.C.*

Figure 4.23 *Thomas Rowlandson, A Little Bigger, 18 May 1791, publ. by S. W. Fores, hand-coloured etching, 39.4 × 31.8 cm, Metropolitan Museum of Art, New York.*

Figure 4.24 *Thomas Rowlandson,* A Little Bigger, *1790, pen, ink and watercolour over pencil, 29.8 × 27.8 cm, National Gallery of Victoria, Victoria.*

Figure 4.25 *Thomas Rowlandson,* A Little Tighter, *1790, pen, ink and watercolour over pencil, 30.8 × 27.8 cm, National Gallery of Victoria, Victoria.*

prints where the lace has been pulled perpendicularly, here, the lace is drawn diagonally through the eyelets and parallel to the back of the wearer, echoing how stays were actually laced. While the staymaker's efforts are still exaggerated, once again using his bodyweight to pull, his turned position, leaning towards the right side of the composition, allows the viewer a full view of his client's width. She stands with legs apart and arms outstretched for balance. Her wide back, shoulders and spanning hips emphasize her bulk not in an objectified way, but one that is ridiculed and grotesque. In the preliminary watercolour, it is difficult to distinguish whether her lips are portrayed in a slight pout as she looks over her shoulder with her eyebrow arched and a beauty mark under her right eye, or if the pouted look is merely the effect of her chubby cheeks and lips (Figure 4.25). In the printed version, her features are heavier – her eyebrows thicker, her forehead wrinkled. The slight upturn of her nose has been replaced with a rounded snout. Overall, her appearance, aided by her wide, muscular back, resonates more with a man's than a woman's.

In *A Little Tighter*, Rowlandson's corpulent woman, who attempts to conform and supress her uncontrollable girth through the use of stays, transcends her gender, becoming visually synonymous with a man. The masculinization of Rowlandson's figure underlines the joke of the print. Rather than lacing a delicate beauty, here, the staymaker's attempts to rein in this woman's masculinized corpulence are as fruitless as adding the feather atop her head to improve her grace. As Hannah Greig has argued, within the elite circles of fashionable society beauty was 'synonymous with being a female member of the beau monde … a fashionable woman could not, by definition, be anything but "beautiful".'[67] The harsh light cast on those lacking the desired appearance was acutely bright within the medium of graphic satire. As has been established in the beginning of this chapter, stays provided a normative shape to the female figure, but as these satires demonstrate, for certain types of female bodies, attempting the normative was itself a cause of anxiety and satirical ridicule. Notably, the poor female body, as well as the non-white female body, is not depicted within the trope of tight lacing, both of whose figures, despite also being shaped by stays, appear beyond the attention of the satirist's stylus.

Foreign anxieties: Stays as the reins of power

Looking to fortify British shores against the waves of revolution and tyranny from France, a political charge and urgency for stability travelled like a current through culture and society, articulated and reinforced by the definition of gender that became highly influential and emblematic of Britain's political and social strength.[68] Dress as a material and visual reinforcement of gender not only signalled steadiness within local society, but also, and perhaps more importantly, became an indicator of the health of the hegemonic structures on which the nation stood. Within the iconography of tight lacing, the stay was transcribed into a politically charged symbol of national stability, or lack thereof. Just as dress was imbued with gendered significance, so too was it imbued with political weight, adapted and adopted to signify political allegiances and agendas.[69] Throughout the 1780s, the wearing of garter-blue and buff, ribbons and fox fur muffs was utilized by Foxite supporters to communicate political allegiance, further emboldening women's participation within politics.[70] Across the Channel, within the turbulence of revolutionary France, the politics surrounding dress became 'a multifarious, ubiquitously assimilated phenomenon that informs revolutionary culture at both individual and collective levels'.[71] While the adoption of these accessories was a conscious choice made by their wearer, the politicization of the stay was not. Unlike fox fur muffs, cockades or embroidered Jacobite garters, stays were not worn to make a political statement or assimilate the wearer with a certain ideological group. Rather, within the medium of graphic satire, the iconographic motif of tight lacing and the control imbued within that action extended beyond a fashionable discourse to communicate political and national concerns.

James Gillray's 1793 print, portraying Britannia being laced into a pair of stays was printed under two concurrent titles: *Britannia in French Stays, or _re_Form, at the Expence of Constitution* and *Fashion before Ease; or, a good constitution sacrificed, for a fantastick form* (Figure 4.26).[72] Published by Hannah Humphrey, both prints date from 2 January 1793. Like the title, *Fashion before Ease*, the composition of the print also echoes John Collet's 1777 print, *Tight Lacing*. Mirroring the fashionable woman clinging to the bedpost, here Gillray presents Britannia, surrounded by her military effects, holding onto a tree trunk while behind her, with one foot on her rump, a red-faced Thomas Paine (1737–1809) laces her into her stays. Wearing her plumed helmet, Britannia, in addition to being named by the second title, is easily identifiable, if a little underdressed. As the allegory of Britain and the British constitution, her shield bearing the crosses of St George and St Andrew rests on the tree trunk and the attributes of the olive branch and spear lie at her feet.[73] Like Figure 4.18, she forlornly gazes over her shoulder, not a victim of fashion, but a victim of politics. Radical author Thomas Paine is identified to the viewer by a sign, which hangs on the wall of the cottage. It reads 'Thomas Paine, Staymaker from Thetford. Paris Modes by Express', alluding to his birthplace and his apprenticeship in his father's staymaking trade before becoming a privateer, a well-known biographical facet of Paine's life.[74] Other tools of his former trade stick out of his back pocket, including a pair of scissors and a tape measure, on which reads, 'Rights of Man', alluding to his publication, *The Rights of Man* (1791).[75] Paine's Jacobin sympathies are expressed sartorially through his liberty cap, worn squarely on his head. In the wake of the French Revolution, the portrayal of the liberty cap 'quickly undermined [previous] patriotic meanings in Britain', and became 'the symbol of revolution, the ensign of French anarchy, the sign under which the Jacobins had orchestrated the terror of 1793–4'.[76] One month prior, in December, Rowlandson's *The Contrast* had depicted Britannia holding a liberty cap on a spear in the crook of her arm, pitted against a raging French Liberty depicted as Medusa (Figure 4.27).[77]

The Motifs and Materiality of Stays 181

Figure 4.26 *James Gillray,* Fashion before Ease, or, A Good Constitution Sacrificed for a Fantastick Form, *2 January 1793, publ. by Hannah Humphrey, hand-coloured etching, 35.3 × 25.1 cm, Courtesy of the Lewis Walpole Library, Yale University.*

Figure 4.27 *Thomas Rowlandson, The Contrast 1792, 1 January 1793, publ. by S. W. Fores, hand-coloured etching, 27.3 × 37.3 cm, Courtesy of the Lewis Walpole Library, Yale University.*

Gillray adapts his composition from Rowlandson's, borrowing the oak, shield and sleeping lion. By transferring the liberty cap from Britannia's regalia to the ruddy-faced head of Thomas Paine, Gillray underscores the cap's position as a symbol of French anarchy.[78]

The threat of constitutional radicalism sparked by the French Revolution, brought to Britain in part through Paine's *Rights of Man,* is expressed sartorially not by the changing status of the liberty cap, but through the tightening Britannia's 'French' stays.[79] The sign on the cottage wall reads 'Paris modes by express', simultaneously referring to the importation of both French goods and political ideas. French had long held sway as a 'byword for style, elegance, and modishness', and news of the latest Paris fashion, knowledge of French construction by well-travelled or well-connected makers, and smuggled French garments had been imported into Britain throughout the period.[80] From 1768, French stays were increasingly advertised by staymakers alongside the newly fashioned, lighter-boned 'corset', which made its first appearance in 1781.[81] With the turmoil of 1789 and the years following, the phrase 'just arrived from Paris' signalled the arrival of the French luxury trades into Britain as French émigré makers found new (living) clientele amongst the British beau monde.[82] Makers like Mrs Mayer, former 'mantua-maker to the French Queen and the Princesses of the Blood Royal' monopolized on their notoriety.[83] Mrs Mayer's business was such a success that she took 'a house to herself entirely' at 12 Dover Street, Piccadilly, as her retail premise within two months of her arrival in London, where she sold French stays, corsets and court dress.[84] The constructional design of 'French' stays remains illusive, as staymakers kept their designs well-guarded, and embodied descriptions of clothing are often fleeting, exaggerated, or non-existent.[85] The extant descriptions of French stays are scant. Within staymaker's advertisements, French stays are often coupled with corsets, and are identified as 'being so light and easy for the wearer'.[86] Whereas, thanks to the popular verses of the prologue to Richard Brinsley Sheridan's *The Camp*, French stays are described as 'stiff' in the press, contributing to a long tradition that emphasizes the stay's constricting nature and detrimental effects.[87] One surviving description by a supposed wearer of French stays is equally problematic. In her loosely autobiographical novel, *The Sylph* of 1779, the Duchess of Devonshire writes that her maid:

> broke two laces in endeavouring to draw my new French stays close. You know I am naturally small at bottom. But now you might literally span me. You never saw such a doll. Then, they are so intolerably wide across the breast, that my arms are absolutely sore with them; and my sides so pinched![88]

Though the Duchess's now iconic words on the price of fashion, that 'it is the *ton;* and pride feels no pain,' is the narrative's most resonant phrase, of perhaps more interest is her description of the wideness across the bust and the apparent pinch at the sides, echoing the wide-fronted shape of fashionable stays at the time. Whether her pinched sides were reflective of her embodied experience, or a narrative device, will never be known.

Of these contrasting accounts, Gillray draws upon the physically constricting nature of French stays, or rather stays in general, to underline the impending threat of Paine's political grip.[89] That they are French stays not only acts as a linguistic reminder of Paine's participation in the French Revolution, but feeds upon the undercurrents of Francophobia, particularly the fear of French influence preying on British women through such influences as dress and fashion, to fuel the sartorial metaphor. Visually, Paine's position pulling two laces from Britannia's stays with his foot pushing against her back mirrors Collet's equine formation and conveys Paine's political dominance over Britannia and her constitution. The visual alignment of the act of tightening stays with the physical (and political) constriction of women as representative of the nation politicizes the familiar gendered hierarchy into a means of conveying complex political fears and anxieties. While stays, and fashion in general, had traditionally been a metaphorical master to which women were bound, here Gillray clearly conveys their potential as a means of political constriction. Drawing on the physical effects of stays – to constrict the body – Gillray transforms a pair of stays into one of political power and influence.

Tightening the reins on Britannia, Gillray politicized a gendered sartorial action, successfully conveying the threat of Paine and his French ideologies. However, when this female-specific act was transcribed onto the male body, the metaphorical significance becomes all the more apparent. When William Heath portrayed the Prince Regent, being laced into a pair of stays by Sir John McMahon depicted as his valet, in *1812, or Regency à la Mode*, Heath was directly questioning the abilities of the Prince as the future head of state (Figure 4.28).[90] Standing at his dressing table, the corpulent future king applies cosmetics to his face while behind him, his personal secretary and keeper of the Privy Purse pulls the laces of his stays.[91] Like his satirical predecessors, McMahon uses his foot for leverage, using a small gold footrest in the shape of a goat's head to separate the sole of his shoe from the Prince's royal rump. Above McMahon's head, a shelf, labelled 'Bills and Recetts' holds a pile of bills: 'hatters Bill, Poulterers Bill, Fishmongers B, Hair Dresser, Taylors Bill, Butchers Bill, Doctors Bill, Silversmiths Bill', evidence of the Prince's indulgent lifestyle, carried on the back of the British taxpayer. Like Paine's influence over Britannia, Heath satirically comments on McMahon's influence over the Regent and his finances through lacing a pair of stays, which particularly resonated with the British public, as the Prince was reputed as wearing stays to hold in his growing belly.[92] Awareness of the Prince Regent's stays and their connection with his ability to rule were remarked upon later by Lord Holland to politician Thomas Creevey in *c.* 1817, 'They say the Prince has left off his stays, and that Royalty, divested of its usual supports, makes a bad figure.'[93] Even at his coronation, two commentators reported that the Prince was faint under the significant weight of his coronation robes, his breadth implicitly inhibited by his stays. Lady Cowper (later Viscountess Palmerston) wrote that the King 'looked more like the Victim than the Hero of the Fete … several times he was at the last Gasp'.[94] In the extensive description of the coronation published in the appendix of Edmund Burke's *The Annual Register, or a View of the History, Politics, and Literature of the Year 1821*, Burke records that during the ceremony, 'his majesty appeared distressed, almost to fainting. It was with uneven steps and evident difficulty, that he made his way up the aisle … the weight of the state cloak alone (which had seven supporters), might have overpowered a man in the most vigorous bodily health'.[95] Material evidence that the Prince wore a form of stays survives in the Museum of London: a paper pattern of a body belt, reinforced with vertical strips of whalebone, laced up the back and sides and fit with button closures in the front.[96]

The gendered act of tight lacing is reinforced with temporal transgressions that permeate throughout the print. Behind the Prince, two timepieces hang on the wall. A large wall clock reads 2:00 on an inverted clock face, above which a figure of father time sits shearing three ostrich plumes with a sickle. A second, smaller pocket watch hangs from a chain next to the mirror, also reading 2:00. Both pieces remind the viewer of the Prince's conspicuous waste of time – dressing in mid-afternoon – cinched into the constricting feminine confines of baleen stays. The Prince, wearing his stays, not only represents a lazy, unproductive future ruler, but one who is submissive within the strata

The Motifs and Materiality of Stays 185

Figure 4.28 William Heath, 1812, or Regency à la Mode, 1 February, c. 1812 [imprint erased], hand-coloured etching, 34.8 × 24.4 cm, British Library, London, UK © British Library Board. All Rights Reserved/Bridgeman Images.

of society, rather than dominant.[97] Instead of a ruler, the Prince Regent is cast as a pawn in the game of politics – already in the clutches of a stronger man, brought down by the weight of his idle, indulgent lifestyle and sartorial routine.

No longer the sartorial archetype illustrating feminine vanity, in a political and nationalistic context, stays articulate the perceived weakness of the burgeoning British Empire, its future king and its dominant sex. The iconographic tradition of stays and tight lacing has been transformed to convey not patriarchal social norms, but pressing social anxieties in the decades following the French Revolution, amidst the turbulent period of the Napoleonic Wars and the political instability of the monarchy. Satirists manipulated a fundamentally feminine garment, which, in turn, articulated male superiority and control, to pointedly convey concerns over the influence of foreign, particularly French, social and political corruption, in a sense, by turning the tools of patriarchal dominance against their sex. Amidst the garments wielded by the satirist's stylus, the stay is perhaps the most versatile and the most symbolic. By lacing a satirical body, satirists effectively conveyed complex social agendas and targeted a pervasive demographic of victims of fashion.

***

The legacy of these prints and the iconography of tight lacing have long outlived the satirists who drew them and the women who wore them. While graphic satires of big bums and enormous breasts have been ruled out for their exaggeration and distortion, this iconographic motif has been taken at its word. Enshrined in the nineteenth century when the material construction of corsets facilitated tight lacing with the invention of metal eyelets and criss-cross lacing in 1828, the introduction of steel boning in addition to pliable baleen, and the moralistic Victorian views on women's bodies, the reputation of stays and corsets as torture devices inflicted upon the female sex was cemented.[98] This perception has been repetitively reinforced in the twentieth and twenty-first centuries through the medium of film, where the action of tight lacing could not only be described in words or depicted in a still image, but viscerally enacted for the viewing public with the pulling of each sharp tug. Yet, the material limitations of stays on an eighteenth-century body, specifically hand-sewn eyelets laced with a single spiral lace, negate the widespread practice of tight lacing. Instead, this iconographic motif is arguably the product of a clandestine union between material garment and the medium of graphic satire. As the construction of the stay evolved in the 1770s and 1780s, widening at the breast and creating a visual appearance of a smaller waist through more severely shaped side panels, so too did the medium of graphic satire. As the stay's prolific representation in graphic satire demonstrates, the stay became one of satire's most malleable and noxious sartorial devices. Manipulating the very associations of femininity and fashionability that promoted the stay in the material world as a positive and necessary garment for the navigation of society, satirists exploited the stay's feminine connotations to articulate anxieties not only about women and fashion, but also about the pressing national fears of foreign influence on king and country, and the resulting weakening of Britain's dominant sex. Subverting the constructions of gender and patriarchy, the stay was employed as a sartorial tool that could transcend the boundaries of society and politics. Within these varied and divergent incarnations, the stay permeated the material and satirical worlds, pulled at the lacing to serve as the eighteenth century's most prolific sartorial motif.

Conclusion
'The fickle Goddess'

On 28 February 1810, Hannah Humphrey, owner of the by-then most fashionable printshop in London located at 27 St. James's Street, published a series of three satirical prints by James Gillray.[1] Publisher and satirist, the pair had enjoyed unrivalled success since their partnership became exclusive in 1791, publishing some of the most cutting and iconic political and social satires ever produced.[2] Made near the end of his career, the tryptic, titled the *Progress of the Toilet,* portrays the evolution of a woman getting dressed (Figures 5.1–5.3).[3] Each print's individual title aligns with the garment it portrays: *The Stays, The Wig,* and *Dress Completed*. Playing upon Hogarthian tradition, the prints depict three moments in time, expressed sartorially as the facets that make up the final ensemble. Staged within a familiar setting – a well-appointed room with a dressing table and mirror framed by the swag of a curtain in the corner – the three prints follow the progress of a tall and slender woman who dons the fashionable attire of the new century.[4] Long gone are the swelling protuberances of the amplified silhouette of the revolutionary years, as the columnar silhouette of the regency mode takes shape within the series. In the first print, a maid laces the woman into her long-line stays, worn over her newly fashioned drawers.[5] A far removed depiction from Gillray's portrayal of Paine tight lacing Britannia nearly twenty years earlier, here, the top of the stay lace gently curls in the maid's hand as the woman calmly and resolutely pushes a busk between her breasts. In the second print, the maid prepares a short-curled wig as the woman relaxed reads the epistolary novel *Delphine* (1802), chosen from the open bookcase behind her – a long cry from the frisseur precariously perched on a cork rump placing ostrich feathers and radishes into a towering coiffeur.[6] And finally, in a softly figure-hugging gown that shows off the petite curve of her backside, the woman pulls on elbow-length gloves over her forearms, while behind her, her maid holds a fan and a paisley-bordered shawl – the diminutive accessories a distant echo of the puffed, buffont handkerchief and enormous muffs that were once seen as the requisite finishing touches to a woman of fashion.

Figure 5.1 *James Gillray,* Progress of the Toilet. The Stays. Plate 1., *26 February 1810, publ. by Hannah Humphrey, etching with stipple, hand-coloured, 28.2 × 2 22.5 cm, Courtesy of the Lewis Walpole Library, Yale University.*

Figure 5.2 James Gillray, Progress of the Toilet. The Wig. Plate 2., *26 February 1810 publ. by Hannah Humphrey, etching with stipple, hand-coloured, 28.2 × 22.1 cm, Courtesy of the Lewis Walpole Library, Yale University.*

Figure 5.3 *James Gillray, Progress of the Toilet. Dress Completed. Plate 3., 26 February 1810, publ. by Hannah Humphrey, etching with stipple, hand-coloured, 28 × 22.1 cm, Courtesy of the Lewis Walpole Library, Yale University.*

We may be satisfied to chart these sartorial differences as coordinates on the trajectory of fashion, whose pendulum of shape and silhouette oscillates from extreme to extreme. Swinging upward, by the following decade big would again be the mode with the puffed sleeves, looped hair and belled skirts of the latter 1820s.[7] However, resisting these macro-fluctuations of 'hemline' histories and fashionable chronologies, Gillray's prints invite us to focus on a smaller increment of time and sartorial change. In the top right-hand corner of each print, a framed picture portrays a woman in varying states of dress, corresponding to the time printed on the frame beneath. Again, building on a rich iconographic tradition of implanting markers of seasonal or diurnal time within graphic satire dating back to Hogarth, the framed pictures depict Morning, Noon and Evening, humorously implying to the viewer that the donning of fashion has occupied an entire day.[8] Amidst this languid progression, Gillray distinguishes three particular stages: underwear, hair and accessories. Clustering hair, or rather headwear and accessories together, these prints visually articulate underwear and accessories as the temporal bookends of the dressed body. They are the garments that underpin and punctuate what constitutes the 'dress completed'.

Taking up the call of that anonymous commentator of August 1785 to consider and meditate on the so-called, 'levities of fashion', this book has encouraged us to ruminate on the peripheral, tangential, underlying and ephemeral. It has explored how a selection of garments, simultaneously distinct yet interrelated, defined the fashioned female body from the mid-1760s to the mid-1790s. As Gillray's prints argue, it is not the gown that is the crucial sartorial moment, but rather the garments that underline and accentuate it that give dress a temporally precise purpose and intention for their wearer. As this book has argued, it is a calash that allows her to maintain her social network, one that has been nurtured through the shared pursuit of the embroidering a muff. It is her stays, bum and buffont handkerchief that sculpt her body into the fashionable silhouette, enabling her to traverse the 'the gardens, the theatres, the watering places' of the emerging, urban landscape of the late eighteenth century.[9] As new fashionable places expanded beyond the ritual and formality of court life, the variety of fashionable dress expounded. In a period defined by development and revolution, that witnessed unparalleled change politically, socially, economically and globally, fashion can be viewed as the most immediate medium women employed to navigate the evolving world.

As Gillray's lady pulls on her gloves and her maid stands ready with her fan and shawl, the sartorial signal that she is ready to leave her dressing room and go out into the world, the supposed source of fashion lays open at her feet. Echoing his predecessors Hogarth and Collet, Gillray depicts an open copy of a copy of Nicolaus Heideloff's *Gallery of Fashion* (1794–1802) in the foreground. Though the British, or more specifically London-centric *Gallery of Fashion*, which Gillray aptly nods to with his subtitle 'dedicated to the Beau Monde', had completed its run eight years prior to Gillray's dressing lady, its inclusion on the floor along with a full-size coloured fashion plate is emblematic of the role that print culture was perceived to hold in the mediation of fashion in women's lives.[10] Gillray's inclusion of material and visual culture throughout the progress is subtle, yet exacting. In plate two, for example, his inclusion of the novel *Delphine*, a commentary on the limited status of women in First Republic French society, underlines the temporally claustrophobic boundaries of the dressing room and the limited nature of this woman's day. To modern audiences, the inclusion of the *Gallery of Fashion* is a rather meta device of the print culture of fashion depicted within print culture of fashion. However, I would argue that the fashion plate here is not the spring of all fashionable knowledge, an accolade that recent scholarship has finally stripped, but rather a branch of the periodical press, which acted as a partner to the production and consumption of fashion itself.[11] Serena Dyer has argued that print culture acts as 'a sartorial timekeeper', a temporal arbitrator of women's material lives.[12] The paths of print and dress are playfully, evocatively and intimately entwined. The haptic exchanges between print and fabric were transmitted and applied through printed patterns, and satin print muffs embodied the cross-over as mediums of self-expression and portable canvases. The printed page was where fashion was reported, discussed, denigrated and promoted. More than a passive timekeeper, this book has positioned print culture as a catalyst and firebrand, echoing the revolutionary sparks of change struck throughout the period. While the fashion magazine on the floor may represent the fashion periodical and press, on whose pages tracked fashion's temporal evolution, it is in their insatiable and unrestrained sister, the satirical print, where spirit, freedom and boldness are allowed to thrive.

Aligning the satirical and the sartorial, this book has championed the genre of graphic satire as the medium in which underwear and accessories were not only portrayed, but flourished as potent motifs of weighted iconography. Fashion's role in graphic satire blossomed over the last four decades of eighteenth century with printsellers and satirists like John Collet, Matthew and Mary Darly, Richard Brindsley Sheridan, Carrington Bowles and Samuel William Fores, whose sharp eyes and wit were as piercing as their styluses. They employed dress as loaded symbols of society, politics, class and gender, and like fashion periodicals, extended the narrow realm of those who could consume fashion. While favouring portrayals of the beau monde, like Gillray's miniature dedication, satires were awash with social climbers, country interlopers and those who wore but did not wield the fashions of the day. The cyclical relationship of dress worn, dress observed, dress satirized and dress made underpins the foundations of this book. Printshops, milliners, staymakers, mantuamakers and the ever-specializing branches of the sartorial trades were nestled within London's streets and townhouses. The proximity between printmakers, the makers and the wearers of fashion was sometimes as close as within the same room, fuelling the fervent dialogues between dress and satirical prints. At a masquerade ball at the London Opera House on 24 April 1775, amidst the 'elegant little shops, in which gloves, ribbons, *feathers* [sic.], jewels and toys of all sorts were to be sold', a columnist in the *The Morning Post and Daily Advertiser* noted 'Mat. Darly selling off his old stock, and taking Caricatures to lay in a new one for the spring trade'.[13] The following day, along with descriptions printed in the newspapers, a pair of satirical prints of the masquerade-goers attired in their masquerade ensembles was published by the Darlys, and two months later reports of the masquerade costumes had crossed the Atlantic and were published in the *Virginia Gazette*.[14] While the heart of satirical and sartorial production is arguably London-centric, satirical prints were carried alongside letters, newspapers and clothes to Calcutta, Virginia, Massachusetts and South Carolina. Like the latest fashions 'just imported from London' so too did images of fashion circulate across the globe.[15] Imported 'humorous prints' were advertised up and down the east coast, and produced alongside America's budding art market.[16] One seller, James McCall in Charlestown, South Carolina advertised 28 January 1773, the 'latest prints plain and coloured … some very humerous … and some drest in the present Taste'.[17] The visual, material and discursive incarnations of fashion reached from the neighbourhoods of the West End and the City to the edges of the empire.

The dialogues and discourses between the material, visual and discursive have informed the methodological frameworks on which this book is built. The melding of the material, representational and critical exchanges unpack the broader position of dress as a medium and mediator in women's lives, establishing how these so-called ephemeral flights of fashion acted as cultural currency in late eighteenth-century society. Interposing material and visual analysis with spatial, temporal, sensorial, immaterial and gendered frameworks demonstrates how articles of dress could act beyond their sartorial function, as timepieces, vehicles or canvases. Methodologically, *The Modern Venus* has challenged traditional approaches of dress history by blending methods of material culture with those of visual and historical analysis, highlighting the benefits of examining the relationships between the material, visual and discursive. In so doing, it has emphasized the possibility and fruitful exploration of graphic satire, not as a taboo exaggeration of dress, but one that is sartorially aware and cognizant not only of material construction, but of the cultural appropriations of dress within society. The inclusion of graphic satire has shaped the focus of this book, inviting the question: why did the period between *c.* 1765 and *c.* 1795 see such extremes in the peripheral garments that shaped the female silhouette? Were these 'drastic' trends in style, such as the cork rump and big hair merely the cyclical products of fashion coming to an extremity at the end of the century before dissipating?[18] Were they moulded by the external social, cultural and political forces of the time, such as the American War of Independence, the growing pains of the expanding empire and the age of revolutions when consumers were more able to buy, industrialization made things more available to sell and print made fashion more accessible to consume?[19] Or could it be due to the influence of graphic satire itself?

In his 1965 tomb of fashion history, writing of the dress worn in the decades just prior to the French Revolution, François Boucher attributes that the 'excessive changeability [of fashion] was a sign of the worldly boredom which was one of the century's ills', implying that the excess of buffonts puffed, hats fashioned, bums stuffed, muffs ornamented and stays laced was merely the result of the desire to fill a languid life, like that portrayed in Gillray's *The Progress of the Toilet*.[20] However, this changeability of fashionable underwear and accessories is not the product of boredom, but rather of keen observation, wit and commerce. As seen with tight lacing, the field of graphic satire was primed, interpreting fashionable change and translating it onto the satirical body within a night. Print culture, and specifically graphic satire itself, was the liquid primer that fuelled fashion's rapid turns. In the so-called golden age of caricature, fashion itself thrived, pushing boundaries, making innovations, expanding the branches of the sartorial trades, and solidifying the temporal rhythm that we would come to recognize as the fashion cycle.[21] Though the medium of graphic satire would continue, the main players of the 1790s and 1800s, including Gillray and Thomas Rowlandson, lost interest in representing the material world, developing a more stylized and abstract manner of depicting figures, and, thereby, aligning their portrayals of dress with the Grecian-lines of the Regency.[22] As one rare female commentator wrote in defence of the shortening and lightening of stays in the early 1790s, fashion was a 'fickle Goddess', whose whims, like Fortune's, were ever-changing.[23] By the late eighteenth century, Venus was no longer the goddess of beauty and love of ancient Greece and Rome, but like the domain she ruled over, she had changed. Tracing her permutations, the modern Venus had become the goddess of sartorial change and innovation, of fashion itself.

Notes

Introduction

1   To Lady Ossory, 27 January 1786. Horace Walpole, *Horace Walpole's Correspondence: The Yale Edition of Horace Walpole's Correspondence*, ed. W. S. Lewis and A. Dayle Wallace (New Haven: Yale University Press, 1965), 33.512.

2   See George E. Haggerty, 'Strawberry Hill: Friendship and Taste', in *Horace Walpole's Strawberry Hill*, ed. Michael Snodin and Cynthia Roman (New Haven: Yale University Press, 2009), 75–9. Walpole sent Lady Ossory another drawing for her daughter to trace in 1788. To Lady Ossory, 9 July 1788. Walpole, *Correspondence*, 34.8.

3   Churchill was Walpole's half-sister.

4   A member of the artistic Hoare family, Mary Hoare was the daughter of portraitist William Hoare, who had painted Churchill prior to her marriage in 1742, and sister to sculptor Prince Hoare. As a young woman she had been encouraged to copy 'suitable' old masters, like Nicholas Poussin's *Hercules between Vice and Vertue* and 'elevating' subjects such as *Vertue and Peace, Health and Temperance*. See Evelyn Newby, *William Hoare of Bath, R. A., 1707–1792* (Bath: Bath Museum Services, 1990); Neil Jeffares, 'Mary Hoare', *Dictionary of Pastellists before 1800* (London: 2006), online edn, http://www.pastellists.com/articles/HOAREM.pdf, (accessed 27 June 2022); Evelyn Newby, 'The Hoares of Bath', https://historyofbath.org/images/BathHistory/Vol%2001%20-%2004.%20Newby%20-%20The%20Hoares%20of%20Bath.pdf (accessed 28 June 2022), 118. See Paris A. Spies-Gans, *A Revolution on Canvas: The Rise of Women Artists in Britain and France, 1760–1830* (London: Paul Mellon Centre for Studies in British Art, 2022), 86–103; Ann Bermingham, *Learning to Draw: Studies in the Cultural History of a Polite and Useful Art* (New Haven: Yale University Press, 2000), Chapter 5. For a comparative discussion of Angelica Kauffman's treatment of antique nudity, see Wendy Wassyng Roworth, 'Anatomy Is Destiny: Angelica Kauffman', in *Femininity and Masculinity in Eighteenth-Century Art and Culture*, ed. Gillian Perry and Michael Rossington (Manchester: Manchester University Press, 1994), 41–62.

5   The circumstances of its creation and Hoare's relationship with Churchill remain veiled, apart from Hoare's father painting Churchill's portrait. For a more typical example, see *Standing Female Nude* by Mary Moser, Acc. No. PD.4-1947, Fitzwilliam Museum, Cambridge.

6   Walpole, *Correspondence*, 33.516.

7   Walpole's interest in satirical prints was substantial. Walpole's interest in graphic satire, or satirical prints, extended to having his own printing press at Strawberry Hill and his accumulation of a significant collection, now largely housed at the New York Public Library. Cynthia Roman, 'A Portfolio of Satires from Horace Walpole's Collection', *Print Quarterly* 25, no. 2 (June 2008): 166–71.

8 The print includes no printed publishing line, but an annotation in Kirgate's hand in the BM version that belonged to Sarah Sophia Banks identifies the Yardley as the publisher.

9 See Neil McKendrick, John Brewer and J. H. Plumb, *The Birth of a Consumer Society: The Commercialization of Eighteenth-Century England* (London: Europa Publications Ltd, 1982); John Brewer and Roy Porter (eds.), *Consumption and the World of Goods* (London: Routledge, 1993); Ben Fine and Ellen Leopold, 'Consumption and the Industrial Revolution', *Social History* 15, no. 2 (1990): 151–79; S. D. Chapman, *The Cotton Industry in the Industrial Revolution*, 2nd edn. (Basingstoke: Macmillan Education, 1987); Beverly Lemire, *Fashion's Favourite: The Cotton Trade and the Consumer in Britain, 1660–1800* (Oxford: Oxford University Press, 1991).

10 *General Advertiser*, 20 August 1785.

11 For example, Lord Chesterfield published an editorial dedicated to its definition. No. 151 Thursday, 20 November 1755. Adam Fitz-Adam, *The World in Three Volumes* (Edinburgh: Printed by and for Martin & Wotherspoon, 1777), 3.48–56. See John Styles, 'Fashion and Innovation in Early Modern Europe', in *Fashioning the Early Modern*, ed. Evelyn Welch (Oxford: Oxford University Press, 2017), 33–7.

12 Hannah Greig, *The Beau Monde: Fashionable Society in Georgian London* (Oxford: Oxford University Press, 2013), 3.

13 Styles, 'Fashion and Innovation', 40–55.

14 Peter McNeil, 'Introduction', in *A Cultural History of Dress and Fashion in the Age of the Enlightenment*, ed. Peter McNeil (London: Bloomsbury Academic, 2017), 1; Peter McNeil, '"Beauty in Search of Knowledge": Eighteenth-Century Fashion and the World of Print', in *Fashioning the Early Modern*, ed. Evelyn Welch (Oxford: Oxford University Press, 2017), 225.

15 *General Advertiser*, 20 August 1785.

16 Ibid.

17 Diana Donald, *Followers of Fashion: Graphic Satires from the Georgian Period* (London: Hayward Gallery Publishing, 2002), 8.

18 See, Viccy Coltman, *Classical Sculpture and the Culture of Collecting in Britain since 1760* (Oxford: Oxford University Press, 2009), 117–58; Brian Allen, 'The Capture of the Westmorland and the Purchase of Art in Rome in the 1770s', in *Art in Rome in the Eighteenth Century: A Study in the Social History of Art*, ed. Edgard Peters Bowron and Joseph J. Rischel (London: Brill, 2019), 187–98. For the development of interest in the antique, see Francis Haskell and Nicholas Penny, *Taste and the Antique: The Lure of Classical Sculpture 1500-1800* (London: Yale University Press, 1981). For a definition of 'genteel', see Amanda Vickery, *The Gentleman's Daughter: Women's Lives in Georgian England* (London: Yale University Press, 1998), 13.

19 See Viccy Coltman, *Fabricating the Antique: Neoclassicism in Britain, 1760–1800* (London: University of Chicago Press, 2006), 10–11.

20 Coltman, *Fabricating*, 123–63. For women on the grand tour, see Brian Dolan, *Ladies of the Grand Tour* (London: Harper Collins, 2001).

21 Hogarth uses the stay and its effect on the female body as evidence of 'how much the form of a woman's body surpasses in beauty that of a man.' William Hogarth, *The Analysis of Beauty* (London: Printed by J. Reeves, 1753), 50; Aileen Ribeiro, *Art of Dress: Fashion in England and France, 1750 to 1820* (London: Yale University Press, 1995), 18.

22 Lady Sabine Winn quoted in Coltman, *Fabricating*, 18.

23 Isabelle Paresys, 'The Body', in *A Cultural History of Dress and Fashion in the Age of the Enlightenment*, ed. Peter McNeil (London: Bloomsbury Academic, 2017), 63–7.

24 The term originated in the 1760s as a style of drawing which shaded in the outline of the body. Georges Vigarello, *The Silhouette: From the 18th Century to the Present Day*, trans. Augusta Dörr (London: Bloomsbury Academic, 2016), 14–21.

25 *General Advertiser*, 20 August 1785. For hierarchies of dress, formality and class, see Anne Buck, *Dress in Eighteenth Century England* (London: B.T. Batsford Ltd, 1979).

26 See Johannes Pietsch, 'Object in Focus 1: A Robe à l'angaise retroussée', in *Fashioning the Early Modern*, ed. Evelyn Welch (Oxford: Oxford University Press, 2017), 83–6.

27 As Tobin argues, these moral concerns were expressed while maintaining class and racial hegemonic social structures. For a discussion of the painting's colonial and class dynamics, see Beth Fowkes Tobin, *Picturing Imperial Power: Colonial Subjects in Eighteenth-Century British Painting* (London: Duke University Press, 1999), 46–55.

28 See Amelia Rauser, *The Age of Undress: Art, Fashion, and the Classical Ideal in the 1790s* (New Haven: Yale University Press, 2020); Hilary Davidson, *Dress in the Age of Jane Austen: Regency Fashion* (New Haven: Yale University Press, 2019).

29 'Underwear' is first published in 1872 and 'accessories' as related to clothing in 1887. *Oxford English Dictionary*.

30 See Susan North, *Sweet and Clean?: Bodies and Clothes in Early Modern England* (Oxford: Oxford University Press, 2020).

31 For example, Mrs Wodrow waits while her friend 'went into another room and put on clean linens.' Robert Wodrow, *Life of James Wodrow, A. M. Professor of Divinity in the University of Glasgow, from MDCXII to MDCCVII* (Edinburgh: William Blackwood and T. Cadell, Strand, London, 1828), 57.

32 See Barbara Burman and Ariane Fennetaux, *The Pocket: A Hidden History of Women's Lives, 1660–1900* (New Haven: Yale University Press, 2019).

33 Robert Campbell, *The London Tradesman. Being a Compendious View of All the Trades, Professions, Arts, Both Liberal and Mechanic, Now Practiced in the Cities of* London *and* Westminster. *Calculated for the Information of PARENTS, and Instruction of YOUTH in Their Choice of Business* (London: Printed by T. Gardner, 1747), 207.

34 Dror Wahrman, *The Making of the Modern Self: Identity and Culture in Eighteenth-Century England* (London: Yale University Press, 2004), 83–126; Robert S. DuPlessis, *The Material Atlantic: Clothing, Commerce, and Colonization in the Atlantic World, 1650–1800* (Cambridge: Cambridge University Press, 2016), 82–5.

35 Robin Mitchell, *Vénus Noire: Black Woman and Colonial Fantasies in Nineteenth-Century France* (Athens: University of Georgia Press, 2020), 34.

36 Mitchell, *Vénus Noire*, 15; Yvette Abrahams, 'Images of Sara Bartman: Sexuality, Race, and Gender in Early-Nineteenth-Century Britain', in *Nation, Empire and Colony: Historicising Gender and Race*, ed. Ruth Roach Pierson and Napur Chaudhuri (Bloomington: Indiana University Press, 1998), 224–7.

37 See Mitchell, *Vénus Noire*, 71–8; Abrahams, 'Images', 220–36; Janell Hobson, *Venus in the Dark: Blackness and Beauty in Popular Culture* (London: Routledge, 2005); Sadiah Qureshi, *Peoples on Parade: Exhibitions, Empire, and Anthropology in Nineteenth-Century Britain* (Chicago: University of Chicago Press, 2011). For the legacies of Sara Baartman, see Samantha Pinto, *Infamous Bodies: Early Black Women's Celebrity and the Afterlives of Rights* (London: Duke University Press, 2020), 105–38.

38 Saidiya Hartman, 'Venus in Two Acts', *Small Axe* 12, no. 2 (June 2008): 1–14.

39 See Jennifer Germann, '"Other Women Were Present": Seeing Black Women in Georgian London', *Eighteenth-Century Studies* 54, no. 3 (Spring 2021): 535–53. See Olivette Otele, *African Europeans: An Untold Story* (London: Hurst & Company, 2020), 95–126.

40 Cheyney Mcknight, 'A Word on African Hair in Eighteenth-Century Europe and the Colonies', in *The American Duchess Guide to 18th Century Beauty: 40 Projects for Period-Accurate Hairstyles, Makeup and Accessories*, ed. Lauren Stowell, Abby Cox and Cheyney McKnight (Salem: Page Street Publishing Co., 2019), 156–7. Rauser, *Age of Undress*, 139–45.

41 Charmaine Nelson, *The Color of Stone: Sculpting the Black Female Subject in Nineteenth-Century America* (Minneapolis: University of Minnesota Press, 2007), 69; Charmaine Nelson, *Representing the Black Female Subject in Western Art* (London: Routledge, 2010), 142. See also, Rauser, *Age of Undress*, 133–53.

42 The term was again used by Romantic poet Robert Southey's description recalling the fashions of the previous century in 1807, which has remained in scholarly circulation largely due to satirical print curator Dorothy George's preliminary description of the 'costume' in 1938. Letter XLIX. Don Manuel Alvarez Espriella, *Letters from England 2nd Edition* (London: Printed for Longman, Hurst, Rees and Orme, 1808), 2.276. Dorothy George, *Catalogue of Political and Personal Satires Preserved in the Department of Prints and Drawings in the British Museum* (London: British Museum, 1938), 6.265.

43 Lemire, *Fashion's Favourite*, 88, 92; John Styles, *Dress of the People* (New Haven: Yale University Press, 2007), 284–98. For a comparative discussion of fashionable 'everyday' dress, see Lizzy Spencer, '"None but Abigails appeared in white aprons": The Apron as an Elite Garment in Eighteenth-Century England', *Textile History* 49, no. 2 (December 2018): 164–90.

44 *Public Advertiser*, 28 December 1787 reported the fashion for 'large plain gauze handkerchief puffed out very much, crossed before and tied behind in the middle'.

45 Handkerchiefs carried in the pocket are most often referred to as pocket handkerchiefs. Those worn about the neck were sometimes referred to as neckerchiefs, or neckcloths. In France, the term fichu was prevalent, though this term was not widely used in Britain until the nineteenth century. Buffonts are first advertised in 1778. *General Evening Post*, 7–9 April 1778.

46 *General Evening Post*, 7–9 April 1778; *Morning Chronicle*, 11 August 1780.

47 MA 7269, Morgan Library; Doc. 67, Downs Collection, Winterthur Museum, Garden and Library.

48 Sonia Ashmore, *Muslin* (London: V&A Publishing, 2012), 27–9.

49 The use of wire to prop the shape of the handkerchief was frequently invoked in satire, like the description of the pouter pigeon itself, published in Robert's Letter. Espriella, *Letters from England*, 2.276.

50 See Elisabeth Gernerd, 'Pulled Tight and Gleaming: The Stocking's Position within Eighteenth-Century Masculinity', *Textile History* 46, no. 1 (May 2015): 10; Susan J. Vincent, *Dressing the Elite: Clothes in Early Modern England* (Oxford: Berg, 2003), 52–4.

51 *Morning Herald*, 14 February 1781; Elizabeth Price, *The New Book of Cookery; or Every Woman a Perfect Cook* (London: Printed for the Authoress, and sold by Alex Hogg, 1782), 106–10; *Morning Herald*, 16 February 1782.

52 *Morning Herald*, 28 May 1783; *Morning Herald*, 30 June 1784.

53 *General Advertiser*, 20 August 1785.

54 The sexualized element of this appeal was illustrated in a print by S. W. Fores, called *The Merry Thought*, where a woman wearing a puffed handkerchief sits suggestively on a couch, legs invitingly open. 16 April 1787, publ. by S. W. Fores, LWL. *Evening Post*, 14–17 October 1786.

55 See Serena Dyer, *Material Lives: Women Makers and Consumer Culture in the 18th Century* (London: Bloomsbury Visual Arts, 2021), 58–78; Timothy Campbell, *Historical Style: Fashion and the New Mode of History, 1740–1830* (Philadelphia: University of Pennsylvania Press, 2016), 79–82.

56 The first flight in Britain was in 1784, whereas in France he flew in 1783.

57 *Morning Post,* 26 August 1784.

58 *London Chronicle,* 22–24 August 1786.

59 For example, *The Inconvenience of Dress,* 19 May 1786, publ. by S. W. Fores, BM; *The Wou'd if the Cou'd,* 20 April 1786, publ. by T. Brandshaw, LOC; *The Bosom Friends,* 28 May 1786, publ. by S. W. Fores, LWL; *The Equilibrium,* 1 February 1786, publ. by S. W. Fores, LWL.

60 *Whitehall Evening Post,* 2–4 May 1786.

61 Sophie von La Roche, *Sophie in London, 1786; Being the Diary of Sophie v. la Roche; Translated from the German with an Introductory Essay by Clare Williams, with a Forward by G. M. Trevelyan* (London: Jonathan Cape, 1933), 95.

62 Ibid.

63 *Morning Herald,* 1 May 1787.

64 Rauser, *Age of Undress,* 64–9; Davidson, *Regency Fashion,* 29–39.

65 Ribeiro, *Art of Dress,* 6. For the development and relationship between dress and art history, see Anne Hollander, *Seeing through Clothes* (New York: The Viking Press, 1975); Lou Taylor, *The Study of Dress History* (Manchester: Manchester University Press, 2002), 116–21; Aileen Ribeiro, 'Re-Fashioning Art: Some Visual Approaches to the Study of the History of Dress', *Fashion Theory* 2, no. 4 (1998): 315–26; Marcia Pointon, *Hanging the Head: Portraiture and Social Formation in Eighteenth-Century England* (London: Yale University Press, 1993), 125–7.

66 For commissioning portraiture, see Pointon, *Hanging the Head,* 184–8. For the conventions of dress in portraiture, see, Carrie Rebora Barratt, 'Oriental Undress and the Artist', *Porticus, Journal of the Memorial Art Gallery of the University of Rochester* 20 (2001): 19–22; Aileen Ribeiro, *The Dress Worn at Masquerades in England, 1730 to 1790, and Its Relation to Fancy Dress in Portraiture* (London: Garland Publishing, Inc., 1984); Leslie Reinhardt, '"The Work of Fancy and Taste": Copley's Invented Dress and the Case of Rebecca Boylston', *Dress* 29, no. 1 (2002): 4–18; Gill Perry, 'Women in Disguise: Likeness, the Grand Style and the Conventions of "Feminine" Portraiture in the Work of Sir Joshua Reynolds', in *Femininity and Masculinity in Eighteenth-Century Art and Culture,* ed. Gillian Perry and Michael Rossington (Manchester: Manchester University Press, 1994), 18–41; Claudia Bush Kidwell, 'Are Those Clothes Real? Transforming the Way Eighteenth-Century Portraits Are Studied', *Dress* 24, no. 1 (1997): 3–15; Susan Sloman, *Gainsborough in London* (London: Modern Art Press, 2021), 164–5.

67 Doris Langley Moore, *Fashion through Fashion Plates 1771–1970* (London: Ward Lock Ltd, 1971), 10. For a re-evaluation of the fashion plate, see Serena Dyer, 'Fashions of the Day: Materiality, Temporality and the Fashion Plate, 1750–1879', in *Disseminating Dress: Britain's Fashion Networks, 1660–1970,* ed. Serena Dyer, Jade Halbert and Sophie Littlewood (London: Bloomsbury Academic, 2022), 73–94.

68 Diana Donald, *The Age of Caricature: Satirical Prints in the Reign of George III* (New Haven: Yale University Press, 1996), 89.

69 Taylor, *Study,* 141.

70 Peter McNeil, 'Macaroni Masculinities', *Fashion Theory* 4, no. 4 (2000): 404. For macaroni dress, see Peter McNeil, '"That Doubtful Gender": Macaroni Dress and Male Sexualities', *Fashion Theory* 3, no. 4 (1999): 411–47; Peter McNeil, *Pretty Gentlemen: Macaroni Men and the Eighteenth-Century Fashion World* (New Haven: Yale University Press, 2018); Philip Carter, 'Men about Town: Representations of Foppery and Masculinity in Early Eighteenth-Century Urban Society', in *Gender in Eighteenth-Century England: Roles Representations, and Responsibilities,* ed. Hannah Barker and Elaine Chalus (London: Addison Wesley Longman Ltd, 1997), 31–57; Gernerd, 'Pulled Tight and Gleaming', 13–15.

71 Styles, 'Fashion and Innovation', 51–5.

72 For the development of fashion-focused periodicals, see Dyer, 'Fashions of the Day', 74–81; Bertha Monica Stearns, 'Early English Periodicals for Ladies (1700–1760)', *Modern Language Association* 48, no. 1 (1933): 38–60; Alison Adburgham, *Women in Print: Writing Women and Women's Magazines from the Restoration to the Accession of Victoria* (London: Allen and Unwin, 1972), Chapter 6; Jennie Batchelor, '"[T]o Cherish Female Ingenuity, and to Conduce to Female Improvement": The Birth of the Woman's Magazine', in *Women's Periodicals and Print Culture in Britain, 1690–1820s: The Long Eighteenth Century*, ed. Jennie Batchelor and Manushag N. Powell (Edinburgh: University of Edinburgh Press, 2018), 382–3.

73 For pocket books, see Anne Buck and Harry Matthews, 'Pocket Guides to Fashion: Ladies' Pocket Books Published in England 1760–1830', *Costume* 18 (1984): 35–58; Dyer, 'Fashions of the Day', 75–8. For *The Lady's Magazine*, see Jennie Batchelor '[T]o Cherish', 377–92; Jennie Batchelor, *The Lady's Magazine (1770–1832) and the Making of Literary History* (Edinburgh: University of Edinburgh Press, 2022); Chloe Wigston Smith, 'Fast Fashion: Style, Text, and Image in Late Eighteenth-Century Women's Periodicals', in *Women's Periodicals and Print Culture in Britain, 1690–1820s: The Long Eighteenth Century*, ed. Jennie Batchelor and Manushag N. Powell (Edinburgh: University of Edinburgh Press, 2018), 440–57.

74 Donald has stressed the chronological importance of George III's reign as the 'age of caricature', when the political climate, emergence of the Royal Academy, and growth in consumption contributed to the boom in the print industry. Cindy McCreery identifies *c*. 1760–1800 as the years most concerned with the satirical representation of women. Donald, *Age of Caricature*, 1–2, 21; Cindy McCreery, *The Satirical Gaze: Prints of Women in Late Eighteenth-Century England* (Oxford: Clarendon, 2004), 6.

75 For the production of satirical prints, see Timothy Clayton, *The English Print 1688-1802* (New Haven: Yale University Press, 1997), 13–16.

76 The term *caricature* derives from the Italian for 'charged' or 'loaded.' Peter McNeil and Patrik Steorn, 'The Medium of Print and the Rise of Fashion in the West', *Konsthistorisk Tidskrift/Journal of Art History* 82, no. 3 (2013): 146. For John Collet, see Caitlin Blackwell, 'John Collet, A Commercial Comic Artist' (PhD thesis, University of York, 2013); Patricia Crown, 'Sporting with Clothes: John Collet's Prints in the 1770s', *Eighteenth-Century Life* 26, no. 1 (Winter 2002): 119–35; David Alexander, 'Prints after John Collet: Their Publishing History and a Chronological Checklist', *Eighteenth-Century Life* 26, no. 1 (Winter 2002): 136–46.

77 See Serena Dyer and Chloe Wigston Smith 'Introduction', in *Material Literacy in Eighteenth-Century Britain: A Nation of Makers*, ed. Serena Dyer and Chloe Wigston Smith (London: Bloomsbury Visual Arts, 2020), 1.

78 Elisabeth Gernerd, 'Fancy Feathers: the Feather Trade in Britain and the Atlantic World', in *Material Literacy in Eighteenth-Century Britain: A Nation of Makers*, ed. Serena Dyer and Chloe Wigston Smith (London: Bloomsbury Visual Arts, 2020), 195–218.

79 McNeil, 'Introduction', 11. The standard price is 1s plain and 2s coloured for prints measuring 10 × 14 inches (25.4 × 35.56 cm). Exceptions to this price include prints by John Collet, for example, which cost 2s plain and 3s coloured, and smaller sizes, measuring 4 ½ × 6 inches (11.43 × 15.24 cm), which cost 6d plain and 1s coloured. E. C. Nicholson has argued for a narrow audience for satires, requiring literacy and iconographic sophistication. Tamara L. Hunt has argued against this scope, evidencing a greater range of literacy among working classes and that the act of viewing could be a collaborative process through reading aloud the texts and sharing allegorical meanings. She also argues that by the end of the century, satires drew from a familiar iconography, making them intelligible to most viewers. E. C. Nicholson, 'Consumers and Spectators: The Public of the Political Print in Eighteenth-Century England', *History* 81, no. 261 (1996): 5–21; Tamara L. Hunt, *Defining John Bull: Political Caricature and National Identity in Late Georgian England* (Aldershot: Ashgate Publishing Ltd, 2003), 9–13.

80 See McNeil, 'Introduction', 5–14; Peter McNeil, 'Beauty in Search of Knowledge', 223–9. For printshop window satires, see Joseph Monteyne, *From Still Life to the Screen: Print Culture, Display, and the Materiality of the Image in Eighteenth-Century London* (New Haven: Yale University Press, 2013), 159–92.

81 Pointon, *Hanging the Head*, 125.

82 For example, of a collection of 200 prints for sale in Williamsburg, Virginia, the advertisement describes them as 'in the hieroglyphick or *caricatura* manner, with the most severe and entertaining satires on some, and the greatest ble [sic.] in others'. *The Virginia Gazette*, 17 October 1766. *The Deplorable State of America or Sc-h Government*, publ. 1 November 1765 is described at length, regarding the Stamp Act, in *The Pennsylvania Gazette*, 21 November 1765, indicating that prints could reach the colonies within a month. In Charles-town, South Carolina, a printseller advertises prints of 'Lord W-ym – the in the character of a drunken Butcher' and 'An excellent *Caricature* of Serjeant N-s singing a Hymn in St. Stephen's Chapel on a Sunday Morning' as imported from London. *The South-Carolina Gazette*, 10 August 1769. For dissemination, see Hunt, *Defining John Bull*, 14–17; McCreery, *Satirical Gaze*, 20–1; McNeil and Steorn, 'Medium of Print', 144–5; Donald, *Age of Caricature*, 19–20; Patrik Steorn, 'Caricature and Fashion Critique on the Move: Establishing European Print and Fashion Culture in Eighteenth-Century Sweden', in *Fashioning the Early Modern*, ed. Evelyn Welch (Oxford: Oxford University Press, 2017), 255–7.

83 Julie Flavell, *When London Was Capital of America* (New Haven: Yale University Press, 2010), 5. For the development of Atlantic history, see Bernard Bailyn, *Atlantic History: Concepts and Contours* (Cambridge: Harvard University Press, 2005), 1–56.

84 Object-based analysis in this book follows a loosely Prownian approach. Jules Prown, 'Mind in Matter: An Introduction to Material Culture Theory and Method', *Winterthur Portfolio* 17, no. 1 (Spring 1982): 1–19. For object-based dress historical approaches, see Valerie Steele, 'A Museum of Fashion Is More Than a Clothes-Bag', *Fashion Theory* 2, no. 4 (1998): 327–36; Ingrid Mida and Alexandra Kim, *The Dress Detective: A Practical Guide to Object-Based Research in Fashion* (London: Bloomsbury Academic, 2015).

85 Burman and Fennetaux, *The Pocket*, 15.

86 Michael Yonan, 'Toward a Fusion of Art History and Material Culture Studies', *West 86th* 18, no. 2 (Fall-Winter 2011): 244.

87 Susan Vincent, *The Anatomy of Fashion: Dressing the Body from the Renaissance to Today* (Oxford: Berg, 2009).

88 Lucrabation (n.) study, or meditation. *General Advertiser*, 20 August 1785.

Chapter 1

1 Campbell, *London Tradesman*, 207.

2 Fiona Clark, *Hats* (London: B. T. Bratsford Ltd, 1982), 17; Georgine De Courtais, *Women's Headdress and Hairstyles in England from AD 600 to the Present Day* (London: B. T. Bratsford Ltd, 1973), 86.

3 Sloman, *Gainsborough*, 165.

4 *The World*, 14 September 1790.

5 *General Advertiser*, 20 August 1785.

6 See Margaret K. Powell and Joseph Roach, 'Big Hair', *Eighteenth-Century Studies* 38, no. 1 (2004): 79–99; Louisa Cross, 'Fashionable Hair in the Eighteenth Century: Theatricality and Display', in *Hair: Styling, Culture and*

Fashion, ed. Sarah Cheang and Geraldine Biddle-Perry (Oxford: Berg, 2008), 15–26; Gill Perry, *Spectacular Flirtations: Viewing the Actress in British Art and Theatre 1768–1820* (London: Yale University Press, 2007); Pointon, *Hanging the Head*; Angela Rosenthal, 'Raising Hair', *Eighteenth-Century Studies* 38, no. 1 (2004): 1–16; Harriet Stroomberg, *High Heads: Spotprenten over Haarmode in de Achttiende Eeuw/Hair Fashions Depicted in Eighteenth-Century Satirical Prints Published by Matthew and Mary Darly* (Enschede: Rijksmuseum Twenthe, 2000).

7 Susan J. Vincent, *Hair: An Illustrated History* (London: Bloomsbury Visual Arts, 2018), 39–40, 66–7.

8 MA 7269, Morgan Library.

9 Pierre-Joseph Buc'hoz, *The Toilet of Flora: Or, a Collection of the Most Simple and Approved Methods of Preparing Baths, Essences, Pomatums, Powders, Perfumes, and Sweet-Scented Waters with Receipts for Cosmetics of Every Kind, That Can Smooth and Brighten the Skin, Give Force to Beauty, and Take Off the Appearance of Old Age and Decay. For Use of the Ladies. A New Edition, Improved* (London: Printed for J. Murray, 1779); James Stewart, *Plocacosmos: Or, The Whole Art of Hair Dressing; Wherein Is Contained, Ample Rules for the Young Artisan, More Particularly for Ladies Women, Valets, &c. &c. as Well as Directions for Persons to Dress Their Own Hair* (London: Printed for the Author, 1782).

10 For reconstructive practices, see Stowell, Cox and McKnight, *The American Duchess*.

11 Richard Corson, *Fashions in Hair: The First Five Thousand Years* (London: Peter Owen Ltd, 1965), 333; Powell and Roach, 'Big Hair', 88, 92; R. Turner Wilcox, *The Mode in Hats and Headdress, Including Hair Styles, Cosmetics and Jewelry* (London: Charles Scribner's Sons, 1959), 151; John Woodforde, *The Strange Story of False Hair* (London: Routledge & Kegan Paul, 1971), 64.

12 See Caitlin Blackwell, '"The Feather'd Fair in a Fright": The Emblem of the Feather in Graphic Satire of 1776', *Journal for Eighteenth-Century Studies* 36, no. 3 (2013): 353–76; Gernerd, 'Fancy Feathers'. For ostrich feathers at court, see Joanna Marschner, 'A Weaving Field of Feathers – Dressing the Head for Presentation at the English Court, 1700–1939', in *Birds of Paradise: Plumes & Feathers in Fashion* (Tielt: Lannoo, 2014), 141–52.

13 Corson, *Fashions in Hair*, 353; De Courtais, *Women's Headdress*, 80.

14 See Dyer, 'Fashions of the Day', 73–94; Campbell, *Historical Style*, 64–6.

15 *The Lady's Magazine, or Entertaining Companion for the Fair Sex,* March 1776, 118.

16 In the 1770s and 1780s, Stanley is the only named correspondent.

17 Dyer, 'Fashions of the Day', 78.

18 See Batchelor, 'To Cherish', 377–92; Smith, 'Fast Fashion', 440–51.

19 *Cabinet des Modes ou Les Modes Nouvelles* was published 1785–9.

20 Collections of numbered fashion cards exist in Winterthur. See Dyer, *Material Lives*, 37–47.

21 Pierres was made Printer Ordinary to Louis XVI in 1779.

22 Dyer, *Material Lives,* 63.

23 French fashion plates identify each hat or style by name, whereas British do not.

24 Clark, *Hats*, 16–17.

25 *Morning Herald,* 11 March 1784; *The Lady's Magazine, or Entertaining Companion for the Fair Sex*, June 1781, 287; *The Lady's Magazine, or Entertaining Companion for the Fair Sex*, July 1774, 379; *Gazetteer and New Daily Advertiser*, 5 February 1784.

26 *Morning Chronicle*, 1 August 1778.

27 Cunnington, *Handbook,* 366; Lady Alice Archer Houblon, *The Houblon Family: Its Story and Times* (London: Constable, 1907), 2.174.

28 *The Lady's Magazine, or Entertaining Companion for the Fair Sex*, June 1781, 287; *The Lady's Magazine, or Entertaining Companion for the Fair Sex,* March 1783, 121; *The Lady's Magazine, or Entertaining Companion for the Fair Sex,* June 1784, 303. In France, the Chapeau Devonshire was illustrated in *Gallerie des Modes et Costumes Français. 41e Cahier des Costumes Français, 11e Suite de coëffures à la mode en 1783*, Acc. No. 44.1551, MFA. Kimberly Chrisman-Campbell, 'French Connections: Georgiana, Duchess of Devonshire, and the Anglo-French Fashion Exchange', *Dress* 31, no. 1 (2004): 7–8; Kimberly Chrisman-Campbell, *Fashion Victims: Dress at the Court of Louis XVI and Marie-Antoinette* (New Haven: Yale University Press, 2015).

29 There is no evidence connecting the Duchess to the design of the hat, or that the portrait by Gainsborough inspired others to buy them. By the time the portrait was painted, Gainsborough had stopped exhibiting at the Royal Academy.

30 *The Lounger*, 1786, partially quoted in C. Willett and Phillis Cunnington, *Handbook of English Costume in the Eighteenth Century* (London: Faber and Faber Ltd, 1972), 364.

31 McNeil, 'Introduction', 11.

32 The 2005 acquisition includes over thirty items of clothing spanning from gowns and outerwear to accessories and underwear, Acc. No. 2005-102, 2–39.

33 For full-size fashionable caps, see Acc. No. M987.32.1-2, McCord Museum. For caps, see Sarah Woodyard, *Martha's Mob Cap? A Milliner's Hand-Sewn Inquiry into Eighteenth-Century Caps c. 1770–1800*, MA Dissertation, 2017, University of Alberta.

34 The calash revived between the 1820s and 1840s. Anne Buck, *Dress*, 49.

35 László Tarr, *The History of the Carriage* (London: Vision Press Ltd, 1969), 267–8. John F. Watson, *Annals of Philadelphia and Pennsylvania, in the Olden Time; Being a Collection of Memoirs, Anecdote, and Incidents of the City and Its Inhabitants from the Days of the Pilgrim Founders* (Philadelphia: E. L. Carey & A. Hart, 1830), 176. Watson's account was the first to assert the popularity of the colour green. Other retrospective catalogues of fashionable dress that describe the calash include: 'Annals of Female Fashion: In Which Every Ancient and Modern Mode is Carefully Traced from the Earliest Ages to the Beginning of the Nineteenth Century,' *The Ladies' Monthly Museum*, April 1820, 196–9. Elisabeth McClellan notes the use of green and pink as described by an unknown source as 'it was like looking down a green lane to see a rose blooming at the end.' Elisabeth McClellan, *Historic Dress in America, 1607–1800: With an Introductory Chapter on Dress in the Spanish and French Settlements in Florida and Louisiana* (Philadelphia: George W. Jacobs & Company, 1904), 214; also eighteenth-century calashes were primarily solid colours. Nineteenth-century calashes were also made of patterned fabrics. For example, see a *c*. 1830 speckled silk taffeta calash in LACMA, Los Angeles, Acc. No. 52.44.18; a plaid cotton calash, early nineteenth century in HD, Deerfield, Acc. No. 2007.28.2; a mid-nineteenth-century checked calash in the MFA, Boston, Acc. No. 52.258; and a floral calash in the FM, Bath, Acc. No. 1.12.775.

36 Alice Morse Earle, *Two Centuries of Costume in America 1620–1820* (Rutland, VT: Charles E. Tuttle Company, 1971), 2.79–82; James Robinson Planché, *A Cyclopaedia of Costume, or Dictionary of Dress. Including Notices of Contemporaneous Fashions on the Continent, and a General Chronological History of the Costume of the Principal Countries of Europe, from the Commencement of the Christian Era to the Accession of George the Third* (London: Chatto and Windus, 1876), 70; François Boucher, *A History of Costume in the West* (London: Thames and Hudson, 1965), 307; Doreen Yarwood, *The Encyclopaedia of World Costume* (London: B. T. Bratsford, 1978), 63.

37 It is difficult to distinguish between flat-cut cane and whalebone unless the boning is visible through a tear in the fabric. However, the weight suggests wood rather than baleen for this example.

38 The opening across the face measures 8 inches (20.32 cm).

39 Former curator of the DWW, Linda Baumgarten, identified that this type of backing construction is the same as the backing construction for hoods of capes. May 2014, Colonial Williamsburg.

40 See Acc. No. 456-1895, V&A. Styles, *Dress of the People*, 122, 127.

41 Due to storage in the museum collection, the calash is now much flatter and wider in front than it would have appeared on the body when worn.

42 Sarah Woodyard made this constructional discovery when examining surviving calashes in the MOL collection, London, May 2014, Colonial Williamsburg.

43 Calashes could be more decorative, including edged ribbon trim around the neck and front, and bows on the back of the calash as well, as seen in a lilac and cream calash in the MET, New York, Acc. No. C.1.45.68.44.

44 *Morning Chronicle and London Advertiser*, 9 August 1779. Many thanks to Jenea Whitacre at Colonial Williamsburg for pointing me to the original source for the song. *Public Advertiser* on 16 September 1779, notes that 'The CALASH, a favourite Rondo, composed by Sig. Kammell, embellished with the Bust of a Lady in that Head Dress, 1S,' is published by Longman and Brooerip, No. 26, Cheapside, Music-sellers to the Royal Family.

45 Cross, 'Fashionable Hair', 15; Powell and Roach, 'Big Hair', 80, 83–4; Perry, *Spectacular Flirtations*, 94; Geraldine Biddle-Perry and Sarah Cheang, 'Introduction: Thinking about Hair', in *Hair: Styling, Culture and Fashion*, ed. Sarah Cheang and Geraldine Biddle-Perry (Oxford: Berg, 2008), 5.

46 Wilcox, *The Mode*, 157; Cunnington, *Handbook*, 350.

47 *Morning Chronicle and London Advertiser*, 9 August 1779.

48 Thank you to John Styles for first bringing a British advertisement of a calash to my attention from the *Manchester Mercury*, sold by milliner Ann Kay, 20 April 1779. *The Lady's Magazine, or Entertaining Companion of the Fair Sex*, March, April, May 1784, 157, 213, 269. *The Lady's Magazine* was published monthly between 1770–1832, covering a wide range of subjects for the betterment of the female mind. Its price indicates the middling class as its target audience. Adburgham, *Women in Print*, 132, 276.

49 *Memoirs and Interesting Adventures of an Embroidered Waistcoat* (London: Printed for and sold by J. Brooke, 1751). An extended version, printed in two volumes, was published in 1760. Though Igor Kopytoff's theory of object biography does not expand to the literary or fictional, his term suits the scope of the poem. Igor Kopytoff, 'The Cultural Biography of Things: Commoditization as Process', in *The Social Life of Things: Commodities in Cultural Perspective*, ed. Arjun Appadurai (Cambridge: Cambridge University Press, 1986), 64–94. For it-narratives, see Mark Blackwell (ed.), *The Secret Life of Things: Animals, Objects, and It-Narratives in Eighteenth-Century England*, ed. Mark Blackwell (Lewisburg: Bucknell University Press, 2007); Chloe Wigston Smith, *Women, Work, and Clothes in the Eighteenth-Century Novel* (Cambridge: Cambridge University Press, 2013), 73–9; Liz Bellamy, 'It-Narrators and Circulation: Defining a Subgenre', in *The Secret Life of Things: Animals, Objects, and It-Narratives in Eighteenth-Century England*, ed. Mark Blackwell (Lewisburg: Bucknell University Press, 2007), 117–46.

50 Whether this poem can be situated within the subgenre of it-narratives is difficult to say. Liz Bellamy has discussed the difficulties of defining it-narratives, which characteristically changed over time and did not comply with a single format or narrative device. Bellamy, 'It-Narrators', 117–46.

51 *The Lady's Magazine, or Entertaining Companion of the Fair Sex*, March 1784, 157.

52 Ibid.

53 Ibid., April 1784, 213.

54 Ibid., May 1784, 269. An ell of fabric was 45 in, or a yard and a quarter (1.143 m). Minerva's measurement for thirty ells would have far exceeded the required amount of fabric, as a calash can be made with under a yard of fabric.

55 Campbell, *London Tradesman*, 208; Elizabeth Kowaleski-Wallace, *Consuming Subjects: Women, Shopping and Business in the Eighteenth Century* (New York: Columbia University Press, 1997), 120. Millinery shops were perceived as being a front for salacious activity. In 1738 Charles Horne warns parents of apprenticing their daughters with milliners, mantuamakers and haberdashers, as they were 'actually seminaries of prostitution'. Charles Horne, *Serious Thoughts on the Miseries of Seduction and Prostitution, with a Full Account of the Evils that Produce Them …* (London: Printed for Swift and Son, 1738), 51; quoted in Tony Henderson, *Disorderly Women in Eighteenth-Century London: Prostitution and Control in the Metropolis 1730–1830* (Harlow: Pearson Educational Ltd, 1999), 14.

56 *The Lady's Magazine, or Entertaining Companion of the Fair Sex*, May 1784, 269.

57 Campbell, *London Tradesman*, 207.

58 *Morning Chronicle*, 11 August 1780.

59 *Manchester Mercury*, 20 April 1779.

60 *The Virginia Gazette*, 24 October 1766.

61 Ibid., 23 December 1773.

62 Though sailing times varied, average voyages took five to seven weeks travelling from Britain to America, and four to five weeks returning. J. P. Marshall, 'Introduction', in *The Oxford History of the British Empire: The Eighteenth Century*, ed. J. P. Marshall (Oxford: Oxford University Press, 1998), 2.13–14.

63 See Mary A. Stephenson, *Milliners of Williamsburg in the Eighteenth Century: Report* (Williamsburg: Colonial Williamsburg Foundation. Early American history research reports, 1951).

64 *The Virginia Gazette*, 31 October 1771.

65 The application of the word 'mechanical' does not refer to a motorized or automatic device, but merely that the object was designed to move between two different points of rest – folded and open.

66 Philip Freneau, *The Miscellaneous Works of Mr. Philip Freneau Containing His Essays, and Additional Poems* (Philadelphia: Francis Bailey, 1788), 380–91.

67 A drawing by Swedish artist, Elias Martin, portrays a young woman blown about by her calash. Elias Martin, *The Artist's Brother and Wife*, c. 1780, Nationalmuseum, Stockholm. Freneau, *Miscellaneous Works*, 382.

68 Freneau, *Miscellaneous Works*, 387.

69 Waterproofing was attempted by oiling the silk.

70 The calash's relationship with the umbrella will be discussed below in detail.

71 McNeil, 'That Doubtful Gender', 154.

72 Mimi Hellman, 'Furniture, Sociability, and the Work of Leisure in Eighteenth Century France', *Eighteenth-Century Studies* 32, no. 4 (1999): 417–34.

73　Ibid., 417.

74　Ibid., 424–8.

75　Ibid., 430–1.

76　Ibid., 430.

77　I have not found another example of a garment used as a name. Double entendre names are common, like Miss Tittup which has obvious sexual connotations, or Miss Brazen, Miss Bruin, Miss Chienne and Miss Renard, which use adjectives or types of animals to describe a woman's personality. The closest similarity would be Miss Hedgehog, which correlates to the specific hairstyle she is portrayed wearing. *A City Officer Taught by Miss Tittup to Cock His Spontoon with Proper Grace,* 10 January 1782, publ. by T. James; *An Actress at Her toilet, or, Miss Brazen Just Breecht,* 24 June 1779, publ. by Carington Bowles; *A Stage Box Scene: Mrs. Bruin, Miss Chienne, Miss Renard,* 1 January 1787, publ. by J. Wicksteed, all in the collection of the LWL, Farmington.

78　This discussion does not follow the chronological order of the five main calash prints, which were published in this order: *The Old Maids Morning Visit or the Calash Lady's,* 11 March 1777; *The Ton at Greenwich. A La Festoon Dans le Park a Greenwich,* 11 August 1777; *Capt. Calipash & Mrs. Calipee,* 28 October 1777; *A Morning Visit – or the Fashionable Dresses for the Year 1777,* 1 January 1778; *Miss Calash: Drawn by Miss Calash 1778,* 14 October 1778; *Miss Calash in Contemplation,* 15 May 1780.

79　The average height of calashes in the DWW collection measures 12.5 in (31.75 cm).

80　It is unclear whether the fabric that extends from her waist around the back of her skirt is part of her dress, or meant to be the apron of the calash, which normally rests around the neck and shoulders.

81　Stroomberg, *High Heads,* 9.

82　The BM has two additional hand-coloured versions, one in which the calash is blue and the second yellow, Acc. Nos. 1935,0522.2.97 and 2010,7081.1963.

83　A lilac calash in the MET, New York, includes a side ribbon; however, due to its darker colour it is most likely a replacement, Acc. No. C.45.68.44. An olive calash in the MFA, Boston, features a ribbon that attaches to both sides of the front, forming a loop to hold onto, Acc. No. 59.273. A green calash, also at the MFA, retains its green silk ribbon, attached to the right side of the front cane, Acc. No. 46.321.

84　Carington Bowles, *Carington Bowles's New and Enlarged Catalogue of Useful and Accurate Maps, Charts, and Plans; Curious and Entertaining Engraved and Mezzotint Prints, Single or in Sets: Writing Books; Including All the Branches of Penmanship: Black-Lines, Letter-File Maps, and Prints, School Pieces, Cards for Schools, &c. &c. Elegant Drawing Books, and Correct Books of Maps, Roads, Perspective, Geometry, &c. Containing a Great Variety of New and Valuable Articles for the Use of the Nobility and Gentry of Great-Britain and Ireland. Merchants Exports, and Shop Keepers Country Trade Which May Be Had Wholesale and Retail at His Map and Print Warehouse, No. 69, St. Paul's Church Yard, London* (London: Printed by Carington Bowles, 1784), 117–18.

85　Though 'pin up' is a twenty-first-century term, the women portrayed in these series are presented as visually consumable, sexualized by the positions of their bodies. Though most are ambiguously presented as suggestively attractive, like the women of these two prints, other are identified directly as sex workers, such as *The Cunning Harlot,* number 441 of Bowles's series.

86　Bowles's version of *A Lady in Waiting,* published 2 September 1780, is depicted in a large bonnet. Sayer's was reprinted on 14 October 1780. Variant titles can be seen in Bowles's *A Man Trap,* published on 6 January 1780, and Sayer & Bennett's *A Military Man Trap,* published on 25 September 1780, both in the BM, London.

87　The print was re-issued on 14 October 1787, a hand-coloured version survives in the BM, London.

88 While Borsay's study primarily focused outside the metropolis of London, his observations are applicable to both urban and provincial sites alike. Peter Borsay, *The English Urban Renaissance: Culture and Society in the Provincial Town, 1660–1770* (Oxford: Clarendon Press, 1989), 117.

89 Examples of public walks in London included Moorfields, Inns of Court and later the London Mall and St. James's Park, and were also constructed in spa towns such as Tumbridge Wells and Bath Spa. Borsay, *English Urban Renaissance*, 141, 162, 168; Vickery, *Gentleman's Daughter*, 248.

90 For a summary of entertainments produced at Vauxhall, see Penelope J. Corfield, *Vauxhall: Sex and Entertainment: London's Pioneering Urban Pleasure Garden* (London: History & Social Action Publications, 2012), 10. Borsay has argued that while the pleasure gardens Vauxhall and Ranelagh have garnered the majority scholarly attention, they were part of a wider trend of 'public or semi-public planted green spaces' that were rooted across Britain. For a thorough list of green spaces across Britain, see Peter Borsay, 'Pleasure Gardens and Urban Culture in the Long Eighteenth Century', in *The Pleasure Garden, from Vauxhall to Coney Island*, ed. Jonathan Conlin (Philadelphia: University of Philadelphia, 2013), 51–60.

91 Corfield, *Vauxhall*, 4; Penelope J. Corfield, 'Walking the City Streets: The Urban Odyssey in Eighteenth-Century England', *Journal of Urban History* 16, no. 2 (1990): 134; Borsay, *English Urban Renaissance*.

92 Vauxhall was re-opened and redesigned by Jonathan Tyres in 1732. Vickery, *Gentleman's Daughter*, 244. Ranelagh was established in 1742. Corfield, *Vauxhall*, 12. While these were not the only metropolitan pleasure gardens and spas, others include those in Islington, Hampstead and Marylebone, they were the most reputed. Elizabeth McKeller, *Landscapes of London: the City, the Country and the Suburbs, 1660–1840* (London: Published for the Paul Mellon Centre for Studies in British Art by Yale University Press, 2013), 111; Borsay, 'Pleasure Gardens', 63–4.

93 Greig, *Beau Monde*, 72. Servants in livery were barred entry from the pleasure gardens. Tickets to the most prominent gardens cost between sixpence at Marylebone and two shillings and sixpence at Ranelagh. Vauxhall cost one shilling after reopening. Borsay, 'Pleasure Gardens', 65.

94 Corfield, *Vauxhall*, 4.

95 Gerald MacLean, Donna Landry and Joseph P. Ward, 'Introduction: The Country and the City Revisited', in *The Country and the City Revisited: England and the Politics of Culture, 1550–1850*, ed. Gerald MacLean, Donna Landry and Joseph P. Ward (Cambridge: Cambridge University Press, 1999), 14. For a study on the shoe and walking, see Giorgio Riello and Peter McNeil, 'The Art and Science of Walking: Mobility, Gender and Footwear in the Long Eighteenth Century', *Fashion Theory* 9, no. 2 (2005): 175–204. For an in-depth study on the eighteenth-century shoe, see Giorgio Riello, *A Foot in the Past: Consumers, Producers and Footwear in the Long Eighteenth Century* (Oxford: Pasold Research Fund/Oxford University Press, 2006). Chris Breward has called for the consideration of this intersection within the urban context of London fashion, whereas Peter McNeil has done so within the interior setting. Chris Breward, *Fashioning London: Clothing and the Modern Metropolis* (Oxford: Berg, 2004); McNeil, 'Doubtful Gender'.

96 *The Gentleman's and London Magazine*, 1777, quoted Cunnington, *Handbook*, 350; *The London Magazine*, 1772, quoted in Althea Mackenzie, *Hats and Bonnets from Snowhill, One of the World's Leading Collections of Costume and Accessories of the 18th and 19th Centuries* (London: National Trust Enterprises Ltd, 2004), 16; *The London Magazine, or, Gentleman's Monthly Intelligencer*, 1778, 406. That it was perceived as a protector of health, also aligns with walking, which Laura Williams has argued was perceived as a benefactor of good health. See Laura Williams, '"To Recreate and Refresh Their Dulled Spirites in the Sweet and Wholesome Ayre": Green Space and the Growth of the City', in *Imagining Early Modern London: Perceptions and Portrayals of the City from Stow to Strype, 1598–1720*, ed. Julia F. Merritt (Cambridge: Cambridge University Press, 2001), 185–213.

97   *The Lady's Magazine, or Entertaining Companion of the Fair Sex*, April 1784, 213.

98   These observations of how the calash interacts with the elements when worn on the body arise from having worn replica calashes made by the Margaret Hunter Millinery Shop, during a fellowship at Colonial Williamsburg, May 2014.

99   *The Lady's Magazine, or Entertaining Companion of the Fair Sex*, April 1784, 213.

100 Corfield, *Vauxhall*, 11–13; Greig, *Beau Monde*, 69. See David H. Solkin, *Painting for Money: The Visual Arts and the Public Sphere in Eighteenth-Century England* (London: Yale University Press, 1993), 135–9; Miles Ogborn, *Spaces of Modernity: London's Geographies, 1680–1780* (London: the Gilford Press, 1998), 128–33.

101 Vauxhall was not open on Sunday, further excluding those of the lower orders. Borsay, 'Pleasure Gardens', 67, 74–5.

102 Bernard Mandeville, *The Fable of the Bees: or, Private Vices, Publick Benefits. With an Essay on Charity and Charity-Schools. And a Search into the Nature of Society* (London: Printed for J. Tonson, 1724), 130. Though written during the first quarter of the century, *Fable of the Bees* was re-printed in 1733, 1757, 1768, 1772, 1795, 1806.

103 McNeil and Riello, 'Art and Science', 180.

104 For the significance of eating turtle, which were imported live from the West Indies, see Krystal McMillen, 'Eating Turtle, Eating the World: Comestible Things in the Eighteenth Century', in *Eighteenth-Century Thing Theory in a Global Context: from Consumerism to Celebrity Culture*, ed. Ileana Baird and Christina Ionescu (Farnham: Ashgate Publishing Company, 2013), 191–208.

105 Stroomberg, *High Heads*, 37; Donald, *Age of Caricature*, 83.

106 Hannah Greig, 'Leading the Fashion: The Material Culture of London's Beau Monde', in *Gender, taste, and material culture in Britain and North America, 1700–1830*, ed. John Styles and Amanda Vickery (London: Yale Centre for British Art, 2006), 308.

107 Greig, *Beau Monde*, 79; Corfield, 'Walking', 140.

108 Jane Austen, *Northanger Abbey: And Persuasion: By the Author of 'Pride and Prejudice;' 'Mansfield-Park,' &c.* (London: John Murray, 1818), 3.42.

109 The polonaise gown was also associated with walking. Kendra van Cleave and Brooke Welborn, '"Very Much the Taste and Variety Are the Makes" Reconsidering the Late-Eighteenth-Century Robe à la Polonaise', *Dress* 39, no. 1 (2013): 19.

110 It is possible that it may be a parasol intended to shade from the sun. Parasols were more decorative and lacked the oiled or waxed finish to make them waterproof. As Jeremy Farrell has noted, the interchange of terms was possible. Jeremy Farrell, *Umbrellas & Parasols* (London: B.T. Batsford Ltd, 1985), 26.

111 Though not the first to invent umbrella's operational design, the first British patent was applied for in 1786 by John Beale. Farrell, *Umbrellas*, 34.

112 For the history of umbrellas, see T. S. Crawford, *A History of the Umbrella* (Newton Abbot: David & Charles Ltd, 1970); Ariel Beaujot, *Victorian Fashion Accessories* (London: Berg, 2012), 105–39; Irene Fizer, 'The Fur Parasol: Masculine Dress, Prosthetic Skins, and the Making of the English Umbrella in Robinson Crusoe', in *Eighteenth-Century Thing Theory in a Global Context: From Consumerism to Celebrity Culture*, ed. Ileana Baird and Christina Ionescu (Farnham: Ashgate Publishing Company, 2013), 209–28; Farell, *Umbrellas*.

113 For a discussion of the umbrella's French origins and production, see Madeleine Delpierre, *Dress in France in the Eighteenth Century* (New Haven: Yale University Press, 1997), 45–6; Cissie Fairchilds, 'The Production and Marketing of Populuxe Goods in Eighteenth-Century Paris', in *Consumption and the World of Goods*, ed. John Brewer and Roy Porter (London: Routledge, 2013), 238. In *The Female Tatler*, on 12 December 1709, the user of an umbrella from a coffee house was accused of wearing the mistress's pattens. In John Gay's *Trivia*, 1716, he attributes it as an accessory for 'good housewives' and 'the walking maid.' Horace Walpole notes that using an umbrella is only done by Frenchmen, rather than English and footman John MacDonald is accused of being a Frenchman when walks with one in London. *The Female Tatler*, 12 December 1709; John Gay, *Trivia*, 1716 quoted in Crawford, *A History*, 106, 116, 124; Farrell, *Umbrellas*, 33; John E. Crowley, 'Homely Pleasures: The Pursuit of Comfort in the Eighteenth Century', in *The Book of Touch*, ed. Constance Classen (Oxford: Berg, 2005), 85.

114 A fashionable woman in profile carries a massive umbrella that shades her coiffeur, as well as a gentleman sitting on the back of her polonaise gown, as a surprised onlooker gawks. The period in which umbrellas became acceptable for men to use is vague and differs in both accounts. Farrell asserts that by the end of the 1830s, umbrellas were universally used by men, however in the meantime, they were adopted by the dandy and presented other issues, such as class, which has made the transition harder to pinpoint. Crawford, *A History*, 114–24; Farrell, *Umbrellas*, 31–7. John Crowley attributes the appearance of the umbrella in the diaries of Reverend James Woodford in the late 1780s as a sign of their acceptance in society. Crowley, 'Homely Pleasures', 86.

115 The pairing of a woman in a calash accompanied by a man carrying an umbrella recurs in the 1781 print *Hyde Park 1780*, in which an elderly calash wearer is accompanied by an Indian serving boy, carrying an umbrella. She walks through the park unaware of her surroundings, causing four men on horseback to nearly collide, one of whom quizzes her through his spy glass. The crook she holds in her left hand strongly suggests that this pair is adaptation from the Darlys'. Henry William Bunbury, *Hyde Park 1780*, 3 February 1781, publ. by James Bretherton, BM, London.

116 Farrell identifies the crook, or tall cane, as a fashionable accessory with pastoral connotations during the 1770s and 80s. Farrell, *Umbrellas*, 26.

117 Warwick Wroth, *The London Pleasure Gardens of the Eighteenth Century* (London: Macmillan and Co Ltd, 1979), 5–7.

118 Of the two, Ranalegh was more expensive. Borsay, 'Pleasure Gardens', 65.

119 Solkin, *Painting for Money*, 108, 110.

120 Stephen Inwood notes that neighbourhoods east and south of the city were unfashionable, of which Greenwich was both, however McKeller observes that Greenwich became 'a desirable suburb for both the gentry and the middling sort'. Stephen Inwood, *Historic London: An Explorer's Companion* (London: Macmillan, 2008), 102; McKeller, *Landscapes*, 6. For fairs, see Anne Wohlcke, *The 'Perpetual Fair': Gender, Disorder, and Urban Amusement in Eighteenth-Century London* (Manchester: Manchester University Press, 2014).

121 'From a young Lady in Town to her Aunt in the Country, describing Greenwich Park, and the Passage to it by Water', *The Instructive Letter-writer, and Entertaining Companion: Containing Letters on the Most Interesting Subjects, in an Elegant and Easy Style; wherein a Peculiar Regard Has Been Had to Select Those, ONLY, Which Are Best Adapted to Inspire NOBLE and MANY SENTIMENTS, and Promote a RATIONAL and VIRTUOUS CONDUCT; Most of Them Being Wrote by the Following Royal and Eminent PERSONAGES, and the Best Authers, Ancient and Modern, viz …. The Second Edition* (London: Printed for W. Nicoll, 1765), 190.

122 Graphic satires which underline Bagnigge Wells's lower reputation include: *Mr. Deputy Dumpling and Family Enjoying a Summer Afternoon, c.* 1780, publ. by Carington Bowles, Guildhall Library, London, which depicts a

distinctly middling family, and *A Bagnigge Wells Scene, or, No Resisting Temptation,* 1776, publ. by Carington Bowles, LWL, Farmington, which depicts two sex workers waiting for custom.

123 Calashes worn on the streets can be seen in Thomas Rowlandson's *Entrance to the Mall, Spring Gardens, c.* 1780, V&A, London and *Place des Victoires, Paris, c.* 1783, YCBA, New Haven. A calash is worn in an assembly room in the spa town of Weymouth in 'Fashionable Dresses in the Rooms at Weymouth 1774' in *The Lady's Magazine, or, Entertaining Companion for the Fair Sex,* February 1775. The back of a pleated calash is also featured 'Twelve of the genteelest Head-dresses of 1772' in the pocket diary belonging to Elizabeth Shakelton reproduced in Vickery, *Gentleman's Daughter,* 176.

124 Ogborn, *Spaces of Modernity,* 75–111; Robert Shoemaker, 'Gendered Spaces: Patterns of Mobility and Perceptions of London's Geography, 1660–1750', in *Imagining Early Modern London: Perceptions and Portrayals of the City from Stow to Strype, 1598–1720,* ed. J. F. Merritt (Cambridge: Cambridge University Press, 2001), 161. Riello and McNeil have attributed the disappearance of pattens to gravel and paving improvements. Riello and McNeil, 'Art and Science', 180.

125 Corfield has argued that women across social classes walked along the streets. While elite women were most often accompanied by a maidservant, as conduct literature stipulates, they were not always as evidenced in illustrations, letters and novels. Corfield, 'Walking', 133–4, 148–51; Borsay, *English Urban Renaissance,* 170–2; Ogborn, *Spaces of Modernity,* 75; Vickery, *Gentleman's Daughter,* 250. For the rise of shopping, see Kowaleski-Wallace, *Consuming Subjects*; Harriet Guest, *Small Change: Women, Learning, Patriotism, 1750–1810* (London: The University of Chicago Press Ltd, 2000), 70–92; Serena Dyer, 'Stitching and Shopping: The Material Literacy of the Consumer', in *Material Literacy in Eighteenth Century Britain,* ed. Serena Dyer and Chloe Wigston Smith (London: Bloomsbury, 2020), 99–116.

126 La Roche, *Sophie in London,* 86; quoted in McNeil and Riello, 'Art and Science', 179.

127 Amanda Flather, *Gender and Space in Early Modern England* (Woodbridge: The Boydell Press, 2007), 122–4; Dyer, 'Stitching and Shopping', 99–116; McKeller, 2013, 113; Vickery, *Gentleman's Daughter,* 9.

128 *The* London *and* Westminster *Guide, Through the Cities and Suburbs …* (London: Printed for W. Nicoll, 1768), xxiv.

129 McKeller, *Landscapes,* 146.

130 Vickery, *Gentleman's Daughter,* 269.

131 *The* London, xxiv.

132 See Vickery, *Gentleman's Daughter,* 206–7.

133 Her porcine appearance recalls the stories of pig-faced ladies, the most famous of which in the long eighteenth century would be the pig-faced lady of Manchester Square, whom Cruikshank would depict on 21 March 1815 in a double print of *The Pig Faced Lady of Manchester Square and the Spanish Mule of Madrid.* See, Jan Bondson, *Freaks: The Pig-Faced Lady of Manchester Square & Other Medical Marvels* (Stroud: Tempus, 2006).

134 The position of the lioness on it hind legs is mirrored by a mouse in the foreground.

135 A German adaptation of the print survives in the BM's collection, *Der Morgen Besuch,* in which the women wear caps instead of calashes. Though the BM dates the print to *c.* 1773, I have been unable to locate an earlier version, other than that of 1777, which suggests that this print is in fact a later date than 1773, and the copy artist chose to replace the calashes with caps, as well as change the title. For a discussion of the adaptation of British prints in continental markets, McNeil and Steorn, 'The Medium of Print', 135–56.

136 'Old maids' were targeted and marginalized for their marital status, linked with themes of vanity, degeneracy and jealousy of the young and fruitful. See McCreery, *Satirical Gaze*, 212–51.

137 For example, *Miss Returning from a Visit, or Thomas Fording a Brook with His Mistress*, 20 August 1774, publ. by R. Sayer & J. Bennett, BM, London. One example of visiting is a mezzotint of two sisters having tea, however their closeness and intimate gaze may suggest the possibility of an alternative relationship between the figures. *The Visit to a Sister*, 1 June 1789, publ. by R. Sayer, BM, London.

138 14 January 1752. Samuel Johnson, *The Rambler* (London: Printed for J. Payne and J. Bouquet, 1762), 6.144–53.

139 Ibid., 149–50.

140 For sending compliments, see Vickery, *Gentleman's Daughter*, 204–5. Though, images of visiting are rare, what does survive in paper are message cards. See Sarah Sophia Bank's collection in the BM.

141 No XXIII, Saturday, 14 August 1756. Nicholas Babble, *The Prater* (London: Printed for T. Lownds, 1756), 182.

142 William Alexander, *The History of Women, from the Earliest Antiquity, to the Present Time: Giving Some Account of Almost Every Interesting Particular Concerning that Sex, among All Nations, Ancient and Modern* (Dublin: Printed by J. A. Husband, 1779), 2.146–7.

143 Hannah Barker and Elaine Chalus, 'Introduction', in *Gender in Eighteenth-Century England*, ed. Hannah Barker and Elaine Chalus (Abingdon: Routledge, 2014), 25–6.

144 Whyman observes that the 'existence of separate gendered visiting patterns has received little attention'. Susan E. Whyman, *Sociability and Power in Late-Stuart England: The Cultural Worlds of the Verneys 1660–1720* (Oxford: Oxford University Press, 1999), 107. See Gudrun Andersson and Jon Stobart, 'Introduction', in *Daily Lives and Daily Routines in the Long Eighteenth Century*, ed. Gudrun Andersson and Jon Stobart (London: Routledge, 2022).

145 Greig, *Beau Monde*, 95, 146–55. For visiting in the seventeenth century, see Felicity Heal, *Hospitality in Early Modern England* (Oxford: Oxford University Press, 1990); Whyman, *Sociability*; Flather, *Gender and Spaces*.

146 Greig, *Beau Monde*, 147–55; Vickery, *Gentleman's Daughter*, 205–8; Amanda Vickery, *Behind Closed Doors: At Home in Georgian England* (London: Yale University Press, 2009), 273–6; Katharine Glover, *Elite Women and Polite Society in Eighteenth-Century Scotland* (Woodbridge: The Boydell Press, 2011), 82–4. For the tea-table see Ann Smart Martin, 'Tea Tables Overturned: Rituals of Power and Place in Colonial America', in *Furnishing the Eighteenth Century: What Furniture Can Tell Us about the European and American Past*, ed. Dena Goodman and Kathryn Norberg (London: Routledge, 2007), 169–82.

147 The first title, which identifies the subject as a visit, echoes the titles of fashion etchings in women's magazines. However, as the calash was still in fashion in 1780, it would have been impractical to back-date the reissue of the print by using the same title. For this discussion, I will draw primarily draw from the hand-coloured version under the second title at the LWL. Though the Walpole's version's date is brandished off, a dated copy exists in the DWW, Williamsburg, with slightly different colouring.

148 Vickery, *Behind Closed Doors*, 14. For recent discussions of women's domestic spaces, Freya Gowrley, *Domestic Space in Britain, 1750–1840: Materiality, Sociability and Emotion* (London: Bloomsbury Visual Arts, 2022).

149 The delicate detail and shading of the calash are arguably more visible in the uncoloured version, indicating the satirist's attention to detail.

150 Donald, *Age of Caricature*, 9,11.

151 See Vickery, *Gentleman's Daughter*, 14–16; Glover, *Elite Women*, 82–3; Stana Nenadic, 'Middle-Rank Consumers and Domestic Culture in Edinburgh and Glasgow 1720–1840', *Past & Present* 145 (1994): 122–56.

152 For the tea table as a construction of politeness and sociability, see Lawrence E. Klein, 'Gender, Conversation and the Public Sphere', in *Textuality and Sexuality: Reading Theories and Practices*, ed. Judith Still and Michael Worton (Manchester: Manchester University Press, 1993), 100–15; Jürgen Habermas, *The Structural Transformation of the Public Sphere: An Inquiry into a Category of Bourgeois Society* (London: Polity Press, 1989); Amanda Vickery, 'Golden Age to Separate Spheres? A Review of the Categories and Chronology of English Women's History', *The Historical Review* 36, no. 2 (June 1993): 383–414.

153 It would reappear in the 1820s–30s, though in smaller proportion.

154 Francis Lathom, *The Dash of the Day, a Comedy, in Five Acts …* (Norwich: J. Payne, 1800), 80.

155 Ibid., 80.

156 *The Tickler, or, Monthly Compendium of Good Things*, 1 February 1819, 37.

157 Carroll Smith-Rosenberg, 'The Female World of Love and Ritual: Relations between Women in Nineteenth-Century America', *Signs* 1, no. 1 (Autumn 1975), 9–10.

158 Lathom, *The Dash*, 80.

159 *The Lady's Magazine, or Entertaining Companion for the Fair Sex*, March 1784, 157.

Chapter 2

1 Ostrich feathers were supposedly introduced by the Duchess of Devonshire and quickly gained popularity in 1774. Powell and Roach, "Big Hair", 89. For more on feathers in hair, see Blackwell, 'The Feather'd Fair in a Fright', 353–76; Gernerd, 'Fancy Feathers', 195–218.

2 The position of this picture foreshadows the satires of Worsley's husband's friend peering in on her in 1782 by James Gillray. Reynolds's portrait was painted *c*. 1776, but not exhibited until 1780, so there is the possibility that it is not a copy, however, it is more likely that the artist of the satire had access to the portrait in Reynolds's studio. For more on Lady Worsley's riding habit, see Cally Blackman, 'Walking Amazons: The Development of the Riding Habit in England during the Eighteenth Century', *Costume* 35, no. 1 (2001): 47–58.

3 The cork rump was referred to as a *cul de paris* and *cul postiche* in French. Norah Waugh, *The Cut of Women's Clothes 1600–1930* (London: Faber and Faber Ltd, 1968), 68; Norah Waugh, *Corsets and Crinolines* (London: B. T. Batsford Ltd, 1987), 47; Alison Carter, *Underwear: The Fashion History* (London: B. T. Batsford Ltd, 1992), 25–6; Ribeiro, *Art of Dress*, 64. As Kendra van Cleave and Brooke Welborn have outlined, the stylistic differences between an English gown, anglaise or nightgown, and a polonaise was in the cut of the robe or jacket. Both featured the looped style of skirt, but the polonaise was distinguished by the inverted 'V' shaped cut of the bodice, which cut away from the centre front of the bust. van Cleave and Welborn, 'Very Much the Taste and Variety are the Makes', 5.

4 This count does not include repeated publications. Depictions in graphic satire appear again in 1785.

5 When the cork rump is mentioned in the fashion chronologies published in the second half of the twentieth century, often adopting the later term bustle, it is done so in passing, in reference to the changing silhouette with little further investigation. For example, F. W. Fairholt, *Costume in England: A History of Dress to the End of*

the Eighteenth Century (London: Chapman and Hall, 1846), 391; C. Willett and Phillis Cunnington, *The History of Underclothes* (London: Faber and Faber, 1981), 60–1; Waugh, *Cut of Women's Clothes*, 68, 72, 120; Waugh, *Corsets and Crinolines*, 47; Carter, *Underwear*, 33; Shelley Tobin, *Inside Out: A Brief History of Underwear* (London: The National Trust, 2000), 8; Elizabeth Ewing, *Dress & Undress: A History of Women's Underwear* (London: B. T. Batsford Ltd, 1978), 39; Aileen Ribeiro, *Dress and Morality* (London: B. T. Batsford Ltd, 1986), 114; Ribeiro, *Art of Dress*, 64. For more recent discussions, see Vincent, *Anatomy of Fashion*, 63; Julie Park, *The Self and It: Novel Objects and Mimetic Subjects in Eighteenth Century Society* (Stanford: Stanford University Press, 2010), 42; Smith, *Women, Work, and Clothes*, 188–93.

6 A pair of hip pads from the MFA is stuffed with wood shavings. Acc. No. 43.1275a.

7 Viccy Coltman, 'Material Culture and the History of Art(efacts)', in *Writing Material Culture History*, ed. Anne Gerristen and Giorgio Riello (London: Bloomsbury Academic, 2014), 26–7.

8 Moore, *Fashion*, 10.

9 *St. James Chronicle, or, the British Evening Post*, 1 April 1780.

10 Jane Tozer and Sarah Levitt, *Fabric of Society: A Century of People and Their Clothes 1770–1870* (Manchester: Laura Ashley Publications, 2010), 12.

11 There is a miniature scaled rump that survives with a 1780 doll in the V&A, which forms a stuffed ring, similar to the bum rolls of the previous century, Acc. No. MISC.339-1984, V&A, London.

12 For a pattern, see Janet Arnold, Jenny Tiramani, Luca Costigliolo, Sébastian Passot, Armelle Lucas and Jonannes Pietsch, *Patterns of Fashion 5: The Content, Cut, Construction and Context of Bodies, Stays, Hoops and Rumps c.1595–1795* (London: The School of Historical Dress, 2018), 150–1. By the 1780s, the rumps and bums were specifically noted as composed with horsehair, as well as wool. *The Public Advertiser* notes 'the ladies who contrived the new invented *wool-rump*, sat so long in contemplation on the proper materials for the purpose that they got the name of the *female rump parliament*', indicating a shift in material composition in the mid 1780s. Horsehair was also named as a material for female padding for the rump and stomach, first published in the 1790s. In addition, the name bustle has become to be adopted to describe a false rump. *The Public Advertiser*, 15 December 1784; *The Times*, 4 May 1793.

13 The tape measures 36½ in (92.71 cm). Linda Baumgarten has observed based on the collection of gowns at the DeWitt Wallace Museum of Decorative Arts, women's average waist spans ranged from 21 to 36 inches (53.34–91.44 cm), meaning the tape would most likely have fit around Elizabeth's waist. Linda Baumgarten, *What Clothes Reveal: The Language of Clothing in Colonial and Federal America: The Colonial Williamsburg Collection* (London: Yale University Press, 2002), 66.

14 For example, see Acc. No. 1949.130, MAG. A pair from *c.* 1800 from MAG includes eyelets higher up on the back, aligned with the elevated waistline, Acc. No. 1947.1625. A pair from the end of the seventeenth century at FM includes two metal hooks about an inch away from the back lacing, which could have hooked onto a bum roll, Acc. No BATMC.1.27.86. A late nineteenth-century ribbon corset at FM includes two buttons spaced evenly on the sides panels, which would have allowed for a wider framed bustle to attach without disturbing the decorative appearance of the ribbon front, Acc. No. I.27.16.

15 *St. James Chronicle, or the British Evening Post*, 1 April 1780.

16 Ibid.

17 See Davidson, *Regency Fashion*, 2019; Rauser, *Age of Undress*, 2020; Waugh, *Cut of Women's Clothes*, 72–135.

18 Clayton, *The English Press*, 220.

19 The curly-hair of the dog indicates that it may be a type of the poodle. The dog acts as an additional appendage to the woman's appearance, a luxury item of display. By 1796, dogs were taxed as a luxury item. Lynn M. Festa, 'Person, Animal, Thing: The 1796 Dog Tax and the Right to Superfluous Things', *Eighteenth-Century Life* 33, no. 2 (2009): 2. For a discussion of the anxieties associated with fashionable dress and lapdogs, see Ingrid H. Tague, *Animal Companions: Pets and Social Change in Eighteenth-Century Britain* (University Park: The Pennsylvania State University Press, 2015), 90–137.

20 The theme of the country girl dressed in metropolitan fashion was a common trope, as well as the country interloper attempting to blend in with the fashionable urban crowd.

21 *St. James Chronicle, or the British Evening Post,* 1 April 1780.

22 Though it is not possible to positively identify the breed of either dog, the second appears to resemble more of an Asian breed, or potentially a mix with a King Charles Spaniel. For a discussion of exotic toy dogs, see Chi-ming Yang, 'Culture in Miniature: Toy Dogs and Object Life', *Eighteenth-Century Fiction* 25, no. 1 (2012): 139–74.

23 The Darlys' inclusion of the rump as a fashionable necessity is affirmed in a column, 'The Man of Pleasure' or a dictionary of 'elegant life', which defines a '*Freight*' as 'A female, pretty or not pretty, who does not improve her complexion by art, does not wear a head above a food high, and has not adopted a cork-rump.' *The Town and Country Magazine*, September 1778, 487.

24 *The Gentleman's Magazine, and Historical Chronicle*, June 1779, 288; Supplement to *The Universal Magazine of Knowledge and Pleasure*, June 1777, 379; *London Chronicle*, 12–14 June 1777. A similar poem, 'Paltry Pride' reads 'There's the ladies of fashion you see, They'll all have a turn at this pride, They must have cork rumps, I declare, And a head as big as a bee-hive'. F. W. Fairholt, *Satirical Songs and Poems on Costume: From the 13th to the 19th Century*, Vol. 27 (London: Printed for the Percy Society, 1849), 247.

25 Judging by the accusatory tone of the last stanza, we can lean towards identifying the author as male. Though magazines, such as *The Lady's Magazine*, had female correspondents, it is most likely that this author is male.

26 For example, Longus's pastoral *Daphnis and Chloe*. The name was also an epithet for the Greek goddess Demeter, referring the young green shoot of a plant, and appears in the New Testament, in Corinthians 1:11. The name's popularity can be attested in 1777 in *The Lady's Magazine, or Entertaining Companion for the Fair Sex* alone, with four different poems using the name throughout the year.

27 Mezzotint prints include *Straphon & Chloe*, 1760, publ. by Robert Sayer, BM, London; *Chloe in the Country*, 1736, publ. by Richard Houston after Henry Pickering, BM, London.

28 *Advice to Chloe*, 1740, G. Bickham, LWL, Farmington; *Advice to Cloe*, 1750, LWL, Farmington; *Cloe as sung at the publick Gardens*, 1750, LWL, Farmington.

29 Jonathan Swift, *The Works of Dr. Jonathan Swift*, Vol. 7. (London: Printed for T. Osborne, W. Bowyer, C. Bathurst, W. Strahan, J. Rivington, J. Hinton, L. Davis and C. Reymers, R. Baldwin, J. Dodsley, S. Crowder, and Co. and B. Collins, 1765), 167–78.

30 The looped styles of the polonaise and English gowns were not explicitly restricted as wedding attire, as a bride would wear what was fashionable rather than the modern concept of a wedding dress. A few surviving polonaise and English gowns that could have been puffed into the looped style, have survived in direct relation with their function as bridal. In the V&A, T.2&A-1947 is an example of a hooped wedding dress, most likely worn for presentation at court. Edwina Ehrman, *The Wedding Dress: 300 Years of Bridal Fashions* (London: V&A Publishing, 2011), 31, 34–7; Shelley Tobin, Sarah Pepper and Margaret Willes, *Marriage à la Mode: Three Centuries of Wedding Dress* (London: National Trust Enterprises Ltd, 2003), 18–21.

31 *Public Advertiser,* 11 October 1776.

32 Ibid.

33 Ibid.

34 Ibid.

35 *Morning Chronicle and London Advertiser*, 22 October 1776.

36 For a discussion of false enhancements, see Aileen Ribeiro, *Facing Beauty: Painted Women & Cosmetic Art* (London: Yale University Press, 2011), 178–97, 342.

37 *The Weekly Miscellany, or Instructive Entertainer*, 16 December 1776, 250.

38 Ibid., 250; *The Seducers*, 1778, iv; *Wits Museum*, 1790, 16–17.

39 Numerous editorials suggest the superficiality of a woman's intellect beneath a painted face and dressed head. *The London Magazine, or Gentleman's Monthly Intelligencer*, February 1777, 85; *General Evening Post*, 16 August 1777; *Public Advertiser*, 29 August 1777; *Public Advertiser*, 15 August 1778. Vincent, *Anatomy of Fashion*, 64.

40 *London Chronicle*, 30 November–3 December 1776, 532.

41 Experimental reproduction has demonstrated that cork can create the desired volume.

42 William Nicholson, *The British Encyclopedia, or Dictionary of Arts and Sciences*, Vol. II (London: C. Whittingham, 1809); Robert Hamilton, *An Introduction to Merchandize* (Edinburgh: Printed for the Author, 1777), 286–8; Lady Mary Walker, *Munster Village, a Novel* (London: Printed for Robson and Co., 1778), 104–5. A cork leg is advertised by 'Jonathan Lightfoot' in *Public Advertiser*, 16 April 1772.

43 An origin story identifies a tailor's surplus of cork soppers as the original design for a cork rump. 'The Observer' attributes the origin of cork rumps to 'Lady Gro – nor', or Lady Grosvenor, who was scared to be near water in fear of falling in at the regatta. *Town and Country Magazine*, December 1776, 650. Peter Pindar appropriated the origin of the cork rump to the French court to cover up the Queen's illegitimate pregnancy in *The Cork Rump, or Queen and Maids of Honour. A Poem*. Peter Pindar, *The Cork Rump, or Queen and Maids of Honour. A Poem* (London: James Johnston, 1815), 10–17.

44 The title also references the Siege of Cork of 1690.

45 *The Feather'd Fair in a Fright*, John Collet, July 1777, publ. by Carrington Bowles, LWL, Farmington.

46 For a discussion of the portrayal of older women in satire, see McCreery, *Satirical Gaze*, 212–51.

47 Thanks to Robin Kipps at Colonial Williamsburg for first bringing the cork jacket to my attention and for pointing me to Dr. Wilkinson's *Tutamen Nauticum*. Costume Accessories from Head to Toe Conference, DWW, March 2011.

48 John Wilkinson, *Tutamen Nauticum: Or, The Seaman's Preservation from Shipwreck, Diseases, and Other Calamities Incident to Mariners*, 4th edn (London: Printed for Dodsley, Lownds, Bristow, Stewart, Willock, Mount, and Page, 1766), 24.

49 John Ward's earliest advertisement appeared in the *Gazetteer and London Daily Advertiser*, 28 March 1764.

50 John Ward exhibited his cork jackets on 15 September 1764, 29 August 1772 and 31 May 1773. *St. James Chronicle, or the British Evening Post*, 15 September 1764; *Public Advertiser*, 29 August 1772; *Public Advertiser*, 31 May 1773. A later cork jacket manufacturer depicted his 1806 exhibition in the Thames in a print *An Exact Representation of Mr. F. C. Daniels, Life Preserver as Exhibited on the 21st of July 1806 Passing through London Bridge to Gun Dock, Wapping*, Acc. No. PAG8189, National Maritime Museum, Greenwich.

51 *Morning Daily Post and Daily Advertiser*, 25 January 1779.

52 *London Evening Post*, 29 January 1743.

53 *Morning Chronicle, and London Advertiser,* 18 May 1775.

54 Vincent, *Anatomy of Fashion*, 64.

55 Another capsized water scene is pictured in 'A Party to Vauxhall by Water', in which the men do not appear in fear of drowning, but instead take the opportunity to assault their female companion. A half submerged man sticks his hand up her skirt between her legs, while one of two voyeurs on another boat masturbates. This kind of semi-pornographic depiction is typical of *The Rambler's* engravings. *The Rambler's Magazine, or Annals of Gallantry, Glee, Pleasure and the Bon Ton,* 1786.

56 *Morning Chronicle, and London Advertiser,* 22 October 1776.

57 *London Chronicle,* 18 November 1776; *Lloyd's Evening Post,* 18 November 1776; *Public Advertiser,* 18 November 1776; *General Evening Post,* 19 November 1776.

58 *Morning Chronicle, and London Advertiser,* 22 October 1776.

59 *Morning Post, and Daily Advertiser,* 4 October 1785.

60 *General Evening Post,* 21 June 1777.

61 Ibid., 27 June 1778.

62 *Town and Country Magazine, or the Universal Repository*, September 1778, 455. For a discussion of dialogues of the dead, see Michael Prince, *Philosophical Dialogue in the British Enlightenment: Theology, Aesthetics, and the Novel* (Cambridge: Cambridge University Press, 1996), 221–6.

63 McNeil, 'Macaroni Masculinities', 404.

64 *Morning Post, and Daily Advertiser,* 24 February 1777.

65 Her large collections of prints, broadsides and clippings, along with other decorative objects, were donated to the British Museum by her sister-in-law in 1818. In addition to the large collection of unbound prints, the Banks collection also includes nine volumes of printed ephemera, held in the BL, LR.301.h.3-11. Another clipping from the *Morning Post, and Daily Advertiser,* dated 6 May 1778 in an eighteenth-century hand, has been pasted on the back of *Miss Dumplin, Ducktail, and Tittup*, published by Matthew and Mary Darly on 13 July 1778, in the collection of the BM. This print was also owned by Sarah Sophia Banks.

66 Walpole's collection of prints is now held in the NYPL. Anne Damer's scrapbook contains engravings from costume books, plates of hairstyles and portraits, Folio 53 D18 828, LWL. For a further discussion of collection practices of satirical prints, see McCreery, *Satirical Gaze,* 30–8. Scafe's scrapbook is a large compendium of annotated newspaper clippings and does not include graphic satires, LWL Mss, Vol. 190, LWL.

67 The reference also assists in dating the print, as the publisher's line has been cut off extant versions in the BM and LOC.

68 The Darlys' font in 1776 and 1777 includes horizontal lines as filler, but also scallops inside the letters. The title does not appear in any newspaper advertisements, announcing the Darlys' publications between 1776 and 1779, which is another indication that the Darlys are not the publisher. The print is comparable in numerous ways to *This Is Something New,* published on 1 September 1777 by John Lockington.

69 Though the series has been acknowledged by McCreery, *The New Rigatta* has not been previously included as part of the set. McCreery, *Satirical Gaze,* 34–5.

70 Richard Brinsley Sheridan is best known for *A Trip to Scarborough* and *The School for Scandal*, which were first acted in February 1777 and May 1777. George, *Catalogue*, 5.239. Thank you to Cindy Roman discussing these prints and the drawings in the DWW, inspiring me to pursue Sheridan's role further as an artist.

71 Further investigation into Sheridan's role as a print designer is needed.

72 Sheridan recycles the text in his concurrent play, *A Trip to Sheridan*: 'Ladies may smile – are they not in the plot? The bounds of nature have they not forgot? Were they design'd to be, when put together, Made up, like shuttlecocks, of cork and feather?' George, *Catalogue*, 5.240; Sheridan, 1781, v.

73 In a later version, the clergyman is off balance, wig falling off.

74 Since Addison and Steele's observations of social life in *The Spectator* and *The Tatler* in the 1710s, a constant commentary on dress has resounded through the print culture. For discussions of dress in *The Spectator* and *The Tatler*, see Erin Skye Mackie, *Market à la mode: Fashion, Commodity, and Gender in the Tatler and the Spectator* (London: Johns Hopkins University Press, 1997).

75 Powell and Roach, 'Big Hair', 95.

76 To Lady Ossory, *Walpole Correspondence*, 32: 317–18.

77 Powell and Roach use this satire as a crescendo of the excess of waist of 'big hair' in connection to the opulent, display of pleasure and leisure in the regatta setting. Powell and Roach, 'Big Hair', 95–7.

78 Ibid., 96.

79 Numerous diatribes criticized high hair at the theatre, for example, an editorial in *Town and Country, or the Universal Repository*, September 1778, 455. This theme was portrayed satirically in satires such as *Optic Curls*, published by Matthew and Mary Darly, 1 April 1777, BM, London.

80 This design is modified and published on 24 April 1777 by William Humphrey in *A Beau at Billingsgate*, LWL, Farmington. The women and cleric are now portrayed as workers of the Billingsgate fish market, throwing a macaroni with exaggerated buttons on his coat high in the air with a blanket. The subtitle reads 'All Fashion', 'No Weight'. The print has been signed with the initials 'WH', for William Humphrey, 'et'. The second contributor's initials have been cut off the page, therefore it remains unknown if Sheridan collaborated; however it is possible as Sheridan designed prints for Humphrey as well, for example, *Titus Shapes Figure Frames*, published by William Humphrey, 19 January 1778, DWW, Williamsburg.

81 The first is from *Satires of Persius*, III.V.82–99. Thanks to Viccy Coltman for the translation.

82 On the copy held at the LWL, the print has been annotated in pencil with the names 'Dr Adey' above the cleric and 'Miss Adeys' above the middle woman. On the right, 'Oxford' has also been written. The handwriting does not suggest that these were contemporary identifications, but later additions. I have been unable to locate references to Dr Adey or Miss Adey in contemporary sources.

83 A similar revenge of women of fashion can be seen in *The Blow Up of the Man Milliner*, 1 February 1787, publ. by J. Wicksteed, LWL, Farmington, where four women of fashion propel a man milliner in a petticoat and cap into the air. It was published one month after *Edwin as Bob in the Man Milliner*, 1 January 1787, publ. by William Holland, BM, London, which portrays the actor John Edwin donning the same petticoat and cap. John Edwin was cast as Bob Dobbin in John O'Keefe's *Man Milliner*, which only preformed once on 27 January 1787. *The Blow Up* is most likely a response to both the earlier print and the play's failure. Shearer West, *The Image of the Actor: Verbal & Visual Representation in the Age of Garrick & Kemble* (New York: St. Martin's Press, Inc., 1991), 48.

84 Though many satirists were male, notable exceptions include Mary Darly, and anonymous female amateurs. Textual diatribes more often than not they were presented in a condescending manner employing the feminine

vices of vanity, fickleness and luxury, which were often compared against an ideal model of feminine virtue, humbleness and grace. The various economic drives for and against fashion were also fervently debated. Kate Haulman, *The Politics of Fashion in Eighteenth-Century America* (Chapel Hill: The University of North Carolina Press, 2011), 1–2.

85   While it is possible that the author was male, writing as a woman, female correspondents did submit editorials to magazines in the last quarter of the century. For example, *The Lady's Magazine* advertised for its female readership to also participate as correspondents. Jennie Batchelor, '"[W]here all things are guided by a fashion": Disseminating Dress in *The Lady's* Magazine (1770–1800)', Disseminating Dress, York University, May 2015.

86   *The Town and Country Magazine*, January 1778, 29.

87   Ibid.

88   Ibid. The designation of 'Amazon', often in reference to riding habits, was frequent at the time, prompted by the concerns surrounding a wave of a masculine femininity. For a further discussion of the implications of Amazons and gender, see Wahrman, *Making of the Modern Self*, 7–44. For a discussion of women's riding habits and their Amazonian connotations, see Blackman, 'Walking Amazons'.

89   *Morning Chronicle, and Daily Advertiser*, 22 October 1776.

90   Textual discussions of the cork rump were fewer in number, but did not disappear altogether during this period.

91   For a discussion on the pouter pigeon silhouette, see Introduction.

92   *The Westminster Magazine, or Pantheon of Taste*, July 1785, 381–2.

93   Ibid.

94   Ibid.

95   *General Advertiser*, 20 August 1785.

96   During the American Revolution, the focus of satirical prints shifted away from fashion towards military and political events. While still present in textual accounts, the cork rump disappeared from the focus of satirical prints from the late 1770s to mid-1780s.

97   Diana Donald identifies William and Hannah Humphrey, William Holland and Samuel W. Fores as the three main printsellers of caricatures in the 1780s and 1790s. The address of Fores's shop is listed as 'Fores, S. W. *Stationer and Printseller*, No. 3, Picadilly' in *Bailey's British Directory*. Fores later expands his title to include 'S. W. Fores: Stationer, Book-Seller, Print-Seller & Publisher, at the City Arms, No. 3, Picadilly near the Hay Market', which survives at the top of a bill to Lady A. Conally, 11 October 1793. Donald, *Age of Caricature*, 3; William Bailey, *Bailey's British Directory; or, Merchant's and Trader's Useful Companion, for the Year 1784 …* (London: Printed by William Bailey, 1784), 89; Print/Bill Head, Heal, 17.53, BM.

98   Donald, *Age of Caricature*, 93. The artist can be identified as Rushworth by two back-to-back R's, followed by 'DELIN.', short for delineate, in the lower left corner of the print.

99   In *c.* 1790, Fores advertised to hold an exhibition for the largest collection of prints ever displayed to the British public. Donald, *Age of Caricature*, 4.

100 *The Westminster Magazine, or Pantheon of Taste*, July 1785, 382.

101 Ibid.

102 The Latin 'aridae nates', translates as dried growth, or birth.

103 Collops are defined by Samuel Johnson as 'A small slice of meat'. *Morning Herald and Daily Advertiser*, 22 June 1781.

104 *Morning Post and Daily Advertiser*, 22 November 1785; *St. James Chronicle, or the British Evening Post*, 15 November 1787.

105 The print is half of a diptych with *The Muff*, which will be addressed in the Chapter 3.

106 For a discussion of the effeminate qualities associated with male milliners, see Kimberly Chrisman-Campbell, 'The Face of Fashion: Milliners in Eighteenth-Century Visual Culture', *British Journal for Eighteenth-Century Studies* 25, no. 2 (Autumn 2002): 157–72; Serena Dyer, 'Mr Calico and Mr Fribble: Queering the Man-Milliner, 1770–1820', forthcoming.

107 An engraving of James Graham's controversial mud baths, or earthbathing, depicted in *The Rambler's Magazine,* in June 1786, portrays rumps with the seemed, section construction. On the right of the print, a woman undresses, pulling the laces from her stays. Her rump, worn over her shift is made of two spherical cushions, seamed into sections. Next to her lie three pairs of discarded rumps, each seamed in equal sections and attached in the centre. Another pair of similar rumps, next to a discarded pair of stays, is pictured in 'The Whores of Kings Place preparing for the meeting of Parliament' and bums are again the focus of 'The Rump Parliament', in which a group of pigeon shaped women, with large bums put forth a 'Bill to Amend the Human Shape' and a 'Bill to naturalize bodily deformity'. Above the caucus of women, a pair of rumps hand beneath an umbrella from the ceiling. All three plates appear in the 1786 volume of *The Rambler's Magazine*. Rumps are also visible in *A Pig in the Poke*, publ. on 6 February 1786 by James Philips; James Gillray's *Contemplations on a Coronet,* published by Hannah Humphrey on 20 March 1797 (though due to the year, this could be a pad worn in front); *Dressing for a Birthday*, 3 March 1789, publ. by S. W. Fores; *Dressing for a Masquerade*, 1 April 1790, publ. by S. W. Fores, all in the collection of the BM, London. In *Dressing for a Birthday*, the petticoat style, and seamed sectioned style are both prominently featured.

108 Though it is possible smaller versions continued to be worn in the 1790s as the waistline raised on the torso, mention of it depletes and attention instead shifts to the pad.

109 Dorothy George and Joseph Grego have identified the printmaker as Thomas Rowlandson, using James Sayer's signature to disguise his identity. LWL Digital Collection.

110 In a letter to 'the Matron', a contributor complains of women 'with their hair curled over their foreheads, and hanging down behind to the bottom of their backs'. *The Lady's Magazine, or Entertaining Companion for the Fair Sex*, November 1789, 597.

111 See Chapter 3.

112 For pouter pigeon silhouettes in 1788 and 89, see, *A Convenience,* 6 March 1788, publ. by S. W. Fores, BM, London; *A Sandwich,* 8 February 1788, publ. by S. W. Fores, BM, London; *A-La-Mode*, John O'Keeffe, 1 January 1789, publ. by S. W. Fores, LWL, Farmington; *Restoration Dressing Room*, Henry Kingsbury, 24 April 1789, publ. by S. W. Fores, LWL, Farmington. For a depiction of the revealing muslin gowns of the turn of the century, see *A Naked Truth, or Nipping Frost*, 2 February 1803, publ. by S.W. Fores, LWL, Farmington.

113 Betsy was twenty-eight, living in London, writing to her sister Alicia, thirty-three, in Dublin. She describes shifts in the handkerchiefs: 'The handkerchiefs are not so much puff'd out and there is now a very pretty sort of handkerchief worn open at the neck and exactly made and trim'd like a Boy's shirt.' She also mentions, hats, caps and hair. Betsy LeFanu [née Sheridan] to Alicia LeFanu [neé Sheridan], Saturday 21 January 1786, Electronic Enlightenment, quoted in Waugh, *Cut of Women's Clothes,* 126.

Chapter 3

1. *Walker's Hibernian Magazine, or Compendium of Entertaining Knowledge,* March 1786, 113.

2. Ibid., December 1785, 617.

3. Ibid., March 1786, 113.

4. Ibid.

5. Ibid.

6. R. Turner Wilcox, *The Mode in Furs: A Historical Survey with 680 Illustrations* (Mineola: Dover Publications, Inc., 2010), 81; Elizabeth Ewing, *Fur in Dress* (London: B. T. Batsford Ltd, 1981), 52.

7. Legislation was abolished in 1604. Ewing, *Fur in Dress,* 35. See Giorgio Riello and Ulinka Rublack, *The Right to Dress: Sumptuary Laws in a Global Perspective, c. 1200–1800* (Cambridge: Cambridge University Press, 2019).

8. Kimberly Chrisman-Campbell, '"He is not dressed without a muff": Muffs, Masculinity and la mode in English Satire', in *Seeing Satire in the Eighteenth Century*, ed. Elizabeth C. Mansfield and Kelly Malone (Oxford: Voltaire Foundation, 2013).

9. See Elisabeth Gernerd, '"Feather Muffs of all Colours": Fashion, Patriotism, and the Natural World in Eighteenth-Century Britain', *Appearance(s): Histoire et culture du paraître* 11 (2022).

10. *Morning Chronicle and London Advertiser,* 17 November 1786.

11. Wilcox, *Mode in Furs,* 49; Chrisman-Campbell, 'Muffs', 134.

12. For the significance of fur in the early modern period, see Philip Zitzlsperger, *Dürers Pelz und das Recht im Bild: Kleiderkunde als Methode der Kunstgeschichte* (Berlin: Akademie Verlag, 2008), 26–7.

13. Andrew Bolton, *Wild: Fashion Untamed* (London: Metropolitan Museum of Art and Yale University Press, 2005), 49.

14. Wilcox, *Mode in Furs,* 78; Julia Emberly, *Venus and Furs: The Cultural Politics of Fur* (London: I.B. Tauris, 2010), 354; Beverly Lemire, *Global Trade and the Transformation of Consumer Cultures: The Material World Remade, c.1500–1820* (Cambridge: Cambridge University Press, 2018), 45.

15. Gernerd, 'Feather Muffs'.

16. Chrisman-Campbell, 'The Face of Fashion', 167–8; Dyer, 'Mr Calico and Mr Fribble'.

17. *The European Magazine and London Review by the Philological Society of London*, Vol. 11, February 1787, 119.

18. A fur muff also appears in *Pamela*. Maurice Johnson, 'The Device of Sophia's Muff in Tom Jones', *Modern Language Notes* 74, no. 8 (1959): 685–9; Carey McIntosh, 'Pamela's Clothes', *ELH* 35, no. 1 (March 1968): 80; Emily A. Hipchen, 'Feilding's Tome Jones', *The Explicator* 53, no. 1 (Fall 1994): 17; Laura Engel, 'The Muff Affair: Fashioning Celebrity in the Portraits of Late-Eighteenth-Century British Actresses', *Fashion Theory* 13, no. 3 (2009): 28; Kelly Fleming, 'The Politics of Sophia Western's Muff', *Eighteenth-Century Fiction* 31, no. 4 (Summer 2019): 659–61.

19. Engel, 'The Muff Affair', 279–98.

20. B. E., *A New Dictionary of the Terms Ancient and Modern of the Canting Crew* (London: W. Hawes, P. Gilbourne and W. Davis, 1699); Francis Grose, *A Classical Dictionary of the Vulgar Tongue* (London: Printed for S. Hooper,

21 Emberly identifies the initial link between fur and women's bodies due to the rising Puritanical views towards material and sexual excess. Emberly, *Venus and Furs*, 55–7, 104. See Joseph Monteyne's discussion of the fur muff as fetishized object in Wenceslaus Hollar's etching. Joseph Monteyne, 'Enveloping Objects: Allegory and Commodity Fetish in Wenceslaus Hollar's Personifications of the Seasons and Fashion Still Lifes', *Art History* 29, no. 3 (2006): 436.

22 John Cleland, *Memoirs of a Woman of Pleasure, Vol. I* (London: Printed for G. Fenton, 1749), 78–9.

23 Ibid.

24 The print most likely refers to Dorothy Jordan in her role as Lucy in Henry Fielding's play, *The Virgin Unmasked* (1782). A fully clothed comic engraving of Jordan in the role was published in 1787, NPG, D4418.

25 Apart from Engel's brief acknowledgment of the LWL version, neither impression has been discussed. A third print under the same name, also held in the LOC, presents two women side by side, one clothed the other not. This pint is most likely by Rowlandson, but includes no muff so will not be discussed here.

26 Humphrey's shop was located at various addresses on Old Bond Street, Bedford Court in Covent Garden, and New Bond Street between 1778 and 1797. Rosie Dias, '"A world of pictures": Pall Mall and the Topography of Display, 1780–99', in *Georgian Geographies: Essays on Space, Place and Landscape in the Eighteenth Century*, ed. Miles Ogborn and Charles W. J. Withers (Manchester: Manchester University Press, 2004), 95.

27 See McNeil, 'Beauty in Search of Knowledge', 223–54.

28 See James Baker, *The Business of Satirical Prints in Late-Georgian England* (Basingstoke: Palgrave Macmillan, 2017).

29 The fur muff was made available to a wider audience through the growing accessibility of consumer products to the middling classes. Maxine Berg, *Luxury & Pleasure in Eighteenth-Century Britain* (Oxford: Oxford University Press, 2005), 9–10, 20. For the commoditization of fashion with the emergence of the middle classes and growth of consumer culture, see Styles, *The Dress of the People*, 1–16.

30 The importation of muffs and other fashionable luxuries was boycotted in Boston on 28 October 1767 in order to wean colonial dependence on British goods and promote the growth of local manufacture. *The Pennsylvania Gazette*, 12 November 1767; *Calcutta Gazette*, 25 October 1792.

31 For the adjacent feather trade, see Gernerd, 'Fancy Feathers', 201–9.

32 *Gazetteer and New Daily Advertiser*, 31 December 1778.

33 *General Advertiser and Morning Intelligencer,* 17 March 1779; *Gazetteer and New Daily Advertiser,* 31 December 1779.

34 *Morning Post and Daily Advertiser,* 28 October 1786.

35 See Serena Dyer, 'Shopping and the Senses: Retail, Browsing and Consumption in 18th-Century England', *History Compass* 12, no. 9 (September 2014): 694–703.

36 *Morning Post*, 26 November 1785.

37 *The World*, 16 November 1787.

38 Mrs Turner followed Dyde when the partnership split. Bill from Dyde and Scribe, 1789, BM, Heal, 86.28.

39 Bill from Dyde, Scribe and Playter, 8 March 1786, RCT, GEO/MAIN29223.

40 Dyde and Scribe even printed their own fans. Paper fan, *c.* 1792, BM, 1891,0713.103.

41 Hester Lynch Piozzi writes to Alexander Leak requesting her bill from Dyde and Scribe on 13 December 1814, nearly twenty years after the company was dissolved. Hester Lynch Piozzi [formerly Mrs Thrale; née Salusbury], 'Hester Lynch Piozzi to Alexander Leak: 13 December 1814,' in *Electronic Enlightenment Scholarly Edition of Correspondence*, edited by Robert McNamee et al. University of Oxford. https://doi.org/10.13051/ee:doc/piozheUD0050309a1c.

42 See David Hope, 'Britain and the Fur Trade: Commerce and Consumers in the North-Atlantic World, 1783–1821,' PhD thesis (University of Northumbria, 2016).

43 A brown 'shaggy fur' muff, *c.* 1785–1810, BK-NM-9708, Rijksmuseum; stripped lynx muff, *c.* 1800, NMS, A.1977.245. Ninke Bloemberg and Bianca M. du Mortier, *Accessorize! 250 Objects of Fashion and Desire* (Amsterdam: Rijksmuseum, Nieuw Amsterdam, 2009), 117–18; Chrisman-Campbell, 'Muffs', 138.

44 Silk velvet muff, 1575–600, MFA, 43.1827.

45 See Rozsika Parker, *The Subversive Stitch: Embroidery and the Making of the Feminine* (London: The Women's Press, 1984); Maureen Daly Goggin and Beth Fowkes Tobin (eds.), *Women and the Material Culture of Needlework and Textiles, 1750–1950* (Farnham: Ashgate, 2009); Crystal B. Lake, 'Needlework Verse', in *Material Literacy in Eighteenth-Century Britain: A Nation of Makers*, ed. Serena Dyer and Chloe Wigston Smith (London: Bloomsbury Visual Arts, 2019), 35–50.

46 Frances Mable Sparrow lived with her aunt and uncle, Ann and Samuel Goodwin. While there is no record of her birth, her parents married in 1760 and the first mention of her appears in 1766, making her age at the date of this letter between fifteen and twenty-one. Letter 665/5942, 7 February 1781, Shropshire Archives.

47 For feminine education and needlework, see Bianca F. C. Calabresi, '"You Sow, Ile Read": Letters and Literacies in Early Modern Samplers', in *Reading Women: Literacy, Authorship, and Culture in the Atlantic World, 1500–1800*, ed. Heidi Brayman Hackel and Catherine E. Kelly (Philadelphia: University of Pennsylvania Press, 2008), 79–104; Heather Pristash, Inez Schaechterle and Sue Carter Wood, 'The Needle as the Pen: Intentionality, Needlework, and the Production of Alternate Discourses of Power', in *Women and the Material Culture of Needlework and Textiles, 1750–1950*, ed. Maureen Daly Goggin and Beth Fowkes Tobin (Farnham: Ashgate, 2009), 17.

48 Browne notes that Mrs Delany worked a selection of accessories including: tippets, mantels, handkerchiefs, muffs and whitework aprons. Claire Browne, 'Mary Delany's Embroidered Court Dress', in *Mrs. Delany and Her Circle*, ed. Mark Laird and Alicia Weisberg-Roberts (London: Yale University Press, 2009), 73. Amanda Vickery, 'The Theory & Practice of Female Accomplishment', in *Mrs. Delany and Her Circle*, ed. Mark Laird and Alicia Weisberg-Roberts (London: Yale University Press, 2009), 102.

49 For embroidered pockets, see Burman and Fenneatux, *The Pocket*, 63–75.

50 For shopping through correspondence, see Trevor Fawcett, 'A Case of Distance Shopping in 1763', *Costume* 25 (1991): 18–20; Miles Lambert, '"Sent from Town": Commissioning Clothing in Britain during the Long Eighteenth Century', *Costume* 43 (2009): 66–82.

51 On 14 October 1776, Sparrow enquires after Whitmore's fashionable hair and informs her cousin she is learning to draw. Letter 665/5934. On 4 April 1778, she asks her cousin about the fashionable headdresses, the types of caps and whether feathers are still the ton. Letter 665/5938. Shropshire Archives.

52 Letter 665/5942, 7 February 1781. Sparrow also mentioned patterns with rode buds and violets intended for a negligee on 4 February 1779. Letter 665/5939. Shropshire Archives.

53 Letter 665/5937, Shropshire Archives.

54 See Greig, *Beau Monde*.

55 For an in-depth discussion on colonial embroidery pattern production, dissemination and practice, see Davida Tenebaum Deutsch, 'Needlework Patterns and Their Use in America', *Magazine Antiques* February (1991): 368–81.

56 *Daily Universal Register*, 4 December 1786.

57 For the use of pattern books in colonial America, see Deutsch, 'Needlework Patterns', 369–70.

58 For the development of patterns, see McNeil, 'Beauty in Search of Knowledge.'

59 Smith, 'Fast Fashion', 441. Passing down pattern books from generation to generation was an established practice throughout the early modern period. Susan Frye, *Pens and Needles: Women's Textuality in Early Modern England* (Philadelphia: University of Pennsylvania Press, 2010), 128–30. Two patterns for muffs survive from the German pattern book, *Continuation of Delights of the Art and Industry of the Practicing Needle, or the Newly Invented Special Sewing Book*, Part III, *c*. 1725, V&A, E.5081-1905, E.5082-1905.

60 *The Lady's Magazine, or Entertaining Companion for the Fair Sex,* August 1770, quoted in Smith, 'Fast Fashion', 440.

61 Jennie Batchelor and Alison Larkin, *Jane Austen Embroidery: Authentic Embroidery Projects for Modern Stitchers* (London: Pavilion, 2020), 10. In addition to patterns for muffs, patterns appear for workbags, aprons, handkerchiefs, shoes, jackets, waistcoats, gowns, cloaks, pockets, shawls and pocket books. Great thanks to Jennie Bachelor for sharing her unpublished quantitative research on *The Lady's Magazine* patterns.

62 Ariane Fennetaux, '"Work'd pockets to my entire satisfaction": Women and the Multiple Literacies of Making', in *Material Literacy in Eighteenth-Century Britain: A Nation of Makers*, ed. Serena Dyer and Chloe Wigston Smith (London: Bloomsbury Visual Arts, 2019), 21; Smith, 'Fast Fashion', 442.

63 Deutsch, 'Needlework Patterns', 374–5; for a discussion of the seventeenth-century sources of Robert Sayer's patterns, see Mary Schoeser, 'A Secret Trade: Plate-printed Textiles and Dress Accessories, *c*. 1620–1820', *Dress* 34, no. 1 (2007): 49–59.

64 Deutsch, 'Needlework Patterns', 370–5.

65 Smith, 'Fast Fashion', 443.

66 See Chloe Wigston Smith and Jennie Batchelor, 27 April 2015, 'Patterns and Posterity: Or, What's Not in the Lady's Magazine', *The Lady's Magazine (1770–1818): Understanding the Emergence of a Genre*, https://blogs.kent.ac.uk/ladys-magazine/2015/04/27/patterns-and-posterity-or-whats-not-in-the-ladys-magazine/ (accessed 19 March 2021).

67 Lack of survival is due to the reader's use and lack inclusion in the annual binding instructions. Smith, 'Fast Fashions', 442 and Batchelor, 'Patterns and Posterity'.

68 That designs for muffs could also be interchangeable for workbags depends on their elemental construction of one rectangular piece of fabric, joined together by a central seam, creating a cylinder. Patterns could also be published demonstrating construction, like the pattern of a workbag or muff in the *London Magazine*, which included instructions in the text as how to construct it. *Walker's Hibernian Magazine, or, Compendium of Entertaining Knowledge,* July 1786; *London Magazine, or Gentleman's Monthly Intelligencer,* June 1771, 292.

69 For example, silk muff, Massachusetts Historical Society, Needlework Misc 009.

70 *The Lady's Magazine, or, Entertaining Companion for the Fair Sex*, December 1779.

71 See silk muff, DWW, 1958-25.

72 For example, silk muff purse, LACMA, M.2007.211.138. See Fennataux and Burman, *The Pocket*, 31. Muffs were also used to hide shoplifted items, for example, Mary Caye, 15 February 1797, t17970215-17, Old Bailey Online.

73 Silk muff, MAG, no accession number.

74 This muff from the 1770s measures 8 ¾ × 16 × 3 ½ inches (22.23 × 40.64 × 8.89 cm).

75 See Gail Marsh, *18th Century Embroidery Techniques* (Lewes: Guild of Master Craftsman Publications Ltd, 2012), 159-61.

76 Maureen Daly Goggin, 'Introduction: Threading Women', in *Women and the Material Culture of Needlework and Textiles, 1750–1950*, ed. Maureen Daly Goggin and Beth Fowkes Tobin (Farnham: Ashgate, 2009), 4.

77 Dyer and Smith, 'Introduction', 1-2.

78 Jenifer Wearden, 2013, 'Samplers, Stitches & Techniques', *Victoria and Albert Museum*, http://www.vam.ac.uk/content/articles/s/samplers-stitches-techniques/ (accessed 19 March 2021).

79 Another late 1770s muff with diagonal embroidered floral chains is in the MET. Silk embroidered muff, 1770s, MET, 1978.280.1.

80 The later muff measures 7 × 15 ½ × 3 ½ inches (17.78 × 39.37 × 8.89 cm).

81 Susan Frye attributes these minor choices as a giving the female maker a 'distinct, if limited agency.' Frye, *Pens and Needles*, 138.

82 Pristash, Schaechterle, and Carter Wood, 'The Needle', 27.

83 Delany produced embroidery, botanical drawings, paper flowers, shellwork, oil paintings, plasterwork, japanning and featherwork. See *Mrs. Delany and Her Circle*, ed. Mark Laird and Alicia Weisberg-Roberts (London: Yale University Press, 2009); Lisa Lynne Moore, 'Queer Gardens: Mary Delany's Flowers and Friendships', *Eighteenth-Century Studies* 39, no. 1 (2005): 49-70; Vickery, 'Theory & Practice', 94-5; Gernerd, 'Feather Muffs', 24-5.

84 Delany refers several times to the patterns she drew, for both herself and her friends, writing in 1724 to her sister, 'You desire some sprigs for working a gown, which I will send you, though my fancy is not a good one.' Letter to her sister, Anne Granville Dewes (1701-61), 16 February 1733. Lady Llanover (ed.), *The Autobiography and Correspondence of Mary Granville, Mrs. Delany: With Interesting Reminiscences of King George the Third and Queen Charlotte, Vol. 1* (London: Richard Bentley, 1861), 429.

85 Letter to her sister, Anne Granville Dewes, 16 February 1733. Llanover, *Autobiography*, 429.

86 Ibid.

87 Letter from Mrs Pendarves to Mrs Anne Granville, 19 December 1733. Llanover, *Autobiography*, 425.

88 Gernerd, 'Feather Muffs', 25.

89 Vickery, 'Theory & Practice', 102. In Lady Llanover's appendix summarizing Mrs Delany's will, she notes that although bequeathing 'all her wearing apparel and body linen that had been washed and once worn' to her maid, Ann Motley, she excluded 'certain exceptions of embroidery and lace and the work of friends', indicating that in addition to giving pieces, Delany also had pieces that she had received from others. Lady Llanover (ed.), *The Autobiography and Correspondence of Mary Granville, Mrs. Delany: With Interesting Reminiscences of King George the Third and Queen Charlotte, Vol. 3* (London: Richard Bentley, 1862), 485.

90 Judy Attfield, *Wild Things: The Material Culture of Everyday Life* (Oxford: Berg, 2000), 130.

91 Lady Llanover notes in the will 'all her fur and father muffs and tippets, which were bequeathed to Mrs. Port, of Illam', who was Frances Mable Sparrow's aunt. Llanover, *Autobiography,* 3.483.

92 Painted medallions imitating satin prints were also produced. Painted satin print muffs include: silk muff, V&A, T.669-1913; silk muff, Albany Institute of History and History of Art, x1940.592.2; silk muff, LACMA, M.79.19.7. For the origins of plate-printed textiles, see Schoeser, 'A Secret Trade', 49–59; Mary Schoeser, *Printed Handkerchiefs* (London: Museum of London, 1988); Mary Schoeser, 'The Mystery of the Printed Handkerchief', in *Disentangling Textiles: Techniques for the Study of Designed Objects*, ed. Mary Schoeser and Christine Boydell (London: Middlesex University Press, 2002), 13–22.

93 See Giorgio Riello, *Cotton: The Fabric That Made the Modern World* (Cambridge: Cambridge University Press, 2013), 179–81; Lemire, *Fashion's Favourite.*

94 See Schoeser, 'A Secret Trade'; Schoeser, 'Printed Handkerchiefs'; and Schoeser, 'The Mystery.'

95 Many thanks to Mary Schoeser and her generous correspondence regarding satin prints and their position as a luxury accessory rather than step towards mass-production and technologically advancing copperplate printed textiles. October 2022.

96 See *A Sunday Concert*, 4 June 1782, publ. by M. Rack, BM, London. More commonly, particular in the later decades of the century, fur muffs were adorned with silk ribbons. For example, Paris fashion plate of 1787, V&A, E.988-1959.

97 *Walkers' Hibernian Magazine, or Compendium of Entertaining Knowledge,* March 1786, 113.

98 Mrs Wells holds a satin print muff of her lover Major Topman in profile in *Under Hoop and Bell,* 26 January 1787, publ. by Boyne & Walker, BM, London.

99 While embroidered muffs continued to be produced throughout the end of the century, as Burman notes, embroidery produced by the wearer was becoming increasingly marginalized as the availability of printed fabrics increased. Barbara Burman and Jonathan White, 'Fanny's Pockets: Cotton, Consumption and Domestic Economy, 1780–1850', in *Women and Material Culture 1660–1830*, ed. Jennie Batchelor and Cora Kaplan (Basingstoke: Palgrave Macmillan, 2007), 36.

100 The cream measures 9 × 16.5 inches (23 × 41.9 cm); the green measures 9 × 21 inches (23 × 53.34 cm).

101 It measures 8.5 × 16.5 inches (21.5 × 42 cm).

102 It is possible that a printer's line may have once been part of the larger printed silk; however, since the medallions were cut down to size, if they did exist, they would have been cut off with the excess fabric. The 'Versailles Sash', MOL, 2000.234a, includes the publisher and date as part of the printed silk design. Edwina Ehrman, 'The Versailles Sash', *Costume* 44 (2010): 66.

103 For Turkish dress, see Aileen Ribeiro, 'Turquerie: Turkish Dress and English Fashion in the Eighteenth Century', *Connoisseur* 201, no. 807 (1979): 16–23; Angela Rosenthal, 'The Inner Orient', in *Angelica Kauffman: Art and Sensibility* (London: Yale University Press, 2006); Onur Inal, 'Women's Fashions in Transition: Ottoman Borderlands and the Anglo-Ottoman Exchange of Costumes', *Journal of World History* 22, no. 2 (2011): 243–72.

104 David Alexander identifies the prints as pendants to two other pairs, published 14 February 1782 and 17 May 1782, after Giovanni Battista Cipriani. David Alexander, 'Kauffman and the Print Market in Eighteenth-Century England', in *Angelica Kauffman: A Continental Artist in Georgian England*, ed. Wendy Wassyng Roworth (London: Reaktion Books, 1992), 183.

105 For the professional relationship between Kauffman and Bartolozzi, see Alexander, 'Kauffman'.

106 Robert Dodsley, *A Collection of Poems in Four Volumes by Several Hands, Vol. IV* (London: Printed by J. Hughs, 1755), 258–9.

107 Benjamin Stillingfleet, *An Essay on Conversation* (London: Printed for L. Gilliver and J. Clarke, 1737), 12–13.

108 *Morning Herald and Daily Advertiser,* 2 December 1782.

109 A representation of a satin print on appears in Ann Frankland Lewis's watercolour, *Morning Dress of the Year 1785*, LACMA, AC1999.154.1-32. *Morning Herald and Daily Advertiser*, 14 February 1783. Walker's advertisements for satin prints appeared subsequently in *Morning Chronicle and London Advertiser, Morning Herald and Daily Advertiser, Morning Post and Daily Advertiser* and *World and Fashionable Advertiser* until 1792.

110 *Morning Chronicle*, 16 July 1792. John Walker announces that his wife will take over the business in December 1791, when his shop moves from No. 106 Bond St to his home No. 7 Cornhill. *Morning Chronicle*, 10 December 1791.

111 Of Walker's fifteen advertisements for satin prints, thirteen advertise Kauffman prints and two mention F. Bartolozzi. The first advertisement for John Walker, carver and printseller appear in the *London Courant and Westminster Chronicle*, 3 July 1780, advertising an Angelica Kauffman print of Diana preparing for Hunting, by F. Bartolozzi (in red chalk).

112 Due to the grain of the silk, it is not possible to difinitively tell whether these were colour stipple engravings, or hand-coloured. Bartolozzi and his circle did practice 'à la poupée', where coloured ink was directly applied to the plate before printing. Roger Baynton-Williams, *The Art of the Printmaker: 1500–1860* (London: A. & C. Black, 2009), 150; Gerald Ward, *The Grove Encyclopedia of Materials and Techniques in Art* (Oxford: Oxford University Press, 2008), 557. For example, a monochrome stipple on silk by Bartolozzi of *Cupid's Manufactory*, 1800, V&A, E.932-2000.

113 Although stipple prepared the copperplate differently, it used the same press as that of other paper printing. As Schoeser has demonstrated, the access to the copperplates was key to the set of London mapmakers in that they could experiment on paper and silk, not restrained through costs of printing through a third party. Schoeser, 'Secret Trade', 51–6; Schoeser, 'The Mystery', 14–21.

114 Walker begins to advertise himself as a 'sattin print manufactury' in November 1784. *Morning Post and Daily Advertiser,* 22 November 1784.

115 Printsellers W. Palmer, J. Bodger, J. Thane, as well as embroiderers, such as Jane White and H. Hass, also advertised satin prints. W. Palmer advertised publishing Kauffman satin prints in *Morning Herald and Daily Advertiser*, 12 March 1783. J. Thane, H. Hass and Jane White also advertised selling satin prints in *Morning Herald and Daily Advertiser* and *Morning Post and Daily Advertiser* between 1784 and 1789.

116 *Abra,* Angelica Kauffman, 15 July 1783, publ. by James Birchall, BM and *Una,* Angelica Kauffman, 2 February 1783, publ. by James Birchall, BM.

117 *Walker's Hibernian Magazine, or Compendium of Entertaining Knowledge,* March 1786, 113–14. *Morning Herald,* 24 March 1786.

118 Silk mezzotint medallions, DWW, 58-(28-36). French satin prints extended to a wide range of subjects, such as the politician Mirabeau as Jupiter abolishing privileges, *Mirabeau- Jupiter foundroyant les abus*, 1789–90, Bibliothèque Nationale de France, RESERVE QB-370 (11)-FT 4. See also, a satin print of *A St. Gilles's Beauty*, engraved by Bartolozzi after John Hodges Benwell, 1783, Acc. No. VP.777, Bryn Mawr College.

119 Fur muffs feature prominently in scenes of winter since Hollar's still lifes of the seasons and continued throughout the eighteenth century. For example, *Hyems/Winter/Three-Quarter-Length Seasons*, Wenceslaus Hollar, 1641, BM and *Winter*, 1 January 1779, publ. by Carington Bowles, BM.

120 A similar extant satin print muff that bares a portrait in profile is in the Snowshill Wade Costume Collection. Silk muff, NT, NT134096.

121 Though satin prints were no longer advertised, they were still produced. For example, a silk workbag from 1827 features an abolitionist satin print of a kneeling enslaved woman made by the Female Society for Birmingham, West Bromwich, Wednesbury, Walsall and their Respective Neighbourhoods for the Relief of British Negro Slaves. Silk workbag, DWW, 2016-166.

122 Alexander, 'Kauffman', 156; Carol Watts, *The Cultural Work of Empire: The Seven Years' War and the Imagining of the Shandean State* (Toronto: University of Toronto Press, 2007), 198. For satin prints for embroidery and needlework pictures, see Deutsch, 'Needlework Patterns', 377–8. For Kauffman needlework pictures, see Parker, *Subversive Stitch*, 134–5; Margaret Swain, *Embroidered Georgian Pictures* (Haverfordwest: Shire Publications Ltd, 1994). Though Tim Clayton's extensive work on English prints briefly recognizes the production of satin prints, he does so again only within their use in needlework and decoupage. Clayton, *The English Print*, 246. Hind also briefly acknowledges satin as a material printed on other than paper or vellum. Arthur Hind, *A History of Engraving and Etching from the 15th Century to the Year 1914* (New York: Dover Publications, Inc., 2011), 17.

123 Alexander, 'Kauffman', 152, 156. For example, needlework picture of *Shakespeare's Tomb,* NT, NT226324.

124 *Morning Post and Daily Advertiser*, 16 February 1789. *Morning Post and Daily Advertiser*, 23 March 1786. A stipple copy survives in the BM's collection. *Autumn*, May 1786, Jane White, BM, London. Two satin prints for fans survive in the French collection at the DWW, each with pencil lines marking out the outline of the fan. One depicts a circus scene with a dancing bear and the other depicts a few animals in landscape. A fan featuring a William Hamilton satin print of Chaucer's *Constantia* survives in the Fan Museum, LDFAN2018.84.

125 For example, John Thane advertised 'NEW PRINTS on SATTIN and PAPER. CUPID REPOSING a small oval after ANGELICA, highly finish, price 2s, 6d, in colours, paper, or sattin, 5s'. *Morning Herald and Daily Advertiser*, 27 January 1784.

126 Wendy Wassyng Roworth, 'Kauffman and the Art of Painting in England', in *Angelica Kauffman: A Continental Artist in Georgian England*, ed. Wendy Wassyng Roworth (London: Reaktion Books, 1992), 13.

127 William T. Whitley, *Artists and Their Friends in England, 1700–1799, Vol. 1* (London: the Medici Society, 1928), 373; Clayton, *English Print*, 246.

128 An allegorical satin print muff depicting Hope, most likely engraved by George Laidler, survives in DWW, Acc. No. 1958–25. For the prominence of allegories on copperplate printed silk, see Schoeser, 'Secret Trade', 55–6.

129 See Rosenthal, *Kauffmann;* Angela Rosenthal, 'Angelica Kauffman Ma(s)king Claims', *Art History* 15, no. 1 (March 1992): 38–59; Oscar Sandner, *Angelika Kauffmann und Rom* (Roma: De Luca, 1998), 91–2.

130 As depicted in numerous paintings and in the existence of accessories like the 'Versailles sash', the wearing of classicized oval motifs and cameos in clothing was a popular and widespread fashion. Classical cameos on belts, or girdles, appear in Kauffman's portraits of *Lady Elizabeth Foster*, 1785; *Self-Portrait as the Muse of Painting*, 1787; *Emma Hart, Lady Hamilton, as Thalia*, 1791; *Fortunata Sulgher Fantastici*, 1792; *Cornelia Knight*, 1793; *Mrs. Henry Benton,* 1794; *Self-Portrait between the Arts of Music and Painting*, 1794–6. Beginning in 1788, Kerr and Co. advertised both 'fine impressions of medallions' as well as the 'Versailles Sash', a silk sash printed with classical motifs. Kerr and Co. advertised satin medallions in conjunction with the 'Versailles Sash' in the *World* and *Morning Post and Daily Advertiser* between 1788 and 1789. See Ehrman, 'Versailles Sash'. For the development of classical fashion in dress, see Rauser, *The Age of Undress*.

131 Ann Frankland, daughter of Admiral Sir Thomas Frankland, married John Lewis, Esq. of Harpton Court, Radnorshire on 24 March 1778. See Dyer, *Material Lives*, 50–8.

132 Dyer, *Material Lives*, 49.

133 Lewis depicted fur muffs for the years: 1781, 1784, 1800 and 1804.

134 *Sylvia Overseen by Daphne Who Edneavor'd to Persuade Her to Love Aminta,* 1787, Angelica Kauffman, publ. by Susanna Viares, BM, London.

135 The appearance of the 'language of flowers' is associated with Lady Mary Wortley Montague. Beverly Seaton, *The Language of Flowers: A History* (Charlottesville: University of Virginia Press, 1995), 62. James Boswell writes in the poem 'A Nosegay', 'The Violet is modesty, For it conceals itself.' *The European Magazine, and London Review,* April 1788, 296; *The Scots Magazine,* July 1788, 344.

136 Malise Adam and Mary Mauchline, 'Kauffman's Decorative Work', in *Angelica Kauffman: A Continental Artist in Georgian England,* ed. Wendy Wassyng Roworth (London: Reaktion Books, 1992), 113.

137 Rosenthal, *Kauffman,* 163–5.

138 Ann Bermingham has argued that within the eighteenth-century patriarchal hierarchy of artistic consumption, the role of connoisseur was traditionally sanctioned to the male sex, leaving women merely as consumers of art, which in turn contributed to their own consumption. Ann Bermingham, 'Elegant Females and Gentleman Connoisseurs: The Commerce in Culture and Self-image in Eighteenth-Century England', in *The Consumption of Culture 1600–1800,* ed. Ann Bermingham and John Brewer (London: Routledge, 1995), 492, 502.

139 For example, feather muff, mid-1800s, V&A, 926-1904. See Gernerd, 'Fancy Feathers'.

140 *Walkers' Hibernian Magazine, or, Compendium of Entertaining Knowledge,* March 1786, 113.

Chapter 4

1 *Whitehall Evening Post,* 3–5 May 1796. 'Lathy consistency', meaning tall and thin, refers to a description of Joe Snip the Tailor in David Garrick's play *Harlequin's Invasion.* David Garrick, *The Plays of David Garrick: Garrick's Own Plays, 1740–1766,* ed. Harry William Pedicord and Frederick Louis Bergmann (Carbondale and Edwardsville: Southern Illinois University Press, 1980), 1: 210, 409.

2 The full text reads 'Just arriv'd Monsr. Titus Shape who has had the Honour of performing on above 2000 Ladies of the first Nobility in France, now in Cock Spur Street, London, has imported a large Assortment of Figure Frames, Sweating Stools, Fumigators, Inflaters, Antiflatulents, and Reducers; by the use of which (in one month only) he forms or alters all manner of Shapes so perfectly as to render Pads, Plumpers, Corks, Tight Stays, and Rollers totally needless. – Those Curves which by Nature the Human Frame (in itself weak) inclines to, he forms into straight Lines and acute Angles. However stiffend by Age, however encumbered with Protuberances Nil desperandum est under the skilful, at the same time Humane and Tender treatment at, Ladies your devoted, Titus Shapes.'

3 Boned bodices as undergarments originated *c.* 1500–1550. Valerie Steele, *The Corset* (New Haven: Yale University Press, 2001), 2–7. For early modern pairs of bodies, see Sarah Bendall, *Shaping Femininity: Foundation Garments, the Body and Women in Early Modern England* (London: Bloomsbury Visual Arts, 2022).

4 For evolutions in terminology see, Waugh, *Corsets and Crinolines,* 75; Carter, *Underwear,* 30.

5 For unfashionable stays, see Peter Mactaggart and R. Ann Mactaggart, 'Some Aspects of the Use of Non-Fashionable Stays', in *Strata of Society Costume Society Conference* (London: Costume Society, 1973), 20–8; Peter Mactaggart and R. Ann Mactaggart, 'Ease, Convenience and Stays, 1750–1850', *Costume* 13 (1979): 41–51.

6 Styles, *Dress of the People*, 32. Beverly Lemire has identified inventories with large quantities of bodices. Sorge-English has also attested to the ubiquity of wearing stays, drawing attention to their perceived value and the risk desperate women went to obtaining them in the records of the Old Bailey. Beverly Lemire, *Dress, Culture and Commerce: The English Clothing Trade before the Factory, 1660–1800* (New York: St. Martin's Press, 1997), 62–3; Lynn Sorge-English, *Stays and Body Image in London: The Staymaking Trade, 1680–1800* (London: Pickering & Chatto, 2011), 165.

7 In a bill from an unidentified staymaker, the Countess is invoiced for '2 pair of black stays 4-00-0', and '1 pair of white stays 2-00-0'. Blenheim Papers, Vol. CCCXL VIII, ADD MS. 61448.

8 Scoring the leather vertically made the stays flexible in one direction, but ridged in another, allowing for movement of the body, while maintaining the structural support. Mactaggart and Mactaggart, 'Some Aspects', 26–7. For a discussion of a surviving material example of a leather stay, see Sorge-English, *Stays and Body Image*, 50–1.

9 *London Evening Post*, 20 August 1754.

10 Mactaggart, 'Some Aspects', 26; Carter, *Underwear*, 29. Ready-made stays, at lower prices were also available, particularly from the mid-1770s onwards. Staymaker Thomas Mills offered a range of to-measure stays as well as ready-made: 'Ladies middle-size French or Italian Stays 1. s. or best rich Sattin, to measure', for two shillings, eight pence or alternatively ready made for one shilling and one pence. *World*, 15 February 1788. For the second-hand and ready-made clothing trades, see Beverly Lemire, 'Developing Consumerism and the Ready-made Clothing Trade in Britain, 1750–1800', *Textile History* 15 (1984): 21–44; Beverly Lemire, 'Consumerism in Preindustrial and Early Industrial England: The Trade in Second Hand Clothes', *Journal of British Studies* 27 (1988): 1–24; Beverly Lemire, 'Peddling Fashion: Salesmen, Pawnbrokers, Taylors, Thieves and the Second-Hand Clothes Trade in England', *Textile History* 22 (1991): 67–82; Miles Lambert, 'Bespoke versus Ready-Made: The Work of the Tailor in Eighteenth-Century Britain', *Costume* 44 (2010): 56–65.

11 Between 1674 and 1819, 619 cases reported thefts of stays in the Old Bailey records. For theft, see Beverly Lemire, 'The Theft of Clothes and Popular Consumerism in Early Modern England', *Journal of Social History* (1990): 255–76; Styles, *Dress of the People*, 42–4; Sorge-English, *Stays and Body Image*, 86–8.

12 See Gernerd, 'Pulled Tight and Gleaming', 18.

13 Vincent, *Anatomy of Fashion*, 97.

14 In addition to the wide piece of boning extending across the top of the bust, two shorter bones have been placed at a diagonal, intersecting with the top bone from beneath the arms. While there is no designated pocket in the front lining, it is possible that in addition to these internal supports, a busk would have also been worn; however, these supports in themselves may have made a busk unnecessary. For a discussion on busks, see Mactaggart, 'Some Aspects', 22–3.

15 Waugh, *Corsets and Crinolines*, 37.

16 Metal eyelets were invented in 1828. Jill Salen, *Corsets Historic Patterns and Techniques* (London: Bratsford, 2008), 7.

17 Stays could be constructed with up to five layers of fabric. Lynn Sorge-English, '"29 Doz and 11 Best Cutt Bone": The Trade in Whalebone and Stays in Eighteenth-Century London', *Textile History* 36 (2005): 31.

18 Waugh, *Corsets and Crinolines*, 167.

19 The effect of body heat and moisture on stays and the body has been discussed with Luca Castiliano of the School for Historical Dress and with Sarah Woodyard, Mark Hutter and Abby Cox at the Margaret Hunter Shop, Colonial Williamsburg. For a further discussion of the use of heat in re-shaping whalebone or plying it,

see Sorge-English, '29 Doz', 34–5. For further differentiation between fully boned, half-boned and jumps, see Mactaggart and Mactaggart, 'Ease, Convenience and Stays', 41–2.

20   Lynn Sorge, 'Eighteenth-Century Stays: Their Origins and Creators', *Costume* 32 (1998): 25; Sorge-English, *Stays and Body Image*, 34.

21   Waugh, *Corsets and Crinolines*, 41. The introduction of horizontal bones across the bust is illustrated in Plate XXII of Diderot's *Encyclopaedia, Patterns of Front and Back French Bodices, Different Operations to Measure Bodices, Jumps, Fully-boned Stays, Inside Arrangement of Quilting and Supporting Whalebones,* which was published between 1751 and 1777. The shift to include horizontal boning was even reflected in staymaker's trade cards. Richard Strange's trade cards changed design when he moved from St. Martin's Lane to Warwick Street, Golden Square. The side silhouette of his later address includes the addition of a visible horizontal bone across the front. Trade cards of Richard Strange, Banks Collection 112.37 and 112.38, Acc. Nos. D,2.3750 and D,2.3757, BM, London.

22   See Waugh, *Corsets and Crinolines*, 41; Carter, *Underwear*, 27–8; Sorge-English, *Stays and Body Image*, 28–45.

23   In recreation circles, this design of stays is called a 'prow front' due to the jutting out of the bust; however, the term was not used in the eighteenth century.

24   For the shift in construction, see Sorge-English, *Stays and Body Image*, 34–42.

25   Petticoats, pockets and stay laces would also be tied around the outside of the stays.

26   An almost identical pair at MAG discussed below also includes eyelets in the same location, Acc. No. 1949.130. A pair from *c.* 1800 from MAG includes eyelets higher up on the back, aligned with the elevated waistline, Acc. No. 1947.1625. A pair from the end of the seventeenth century at FM includes two metal hooks about an inch away from the back lacing, which could have hooked onto a bum roll, Acc. No BATMC.1.27.86. A late nineteenth-century ribbon corset at FM includes two buttons spaced evenly on the sides panels, which would have allowed for a wider framed bustle to attach without disturbing the decorative appearance of the ribbon front, Acc. No. I.27.16.

27   Hooks, which have fallen off, can be seen on a pair of pink woollen stays, also at MAG, Acc. No. 1947.1623. Two rust stains act as visual indentations above the first fingers next to centre front, indicating the presence of metal hooks. Unusually, the directional loops are not attached at the top back panels, but aligned with the curving seams attaching the front panels with the side panels. A pair of satin stays in the DWW without tapes includes ribbon loops at the top of the shoulders, Acc. No.1960-729. While there is no evidence of hooks, the stays include two twill loops at the bottoms of the back centre panels. These loops could either have served to aid in the tying of straps, or possibly the attachment of a rump.

28   Mark Hutter has identified a pair in a private collection as riding stays as they were accompanied by a matching riding habit when purchased, which he asserts were intended to be worn together. Curators at MCM and DWW have identified both pairs as riding stays, as have the School for Historical Dress. Conversations with MCM curator Cynthia Cooper, July 2014, and DWW curator Linda Baumgarten, May 2014. A third pair of very lightly boned stays exists in the DWW collection, which Baumgarten has identified as riding stays. This pair has a working gusset without the linen panel behind and has sewn straps extending from the front of the stays and attaching on the back, further demonstrating that tapes do not distinguish riding stays, Acc. No. G1990.9. Discussion with Mark Hutter and examination of the pair in the private collection, May 2014, Colonial Williamsburg. Arnold, Tiramani, Costigliolo, Passot, Lucas and Pietsch, *Patterns of Fashion 5,* 108–9.

29   *Morning Post and Daily Advertiser,* 11 February 1778.

30   *Public Advertiser*, 8 March 1755.

31 See Dyer and Smith, 'Introduction'.

32 *World*, 25 May 1791.

33 This is most likely William Saltzman of Henrietta Street, Covent Garden. MA 7269, Morgan Library.

34 Austen changes staymakers to Dietrichsen in June 1780. MA 7269, Morgan Library.

35 Doc. 67, Downs Collection, Winterthur.

36 For example, brown linen stays that have lost their tape traps, but retain hooks at the centre front and linen tape loops on the back shoulders, Acc. No. T.913-1913, V&A; fully boned, grey cotton warp/wool weft glazed cotton stays with tape straps, Acc. No. 139940, NT; fully boned satin stays, tapes missing, but silk ribbon loops in back, Acc. No. 1960-729, DWW, Williamsburg; pink stays with tape straps and loops, rust stains where hooks used to be, and a removable busk at the bottom front beneath the gusset, Acc. No. 1947.1623, Manchester; brown twill stays with tape straps and tape loops, Acc. No. 1940.157, Manchester.

37 The 2005 acquisition includes over thirty items of clothing spanning from gowns and outerwear to accessories and underwear, Acc. No. 2005-102, 2–39. I would like to thank Mark Hutter for originally bringing this doll to my attention.

38 Sorge-English has attributed this shift in shape around 1775 to the growth and influence of female staymakers. Sorge-English, *Stays and Body Image*, 187–90.

39 Conversation with Mark Hutter, May 2014, Colonial Williamsburg.

40 Scenes of female undress were a popular trope in French painting, however, never translated into a British genre. An unusual example can be seen in two stipple engravings by Charles Ansell, *Dressing Room a l'Anglaise* and *Dressing Room a la Française,* 7 April 1789, publ. by Ino. Matthews, LWL, Farmington.

41 Steele, *Corset*, 25; Vincent, *Anatomy of Fashion*, 43.

42 *Walker's Hibernian Magazine, or, Compendium of Entertaining Knowledge*, May 1786, 258–9.

43 Johann Georg Zimmermann, *A Treatise on Experience in Physic* (London: Printed for J. Wilkie, 1778), 2.317–8.

44 'Emperor's Edict against wearing Stays', *Hibernian Magazine, or, Compendium of Entertaining Knowledge*, November 1783, 563; Erasmus Darwin, *A Plan for the Conduct of Female Education* (Derby: Printed by J. Drewry, 1797), 177; R. Phillips, *The Medical and Physical Journal; Containing the Earliest Information on Subjects of Medicine, Surgery, Pharmacy, Chemistry, and Natural History …* (London: Printed by William Thorne, 1799), 2.47–8.

45 In a hand-coloured version in the MET, New York, the carpet has been coloured over, the floor resembling a series of wooden floor boards, receding towards the back of the print. Both prints have the same publication date of 1 March 1777, Acc. No. 41.25.5.

46 See Stroomberg, *High Heads*; Powell and Roach, 'Big Hair'.

47 This print is referenced in an endnote (Chapter 5, Number 12) in David Kunzle's *Fashion and Fetishism*, but has never been discussed within the eighteenth-century iconographic stay tradition. David Kunzle, *Fashion & Fetishism: Corsets, Tight-Lacing & Other Forms of Body-Sculpture* (Stroud: Sutton Publishing, 2006), 353.

48 The version examined here is labelled as published by Bowles and Carver, hence it is a later reissued version. An original issued version with Carington Bowles identified as publisher exists in the collection of the YCBA; however, the date has also been burnished out. The date was burnished out from the copper plates of the initial and the re-issued version. The LWL has dated the print to 'after June 1777', based on George's chronological

appendix, which identified number 352 *Six Weeks after Marriage* (25 June 1777) as the closest number to *Tight Lacing*. However, due to its issue number, 362 on the bottom left-hand corner, it is possible to narrow it further between 24 July and 10 November 1777. The two closest adjacent prints surviving in the series are numbers 361 and 365, *The Unfortunate Discovery* and *Bachelor's Fare, or, Bread and Cheese with Kisses* respectively, which both survive with dates intact. Blackwell suggests that the artist of the Darly print, whom she identifies as a 'sloppy amateur', could have seen a version of Collet's print first, as she demonstrated was the case with *Grown Gentlemen Learning to Dance* and *Grown Citizens Learning to Dance*. Alexander, 'Kauffman and the Print Market', 138; George, *Catalogue*, 5.786; Blackwell, 'John Collet', 17, 214.

49   Steele has identified this print and the trope of tight lacing as primarily articulating concerns over female vanity. Steele, *The Corset*, 2, 21–6.

50   Various versions exist, which vary the colours of each article of clothing. I have chosen to work with the DWW's print as my primary example, despite that it is a reissued version, published in 1793.

51   See Fowkes Tobin, *Picturing Imperial Power,* 27–55; Freya Gowrley, 'Taste à-la-Mode: Consuming Foreignness, Picturing Gender', in *Materializing Gender in Eighteenth-Century Europe*, ed. J. G. Germann and H. A. Strobel (Abingdon: Routledge, 2016), 73–80.

52   The Mactaggarts argue that it would have been necessary for a woman to hold on to a bedpost, not only to lift the ribcage into an open position under the stays, but also because when laced using one lace, which zigzagged across, the woman would have been physically pulled side to side. Mactaggart and Mactaggart, 'Ease, Convenience and Stays', 45.

53   This print, like others by Collet's hand, is identified as a printed reproduction of a painting, 'in possession of the Publisher', Carington Bowles. While some of Collet's paintings survive, for example five in the DWW collection, many of their whereabouts are still unknown.

54   John Collet, *The Victim*, 1780, publ. by Carington Bowles, hand-coloured mezzotint, 35.5 cm × 25.2 cm, BM, London.

55   Llanover, *Autobiography,* 3.160; previously quoted in Waugh, *Corsets and Crinolines*, 60; Steele, *Corset*, 25.

56   Steele, *Corset*, 26.

57   For example, Mrs Delany writes to her niece of Miss Sparrow that 'she is attentive to all studies going forward, and seems desirous of information, and speak and understand French much better than she expected to find she did; as to manner she is *gauch*, and will, I fear, always be so; but as she does not want for sense and good nature, I hope those faults that have been gain'd ground for want of *early* good habits will be conquer'd for her own sake as well as for her friends, and I most heartily wish they may.' Mrs Delany to Mrs Port, of Ilam, 16 April 1776. Delany, *Autobiography*, 3.209.

58   Steele has addressed this quotation as if the subjects were strangers, using Miss Sparrow as an example of mockery, rather than concern. Steele, *Corset*, 26.

59   The anonymous print, ridiculing high coiffeurs, was published on 1 July 1778 at No. 27 Great Castle Street, Oxford. The woman on the left is reminiscent of the Farnese Hercules, while the beauty in the centre draws upon the position of the *Venus de' Medici*. Rasche and Wolter observe the outdated headdress of the woman on the right. Adelheid Rasche and Gundula Wolter (eds.), *Ridikül! Mode in Der Karikatur 1600 bis 1900* (Berlin: SMB, Staatliche Museen zu Berlin, Dumont, 2003), 175.

60   Sheridan produced numerous satirical prints between 1776 and 1777, primarily for the Darlys. See Chapter 2.

61   In a sketch at DWW, which may be preliminary or a copy, the method of lacing in the spiral zig-zag pattern is visible.

62 McCreery, *Satirical Gaze*, 229–48.

63 Macauley died in 1791 at the age of sixty. Ribeiro notes that the cause of death in the satire is attributed to the lead-based makeup, which she is applying to her face. Ribeiro, *Facing Beauty*, 191.

64 Based on an inscription by Sarah Sophia Banks, the original owner of the print in the British Museum, the woman is identified as Mrs Catherine Macaulay, who was well-known for her use of cosmetics. George, *Catalogue*, 5.268–9.

65 While George does not identify this print as the hand of Sheridan, as his signature 'RS' does not appear in the bottom left-hand corner, if the collection of sketches at DWW are preliminary, rather than copies, then it affirms that this satire was made by the same hand. However, further investigation into artist of these sketches is required.

66 Steele identifies this print as a failed attempt 'to conceal her obesity', Steele, *Corset*, 26.

67 Greig, *Beau Monde*, 169.

68 Dror Wahrman has identified this tightening of previous fluidity of gender as 'gender panic', or, 'a pattern of change that decisively reversed, over a short period of time, a variety of interconnected cultural forms through which eighteenth-century Britons signalled their recognition of the potential limitations of gender categories'. Dror Wahrman, 'Percy's Prologue: From Gender Play to Gender Panic in Eighteenth-Century England', *Past and Present* 159, no. 1 (1998): 123–8; Wahrman, *The Making of the Modern Self*, 21, 33–4; Linda Colley, *Britons: Forging the Nation 1707–1837* (London: Yale University Press, 1992), 242–50.

69 For Jacobite and Jacobin dress, see Michael Darby, 'Jacobite Garters', *Victoria and Albert Museum Bulletin* 2, no. 4 (1966): 157–63; Murray Pittock, 'Treacherous Objects: Towards a Theory of Jacobite Material Culture', *Journal for Eighteenth-Century Studies* 34, no. 1 (2011): 39–63; Richard Wrigley, 'The Formation and Currency of a Vestimentary Stereotype: The *Sans-culotte* in Revolutionary France', in *Fashioning the Body Politic: Dress, Gender, Citizenship*, ed. Wendy Parkins (Oxford: Berg, 2002), 19–48; Richard Wrigley, *The Politics of Appearances: Representations of Dress in Revolutionary France* (Oxford: Berg, 2002), 19–48.

70 See Elaine Chalus, 'Fanning the Flames: Women, Fashion, and Politics', in *Women, Popular Culture, and the Eighteenth Century*, ed. Tiffany Potter (London: University of Toronto Press, 2012), 92–112; Katrina Navickas, '"That sash will hang you": Political Clothing and Adornment in England, 1780–1840', *The Journal of British Studies* 49, no. 3 (2010): 542, 564.

71 Wrigley, 'Politics', 5–6.

72 This print has been briefly addressed by Steele, *Corset*, 25; Blackwell, 'John Collet', 266.

73 The crosses appeared on her shield in 1672. The olive branch appeared during Charles II's reign. For a thorough discussion of the evolution of Britannia's image from a conquered warrior in the Roman period to her identification with Margaret Thatcher, see Marina Warner, *Monuments and Maidens: The Allegory of the Female Form* (London: Vintage, 1985), 45–9.

74 Paine was born in Thetford, Norfolk on 29 January 1737 to Joseph Pain and Frances Cocke. According to his biographers, he also worked as a staymaker for John Morris on Hanover Street, Longe Acre, Benjamin Grace in Dover and eventually in Sandwich. On one version of the print, a handwritten note has been attached, stating 'Thomas Paine was born at Thetford in Norforlk on the 29th of January 1737. His father was a Quaker and by trade a staymaker, and when his son was thirteen years old he was apprenticed to him in order to learn that trade.' BM, London, No. 1851,0901.638. Mark Philip, *Thomas Paine* (Oxford: Oxford University Press, 2007).

75 Gillray portrays Paine with a large pair of scissors attached to his waist as the 'little American Taylor' measuring the crown for a pair of breeches in *The Rights of Man, or Tommy Paine, the Little American Taylor, Taking the*

Measure of the Crown for a New Pair of Revolution-Breeches, 23 May 1791, publ. by Hannah Humphrey, BM, London. John Brewer, *The Common People and Politics 1750–1790s* (Cambridge: Chadwyck-Healey Ltd, 1986), 39.

76   James Epstein, 'Understanding the Cap of Liberty: Symbolic Practice and Social Conflict in Nineteenth-Century England', *Past & Present* 122 (February 1989): 74, 88.

77   Donald, *Age of Caricature*, 152–3.

78   This print illustrates John Brewer's assertion that Gillray's fierce depictions of French and British radicals, such as Thomas Paine, wearing liberty caps most likely aided the cap's drastic change in meaning. Brewer, *Common People*, 39–40.

79   For a broader discussion of the fear of French influence spreading in Britain, see John Barrell, *The Spirit of Despotism: Invasions of Privacy in the 1790s* (Oxford: Oxford University Press, 2006).

80   Dyer, 'Fashioning Consumers', 483. For example, Brickman, '*French* Stay-Maker' in Bristol advertised his recent return from Paris and John Burchett, 'Stay-maker, from Paris' advertised 'having received some new fashioned patterns from Paris'. *Felix Farley's Bristol Journal*, 27 September 1783; *Morning Post*, 11 February 1778.

81   French stays were also advertised in colonial America. Sebastian Finlass advertised 'French and English' stays, along with 'riding stays, turned stays, and jumps, half-bone and whole-bone'. *Pennsylvania Gazette*, 6 June 1787. Corsets were described as lighter boned, 'quilted waistcoat', and even elastic by the early 1790s. *The Lady's Magazine, or Entertaining Companion for the Fair Sex*, May 1785, 263. For the increasing use of the term corset over the regency period, see Davidson, *Regency Fashion*, 64.

82   See Juliette Reboul, *French Emigration to Great Britain in Response to the French Revolution* (Cham: Springer International Publishing AG, 2017), chapter 5; Kimberly Chrisman-Campbell, 'Rose Bertin in London?', *Costume* 32, no. 1 (1998): 45–51; Macushla Baudis, '"Smoking hot with fashion from Paris": The Consumption of French Fashion in Eighteenth-Century Ireland', *Costume* 48, no. 2 (2014): 141–59.

83   Invoking royal patronage was an established retail tactic. An advertisement for Dyde and Scribe, who were discussed in Chapter 3, beneath the advert for Mrs Mayer, identify themselves as 'Furriers to their Royal Highnesses the Prince of Wales and Duke of York.' *Oracle*, 20 October 1789.

84   *Oracle*, 25 December 1789.

85   Lynn Sorge-English implies that this type of construction could be 'French' stays with a pair, 1775–85, Acc. No. 57.200, Worthing Museum & Art Gallery, Worthing. Sorge-English, *Stays and Body Image*, 38–9.

86   *Morning Herald*, 24 October 1783.

87   Prologue written by Richard Ticknell to Richard Brindsley Sheridan's *The Camp: A Musical Entertainment*, *Public Advertiser*, 23 October 1778. See also George Coleman, Prologue to *Bon Ton; or, High Life above Stairs. In Two Acts*. Anonymous, *Supplement to Bell's British Theatre, Consisting of the Most Esteemed Farces and Entertainments Now Performing on the British Stage. Vol. IV* (London: Printed for Joh Bell, 1784); Anonymous, *Fashion: A Poem Addressed to the Ladies of Great Britain. In Two Books. Book First. The Second Edition* (London: Printed for J. Williams, 1778).

88   Georgiana Cavendish, Duchess of Devonshire, *The Sylph; a Novel in Two Volumes* (London: Printed for T. Lowndes, 1779), 69.

89   Cavendish, *Sylph*, 69. This phrase has often been used to demonstrate the necessary discomfort of fashion. A second example where the ton is described as the physical manipulation of a woman's torso by her stays can be found in Christopher Antsley's poem of a father describing his daughter's appearance. He writes 'Lack a day!

how her Throat doth our MARGERY raise, How *shove up* her Bosom, and *shove down* her Stays? For to make a young Lady a true polite Figure You must cramp up her Sides that her Breast may look bigger.' Christopher Anstley, *An Election Ball in Poetical Letters from Mr. Inkle at Bath, to His Wife at Glocester: With a Poetical Address to* John Miller, Esq. *at Batheaston Villa. Third Edition* (Bath: Printed for the Author, by S. Hazard, 1776), 42; quoted as evidence of women's objectification through stays by Fiona Haslam, *From Hogarth to Rowlandson: Medicine in Art in Eighteenth-Century Britain* (Liverpool: Liverpool University Press, 1996), 230.

90   George, *Catalogue*, 9.84–5.

91   The cosmetics bottles read: Tooth Powder, Rouge, Otto of Roses, and Secilian Wash for the Skin.

92   Influence over the Prince Regent is depicted as having shifted to McMahon from Yarmont, as denoted by the poodle pissing on the 'Striped Poem'.

93   Lord Holland to Mr. Creevey, undated, The Right Hon. Sir Herbert Maxwell (ed.), *The Creevey Papers: A Selection from the Correspondence & Diaries of the Late Thomas Creevey, M. P. Born 1768 – Died 1838* (New York: E. P. Dutton & Company, 1904), 264.

94   Lady Cowper, 20 July 1821, in Tresham Lever (ed.), *The Letters of Lady Palmerston: Selected and Edited from the Originals at Broadlands and Elsewhere …* (London: John Murray Ltd, 1957), 86.

95   *The Annual Register, or a View of the History, Politics, and Literature of the Year 1821* (London: Printed for Baldwin, Cradock and Joy, 1822), 365.

96   This pattern was copied and replicated in 2012 for Brighton Museum's exhibition, 'Dress for Excess'. Records for belts and fitted linings also appear in the Prince's expenditures in the Royal Archives. For a wider discussion of his apparel see Ribeiro, *Art of Dress*, 99–100. See Davidson, *Regency Fashion,* 64–5.

97   The connection between stays and effeminacy is underlined in the portrayal of dandies in stays. For example, *Laceing a Dandy,* 26 January 1819, publ. by Thomas Tegg, LWL, Farmington and George Cruikshank, *The Dandies Coat of Arms,* 28 March 1819, publ. by Thomas Tegg, MET, New York. For dandies, see Cole Shaun and Miles Lambert, *Dandy Style: 250 Years of British Men's Fashion* (New Haven: Yale University Press, 2021).

98   See Steele, *The Corset,* 2001; Kunzle, *Fashion & Fetishism,* 2006.

Conclusion

1   Dias, 'A world of pictures,' 95.

2   Gillray had been producing prints for Humphrey non-exclusively since 1779.

3   Gillray produced his last print on 9 January 1811 due to failing eyesight and mental health, dying in 1815.

4   Similar to other dressing rooms within satirical prints, like Figure 2.2. For the material culture of the dressing room, see Kimberley Chrisman-Campbell, 'Dressing to Impress: The Morning Toilette and the Fabrication of Femininity', in *Paris: Life & Luxury in the Eighteenth Century*, ed. Charissa Bremer-David (Los Angeles: J. Paul Getty Museum, 2011), 53–74.

5   Women started wearing drawers around 1810 due to the transparency of clinging muslin gowns.

6   *Delphine* by Germaine de Staël was published in France in 1802, and published in English by 1803.

7   For examples extant sleeve puffs, see Acc. No. 2017-258,1&2, DWW, Williamsburg; Acc. No. 1996.0093.015 and Acc. No. 1997.0003.006.002, Winterthur Museum, Garden and Library, Winterthur.

8   See Elisabeth Gernerd, 'Subverting Time: The Banyan, Temporality, and Graphic Satire,' *Eighteenth-Century Studies* 56, no. 3 (Spring 2023): 395–423.

9   *General Advertiser*, 20 August 1785.

10 The fashion plates of *Gallery of Fashion* claimed to be based on the aristocratic fashions of beau monde London. See Dyer, 'Fashions of the Day,' 79–81.

11 See Dyer, 'Fashions of the Day.'

12 Dyer, *Material Lives*, 191.

13 *The Morning Post and Daily Advertiser*, 25 April 1775.

14 Duke and Duchess of Gordon were portrayed in *The Petticoat in the Fiera Maschereta* and *The Breeches in the Fiera Maschereta*. Gernerd, 'Fancy Feathers,' 195–9. *The Virginia Gazette*, 24 June 1776.

15 Peter McNeil and Patrik Steorn have addressed the dissemination of fashion through print culture transnationally between London and continental Europe. This pattern of dissemination extended transatlantically as part of a wider network of material exchange between London and British America, which has been recently explored by authors such as Zara Anishanslin and Jenifer van Horn. McNeil and Steorn, 'The Medium of Print,' 135–56; Zara Anishanslin, *Portrait of a Woman in Silk: Hidden Histories of the British Atlantic World* (London: Yale University Press, 2016); Jennifer van Horn, *The Power of Objects in Eighteenth-Century British America* (Chapel Hill: University of North Carolina Press, 2017).

16 For example, Nicholas Brooks sold both imported prints and prints published at his printshop, including a mezzotint of John Hancock. *The Pennsylvania Gazette*, 23 June 1773; *The Pennsylvania Gazette*, 1 November 1775. *The South Carolina Gazette*, 10 August 1769.

17 *The South Carolina Gazette*, 28 January 1773.

18 Bustles appear in women's fashion, roughly every hundred years towards the end of the century, which Shearer West attributed to a *fin de siècle* phenomenon and millenarianism characteristic at the end of centuries. Shearer West, *Fin De Siecle: Art and Society in an Age of Uncertainty* (London: Bloomsbury Publishing Ltd, 1993), 1–15.

19 Wahrman, 'Percy's Prologue,' 123–8; Wahrman, *Making of the Modern Self*, 21, 33–4; Colley, *Britons*, 242–50. For consumption see, McKendrick, Brewer and Plumb, *Birth of a Consumer Society*, 34–66.

20 Boucher, *History of Costume*, 330.

21 Styles, 'Fashion and Innovation,' 44–55.

22 Rauser argues that in the 1780s a stylistic shift occurred from emblematic to naturalistic, or caricatural expression that focuses on the self instead of symbols, building upon Dror Wahrman's theory of sudden emersion of the self in the late eighteenth century. She has expanded this argument to the naturalistic dress of the 1790s. Amelia Rauser, *Caricature Unmasked: Irony, Authenticity, and Individualism in Eighteenth-Century English Prints* (Newark: University of Delaware Press, 2008), 19–21, 25; Wahrman, *Making of the Modern Self*; Rauser, *Age of Undress*.

23 *Morning Chronicle*, 19 September 1794. Fickle goddess normally refers to Fortune. For example, see *The World*, 17 September 1787. For similar advocacy favouring simplicity of dress and short stays, see *Courier*, 29 October 1800. For regency stays, see Davidson, *Regency Fashion*, 62–6.

Bibliography

Published primary sources before 1850

Alexander, William. *The History of Women, from the Earliest Antiquity, to the Present Time: Giving Some Account of Almost Every Interesting Particular Concerning That Sex, among All Nations, Ancient and Modern*. Dublin: Printed by J. A. Husband, 1779.

Anstley, Christopher. *An Election Ball in Poetical Letters from Mr. Inkle at Bath, to His Wife at Glocester: With a Poetical Address to John Miller, Esq. at Batheaston Villa. Third Edition*. Bath: Printed for the Author, by S. Hazard, 1776.

Austen, Jane. *Northanger Abbey: And Persuasion: By the Author of 'Pride and Prejudice;' 'Mansfield-Park,' &c*. London: John Murray, 1818.

Babble, Nicholas. *The Prater*. London: Printed for T. Lownds, 1756.

Bailey, William. *Bailey's British Directory; or, Merchant's and Trader's Useful Companion, for the Year 1784 …* London: Printed by William Bailey, 1784.

Bowles, Carrington. *Carington Bowles's New and Enlarged Catalogue of Useful and Accurate Maps, Charts, and Plans; Curious and Entertaining Engraved and Mezzotint Prints, Single or in Sets: Writing Books; Including All the Branches of Penmanship: Black-Lines, Letter-File Maps, and Prints, School Pieces, Cards for Schools, &c. &c. Elegant Drawing Books, and Correct Books of Maps, Roads, Perspective, Geometry, &c. Containing a Great Variety of New and Valuable Articles for the Use of the Nobility and Gentry of Great-Britain and Ireland. Merchants Exports, and Shop Keepers Country Trade Which May Be Had Wholesale and Retail at His Map and Print Warehouse, No. 69, St. Paul's Church Yard, London*. London: Printed by Carington Bowles, 1784.

Buc'hoz, Pierre-Joseph. *The Toilet of Flora: or, A Collection of the Most Simple and Approved Methods of Preparing Baths, Essences, Pomatums, Powders, Perfumes, and Sweet-scented Waters with Receipts for Cosmetics of Every Kind, that Can Smooth and Brighten the Skin, Give Force to Beauty, and Take Off the Appearance of Old Age and Decay. For Use of the Ladies. A New Edition, Improved*. London: Printed for J. Murray, 1779.

Campbell, Robert. *The London Tradesman. Being a Compendious View of All the Trades, Professions, Arts, Both Liberal and Mechanic, Now Practiced in the Cities of* London *and* Westminster. *Calculated for the Information of PARENTS, and Instruction of YOUTH in Their Choice of Business*. London: Printed by T. Gardner, 1747.

Cavendish, Georgiana, Duchess of Devonshire. *The Sylph; A Novel in Two Volumes*. London: Printed for T. Lowndes, 1779.

Cleland, John. *Memoirs of a Woman of Pleasure, Vol. I*. London: Printed for G. Fenton, 1749.

Darwin, Erasmus. *A Plan for the Conduct of Female Education*. Derby: Printed by J. Drewry, 1797.

Dodsley, Robert. *A Collection of Poems in Four Volumes by Several Hands, Vol. IV*. London: Printed by J. Hughs, 1755.

E., B. *A New Dictionary of the Terms Ancient and Modern of the Canting Crew*. London: W. Hawes, P. Gilbourne and W. Davis, 1699.

Espriella, Don Manuel Alvarez. *Letters from England 2nd Edition*. London: Printed for Longman, Hurst, Rees and Orme, 1808.

Fairholt, F. W. *Costume in England: A History of Dress to the End of the Eighteenth Century*. London: Chapman and Hall, 1846.

Fairholt, F. W. *Satirical Songs and Poems on Costume: From the 13th to the 19th Century*. Vol. 27. London: Printed for the Percy Society, 1849.

Fashion: A Poem Addressed to the Ladies of Great Britain. In Two Books. Book First. The Second Edition. London: Printed for J. Williams, 1778.

Fitz-Adam, Adam. *The World in Three Volumes*. Edinburgh: Printed by and for Martin & Wotherspoon, 1777.

Freneau, Philip. *The Miscellaneous Works of Mr. Philip Freneau Containing His Essays, and Additional Poems*. Philadelphia: Francis Bailey, 1788.

Grose, Francis. *A Classical Dictionary of the Vulgar Tongue*. London: Printed for S. Hooper, 1785.

Hamilton, Robert. *An Introduction to Merchandize*. Edinburgh: Printed for the Author, 1777.

Hogarth, William. *The Analysis of Beauty*. London: Printed by J. Reeves, 1753.

Horne, Charles. *Serious Thoughts on the Miseries of Seduction and Prostitution, with a Full Account of the Evils That Produce Them …* London: Printed for Swift and Son, 1738.

The Instructive Letter-Writer, and Entertaining Companion: Containing Letters on the Most Interesting Subjects, in an Elegant and Easy Style; wherein a Peculiar Regard Has Been Had to Select Those, ONLY, Which Are Best Adapted to Inspire NOBLE and MANY SENTIMENTS, and Promote a RATIONAL and VIRTUOUS CONDUCT; Most of Them Being Wrote by the Following Royal and Eminent PERSONAGES, and the Best Authers, Ancient and Modern, viz …. The Second Edition. London: Printed for W. Nicoll, 1765.

Lathom, Francis. *The Dash of the Day, a Comedy, in Five Acts …* Norwich: J. Payne, 1800.

The London and Westminster Guide, through the Cities and Suburbs … London: Printed for W. Nicoll, 1768.

Mandeville, Bernard. *The Fable of the Bees: or, Private Vices, Publick Benefits. With an Essay on Charity and Charity-Schools. And a Search into the Nature of Society*. London: Printed for J. Tonson, 1724.

Memoirs and Interesting Adventures of an Embroidered Waistcoat. London: Printed for and sold by J. Brooke, 1751.

Nicholson, William. *The British Encyclopedia, or Dictionary of Arts and Sciences*. Vol. II. London: C. Whittingham, 1809.

Phillips, R. *The Medical and Physical Journal; Containing the Earliest Information on Subjects of Medicine, Surgery, Pharmacy, Chemistry, and Natural History …* London: Printed by William Thorne, 1799.

Pindar, Peter. *The Cork Rump, or Queen and Maids of Honour. A Poem*. London: James Johnston, 1815.

Price, Elizabeth. *The New Book of Cookery; or Every Woman a Perfect Cook*. London: Printed for the Authoress, and sold by Alex Hogg, 1782.

Stewart, James. *Plocacosmos: or, The Whole Art of Hair Dressing; Wherein Is Contained, Ample Rules for the Young Artisan, More Particularly for Ladies Women, Valets, &c. &c. as Well as Directions for Persons to Dress Their Own Hair*. London: Printed for the Author, 1782.

Stillingfleet, Benjamin. *An Essay on Conversation*. London: Printed for L. Gilliver and J. Clarke, 1737.

Supplement to Bell's British Theatre, Consisting of the Most Esteemed Farces and Entertainments Now Performing on the British Stage. Vol. IV. London: Printed for John Bell, 1784.

Walker, Lady Mary. *Munster Village, a Novel*. London: Printed for Robson and Co., 1778.

Watson, John F. *Annals of Philadelphia and Pennsylvania, in the Olden Time; Bring a Collection of Memoirs, Anecdote, and Incidents of the City and Its Inhabitants from the Days of the Pilgrim Founders*. Philadelphia: E. L. Carey & A. Hart, 1830.

Wilkinson, John. *Tutamen Nauticum: Or, The Seaman's Preservation from Shipwreck, Diseases, and Other Calamities Incident to Mariners*. 4th edn. London: Printed for Dodsley, Lownds, Bristow, Stewart, Willock, Mount, and Page, 1766.

Wodrow, Robert. *Life of James Wodrow, A. M. Professor of Divinity in the University of Glasgow, from MDCXII to MDCCVII*. Edinburgh, William Blackwood and T. Cadell, Strand, London, 1828.

Zimmermann, Johann Georg. *A Treatise on Experience in Physic*. London: Printed for J. Wilkie, 1778.

Secondary sources after 1850

Abrahams, Yvette. 'Images of Sara Bartman: Sexuality, Race, and Gender in Early-Nineteenth-Century Britain'. In *Nation, Empire and Colony: Historicising Gender and Race*, edited by Ruth Roach Pierson and Napur Chaudhuri, 220–36. Bloomington: Indiana University Press, 1998.

Adam, Malise and Mary Mauchline. 'Kauffman's Decorative Work'. In *Angelica Kauffman: A Continental Artist in Georgian England*, edited by Wendy Wassyng Roworth, 113–40. London: Reaktion Books, 1992.

Adburgham, Alison. *Women in Print: Writing Women and Women's Magazines from the Restoration to the Accession of Victoria*. London: Allen and Unwin, 1972.

Allen, Brian. 'The Capture of the Westmorland and the Purchase of Art in Rome in the 1770s'. In *Art in Rome in the Eighteenth Century: A Study in the Social History of Art*, edited by Edgard Peters Bowron and Joseph J. Rischel, 187–98. London: Brill, 2019.

Alexander, David. 'Kauffman and the Print Market in Eighteenth-Century England'. In *Angelica Kauffman: A Continental Artist in Georgian England*, edited by Wendy Wassyng Roworth, 141–78. London: Reaktion Books, 1992.

Alexander, David. 'Prints after John Collet: Their Publishing History and a Chronological Checklist'. *Eighteenth-Century Life* 26, no. 1 (Winter 2002): 136–46.

Anishanslin, Zara. *Portrait of a Woman in Silk: Hidden Histories of the British Atlantic World*. London: Yale University Press, 2016.

Arnold, Janet, Jenny Tiramani, Luca Costigliolo, Sébastian Passot, Armelle Lucas and Jonannes Pietsch. *Patterns of Fashion 5: The Content, Cut, Construction and Context of Bodies, Stays, Hoops and Rumps c.1595–1795*. London: The School of Historical Dress, 2018.

Ashmore, Sonia. *Muslin*. London: V&A Publishing, 2012.

Attfield, Judy. *Wild Things: the Material Culture of Everyday Life*. Oxford: Berg, 2000.

Baker, James. *The Business of Satirical Prints in Late-Georgian England*. Basingstoke: Palgrave Macmillan, 2017.

Bailyn, Bernard. *Atlantic History: Concepts and Contours*. Cambridge: Harvard University Press, 2005.

Barratt, Carrie Rebora. 'Oriental Undress and the Artist'. *Porticus, Journal of the Memorial Art Gallery of the University of Rochester* 20 (2001): 18–31.

Barrell, John. *The Spirit of Despotism: Invasions of Privacy in the 1790s*. Oxford: Oxford University Press, 2006.

Barker, Hannah and Elaine Chalus. 'Introduction'. In *Gender in Eighteenth-Century England*, edited by Hannah Barker and Elaine Chalus, 1–28. Abingdon: Routledge, 2014.

Batchelor, Jennie. '"[T]o Cherish *Female* Ingenuity, and to Conduce to *Female* Improvement": The Birth of the Woman's Magazine'. In *Women's Periodicals and Print Culture in Britain, 1690–1820s: The Long Eighteenth Century*, edited by Jennie Batchelor and Manushag N. Powell, 377–92. Edinburgh: University of Edinburgh Press, 2018.

Batchelor, Jennie. *The Lady's Magazine (1770–1832) and the Making of Literary History*. Edinburgh: University of Edinburgh Press, 2022.

Batchelor, Jennie and Alison Larkin. *Jane Austen Embroidery: Authentic Embroidery Projects for Modern Stitchers*. London: Pavilion, 2020.

Baudis, Macushla. '"Smoking hot with fashion from Paris": The Consumption of French Fashion in Eighteenth-Century Ireland'. *Costume* 48, no. 2 (2014): 141–59.

Baumgarten, Linda. *What Clothes Reveal: The Language of Clothing in Colonial and Federal America: The Colonial Williamsburg Collection*. London: Yale University Press, 2002.

Baynton-Williams, Roger. *The Art of the Printmaker: 1500–1860*. London: A. & C. Black, 2009.

Beaujot, Ariel. *Victorian Fashion Accessories*. London: Berg, 2012.

Bellamy, Liz. 'It-Narrators and Circulation: Defining a Subgenre'. In *The Secret Life of Things: Animals, Objects, and It-Narratives in Eighteenth-Century England*, edited by Mark Blackwell, 117–46. Lewisburg: Bucknell University Press, 2007.

Bendall, Sarah. *Shaping Femininity: Foundation Garments, the Body and Women in Early Modern England*. London: Bloomsbury Visual Arts, 2022.

Berg, Maxine. *Luxury & Pleasure in Eighteenth-Century Britain*. Oxford: Oxford University Press, 2005.

Bermingham, Ann. 'Elegant Females and Gentleman Connoisseurs: The Commerce in Culture and Self-image in Eighteenth-Century England'. In *The Consumption of Culture 1600–1800*, edited by Ann Bermingham and John Brewer, 489–513. London: Routledge, 1995.

Bermingham, Ann. *Learning to Draw: Studies in the Cultural History of a Polite and Useful Art*. New Haven: Yale University Press, 2000.

Blackman, Cally. 'Walking Amazons: The Development of the Riding Habit in England during the Eighteenth Century'. *Costume* 35, no. 1 (2001): 47–58.

Blackwell, Caitlin. '"The Feather'd Fair in a Fright": The Emblem of the Feather in Graphic Satire of 1776'. *Journal for Eighteenth-Century Studies* 36, no. 3 (2013): 353–76.

Blackwell, Caitlin. 'John Collet, A Commercial Comic Artist'. PhD thesis, University of York, 2013.

Blackwell, Mark. *The Secret Life of Things: Animals, Objects, and It-Narratives in Eighteenth-Century England*, edited by Mark Blackwell. Lewisburg: Bucknell University Press, 2007.

Bloemberg, Ninke and Bianca M. du Mortier. *Accessorize! 250 Objects of Fashion and Desire*. Amsterdam: Rijksmuseum, Nieuw Amsterdam, 2009.

Biddle-Perry, Geraldine and Sarah Cheang. 'Introduction: Thinking about Hair'. In *Hair: Styling, Culture and Fashion*, edited by Sarah Cheang and Geraldine Biddle-Perry, 3–12. Oxford: Berg, 2008.

Bolton, Andrew. *Wild: Fashion Untamed*. London: Metropolitan Museum of Art and Yale University Press, 2005.

Bondson, Jan. *Freaks: The Pig-Faced Lady of Manchester Square & Other Medical Marvels*. Stroud: Tempus, 2006.

Borsay, Peter. *The English Urban Renaissance: Culture and Society in the Provincial Town, 1660–1770*. Oxford: Clarendon Press, 1989.

Borsay, Peter. 'Pleasure Gardens and Urban Culture in the Long Eighteenth Century'. In *The Pleasure Garden, from Vauxhall to Coney Island*, edited by Jonathan Conlin, 49–77. Philadelphia: University of Philadelphia, 2013.

Boucher, François. *A History of Costume in the West*. London: Thames and Hudson, 1965.

Breward, Chris. *Fashioning London: Clothing and the Modern Metropolis*. Oxford: Berg, 2004.

Brewer, John. *The Common People and Politics 1750–1790s*. Cambridge: Chadwyck-Healey Ltd, 1986.

Brewer, John and Roy Porter (eds.). *Consumption and the World of Goods*. London: Routledge, 1993.

Browne, Claire. 'Mary Delany's Embroidered Court Dress'. In *Mrs. Delany and Her Circle*, edited by Mark Laird and Alicia Weisberg-Roberts, 66–79. London: Yale University Press, 2009.

Buck, Anne. *Dress in Eighteenth Century England*. London: B.T. Batsford Ltd, 1979.

Buck, Anne. and Harry Matthews. 'Pocket Guides to Fashion: Ladies' Pocket Books Published in England 1760–1830'. *Costume* 18 (1984): 35–58.

Burman, Barbara and Ariane Fennetaux. *The Pocket: A Hidden History of Women's Lives, 1660–1900*. New Haven: Yale University Press, 2019.

Burman, Barbara and Jonathan White. 'Fanny's Pockets: Cotton, Consumption and Domestic Economy, 1780–1850.' In *Women and Material Culture 1660–1830*, edited by Jennie Batchelor and Cora Kaplan, 31–51. Basingstoke: Palgrave Macmillan, 2007.

Calabresi, Bianca F. C. '"you sow, Ile read": Letters and Literacies in Early Modern Samplers'. In *Reading Women: Literacy, Authorship, and Culture in the Atlantic World, 1500–1800*, edited by Heidi Brayman Hackel and Catherine E. Kelly, 79–104. Philadelphia: University of Pennsylvania Press, 2008.

Campbell, Timothy. *Historical Style: Fashion and the New Mode of History, 1740–1830*. Philadelphia: University of Pennsylvania Press, 2016.

Carter, Alison. *Underwear: The Fashion History*. London: B. T. Batsford Ltd 1992.

Carter, Philip. 'Men about Town: Representations of Foppery and Masculinity in Early Eighteenth-Century Urban Society'. In *Gender in Eighteenth-Century England: Roles Representations, and Responsibilities*, edited by Hannah Barker and Elaine Chalus, 31–57. London: Addison Wesley Longman Ltd, 1997.

Chalus, Elaine. 'Fanning the Flames: Women, Fashion, and Politics'. In *Women, Popular Culture, and the Eighteenth Century*, edited by Tiffany Potter, 92–112. London: University of Toronto Press, 2012.

Chapman, S. D. *The Cotton Industry in the Industrial Revolution*, 2nd edn. Macmillan Education: 1987.

Chrisman-Campbell, Kimberly. 'Rose Bertin in London?' *Costume* 32, no. 1 (1998): 45–51.

Chrisman-Campbell, Kimberly. 'The Face of Fashion: Milliners in Eighteenth-Century Visual Culture'. *British Journal for Eighteenth-Century Studies* 25, no. 2 (Autumn 2002): 157–72.

Chrisman-Campbell, Kimberly. 'French Connections: Georgiana, Duchess of Devonshire, and the Anglo-French Fashion Exchange'. *Dress* 31, no. 1 (2004): 3–14.

Chrisman-Campbell, Kimberley. 'Dressing to Impress: The Morning Toilette and the Fabrication of Femininity'. In *Paris: Life & Luxury in the Eighteenth Century*, edited by Charissa Bremer-David, 53–74. Los Angeles: J. Paul Getty Museum, 2011.

Chrisman-Campbell, Kimberley. '"He is not dressed without a muff": Muffs, Masculinity and *la mode* in English Satire'. In *Seeing Satire in the Eighteenth Century*, edited by Elizabeth C. Mansfield and Kelly Malone, 131–48. Oxford: Voltaire Foundation, 2013.

Chrisman-Campbell, Kimberly. *Fashion Victims: Dress at the Court of Louis XVI and Marie-Antoinette*. New Haven: Yale University Press, 2015.

Clark, Fiona. *Hats*. London: B. T. Bratsford Ltd, 1982.

Clayton, Timothy. *The English Print 1688–1802*. New Haven: Yale University Press, 1997.

Colley, Linda. *Britons: Forging the Nation 1707–1837*. London: Yale University Press, 1992.

Coltman, Viccy. *Fabricating the Antique: Neoclassicism in Britain, 1760–1800*. London: University of Chicago Press, 2006.

Coltman, Viccy. *Classical Sculpture and the Culture of Collecting in Britain since 1760*. Oxford: Oxford University Press, 2009.

Coltman, Viccy. 'Material Culture and the History of Art(efacts)'. In *Writing Material Culture History*, edited by Anne Gerristen and Giorgio Riello, 17–31. London: Bloomsbury Academic, 2014.

Corfield, Penelope J. 'Walking the City Streets: The Urban Odyssey in Eighteenth-Century England'. *Journal of Urban History* 16, no. 2 (1990): 132–74.

Corfield, Penelope J. *Vauxhall: Sex and Entertainment: London's Pioneering Urban Pleasure Garden*. London: History & Social Action Publications, 2012.

Corson, Richard. *Fashions in Hair: The First Five Thousand Years*. London: Peter Owen Ltd, 1965.

Crawford, T. S. *A History of the Umbrella*. Newton Abbot: David & Charles Ltd, 1970.

Cross, Louisa. 'Fashionable Hair in the Eighteenth Century: Theatricality and Display'. In *Hair: Styling, Culture and Fashion*, edited by Sarah Cheang and Geraldine Biddle-Perry, 15–26. Oxford: Berg, 2008.

Crowley, John E. 'Homely Pleasures: the Pursuit of Comfort in the Eighteenth Century'. In *The Book of Touch*, edited by Constance Classen, 82–91. Oxford: Berg, 2005.

Crown, Patricia. 'Sporting with Clothes: John Collet's Prints in the 1770s'. *Eighteenth-Century Life* 26, no. 1 (Winter 2002): 119–35.

Cunnington, C. Willett and Phillis Cunnington. *Handbook of English Costume in the Eighteenth Century*. London: Faber and Faber Ltd, 1972.

Cunnington, C. Willett and Phillis Cunnington. *The History of Underclothes*. London: Faber and Faber, 1981.

Darby, Michael. 'Jacobite Garters'. *Victoria and Albert Museum Bulletin* 2, no. 4 (1966): 157–63.

Davidson, Hilary. *Dress in the Age of Jane Austen: Regency Fashion*. New Haven: Yale University Press, 2019.

De Courtais, Georgine. *Women's Headdress and Hairstyles in England from AD 600 to the present day*. London: B. T. Bratsford Ltd, 1973.

Delpierre, Madeleine. *Dress in France in the Eighteenth Century*. New Haven: Yale University Press, 1997.

Deutsch, Davida Tenenbaum. 'Needlework Patterns and Their Use in America'. *The Magazine Antiques* (February 1991): 368–81.

Dias, Rosie. '"A world of pictures": Pall Mall and the Topography of Display, 1780–99'. In *Georgian Geographies: Essays on Space, Place and Landscape in the Eighteenth Century*, edited by Miles Ogborn and Charles W. J. Withers, 92–113. Manchester: Manchester University Press, 2004.

Dolan, Brian. *Ladies of the Grand Tour*. London: Harper Collins, 2001.

Donald, Diana. *The Age of Caricature: Satirical Prints in the Reign of George III*. New Haven: Yale University Press, 1996.

Donald, Diana. *Followers of Fashion: Graphic Satires from the Georgian Period*. London: Hayward Gallery Publishing, 2002.

DuPlessis, Robert S. *The Material Atlantic: Clothing, Commerce, and Colonization in the Atlantic World, 1650–1800*. Cambridge: Cambridge University Press, 2016.

Dyer, Serena. 'Shopping and the Senses: Retail, Browsing and Consumption in 18th-Century England'. *History Compass* 12, no. 9 (September 2014): 694–703.

Dyer, Serena. 'Fashioning Consumers: Ackermann's *Repository of Arts* and the Cultivation of the Female Consumer'. In *Women's Periodicals and Print Culture in Britain, 1690–1820s: The Long Eighteenth Century*, edited by Jennie Batchelor and Manushag N. Powell, 474–87. Edinburgh: University of Edinburgh Press, 2018.

Dyer, Serena. 'Stitching and Shopping: The Material Literacy of the Consumer'. In *Material Literacy in Eighteenth Century Britain*, edited by Serena Dyer and Chloe Wigston Smith, 99–116. London: Bloomsbury Visual Arts, 2020.

Dyer, Serena. *Material Lives: Women Makers and Consumer Culture in the 18th Century*. London: Bloomsbury Visual Arts, 2021.

Dyer, Serena. 'Fashions of the Day: Materiality, Temporality and the Fashion Plate, 1750–1879'. In *Disseminating Dress: Britain's Fashion Networks, 1660–1970*, edited by Serena Dyer, Jade Halbert and Sophie Littlewood, 73–94. London: Bloomsbury Academic, 2022.

Dyer, Serena and Chloe Wigston Smith. 'Introduction'. In *Material Literacy in Eighteenth-Century Britain: A Nation of Makers*, edited by Serena Dyer and Chloe Wigston Smith, 1–16. London: Bloomsbury Visual Arts, 2020.

Ehrman, Edwina. 'The Versailles Sash'. *Costume* 44 (2010): 66–74.

Ehrman, Edwina. *The Wedding Dress: 300 Years of Bridal Fashions*. London: V&A Publishing, 2011.

Emberly, Julia. *Venus and Furs: The Cultural Politics of Fur*. London: I.B. Tauris, 2010.

Engel, Laura. 'The Muff Affair: Fashioning Celebrity in the Portraits of Late-Eighteenth-Century British Actresses'. *Fashion Theory* 13, no. 3 (2009): 279–98.

Engel, Laura. *Fashioning Celebrity: Eighteenth-Century British Actresses and Strategies for Image Making*. Columbus: Ohio State University Press, 2011.

Epstein, James. 'Understanding the Cap of Liberty: Symbolic Practice and Social Conflict in Nineteenth-Century England'. *Past & Present* 122 (February 1989): 75–118.

Ewing, Elizabeth. *Dress & Undress: A History of Women's Underwear*. London: B. T. Batsford Ltd, 1978.

Ewing, Elisabeth. *Fur in Dress*. London: B. T. Batsford Ltd, 1981.

Fairchilds, Cissie. 'The Production and Marketing of Populuxe Goods in Eighteenth-Century Paris'. In *Consumption and the World of Goods*, edited by John Brewer and Roy Porter, 228–48. London: Routledge, 2013.

Farrell, Jeremy. *Umbrellas & Parasols*. London: B.T. Batsford Ltd, 1985.

Fawcett, Trevor. 'A Case of Distance Shopping in 1763'. *Costume* 25 (1991): 18–20.

Fennetaux, Ariane. '"Work'd pockets to my entire satisfaction": Women and the Multiple Literacies of Making'. In *Material Literacy in Eighteenth-Century Britain: A Nation of Makers*, edited by Serena Dyer and Chloe Wigston Smith, 17–34. London: Bloomsbury Visual Arts, 2019.

Festa, Lynn M. 'Person, Animal, Thing: The 1796 Dog Tax and the Right to Superfluous Things'. *Eighteenth-Century Life* 33, no. 2 (2009): 1–44.

Fine, Ben and Ellen Leopold. 'Consumption and the Industrial Revolution'. *Social History* 15, no. 2 (1990): 151–79.

Fizer, Irene. 'The Fur Parasol: Masculine Dress, Prosthetic Skins, and the Making of the English Umbrella in Robinson Crusoe'. In *Eighteenth-Century Thing Theory in a Global Context: From Consumerism to Celebrity Culture*, edited by Ileana Baird and Christina Ionescu, 209–28. Farnham: Ashgate Publishing Company, 2013.

Flather, Amanda. *Gender and Space in Early Modern England*. Woodbridge: The Boydell Press, 2007.

Flavell, Julie. *When London Was Capital of America*. New Haven: Yale University Press, 2010.

Fleming, Kelly. 'The Politics of Sophia Western's Muff'. *Eighteenth-Century Fiction* 31, no. 4 (Summer, 2019): 659–61.

Frye, Susan. *Pens and Needles: Women's Textuality in Early Modern England*. Philadelphia: University of Pennsylvania Press, 2010.

Garrick, David. *The Plays of David Garrick: Garrick's Own Plays, 1740–1766*, edited by Harry William Pedicord and Frederick Louis Bergmann. Carbondale and Edwardsville: Southern Illinois University Press, 1980.

George, Dorothy. *Catalogue of Political and Personal Satires Preserved in the Department of Prints and Drawings in the British Museum, Vol. V*. London: British Museum, 1935.

George, Dorothy. *Catalogue of Political and Personal Satires Preserved in the Department of Prints and Drawings in the British Museum, Vol. VI*. London: British Museum, 1938.

George, Dorothy. *Catalogue of Political and Personal Satires Preserved in the Department of Prints and Drawings in the British Museum, Vol. IX*. London: British Museum, 1949.

Germann, Jennifer. '"Other Women Were Present": Seeing Black Women in Georgian London'. *Eighteenth-Century Studies* 54, no. 3 (Spring 2021): 535–53.

Gernerd, Elisabeth. 'Pulled Tight and Gleaming: The Stocking's Position within Eighteenth-Century Masculinity'. *Textile History* 46, no. 1 (May 2015): 3–27.

Gernerd, Elisabeth. 'Fancy Feathers: The Feather Trade in Britain and the Atlantic World'. In *Material Literacy in Eighteenth-Century Britain: A Nation of Makers*, edited by Serena Dyer and Chloe Wigston Smith, 195–218. London: Bloomsbury Visual Arts, 2020.

Gernerd, Elisabeth. '"Feather Muffs of all Colours": Fashion, Patriotism, and the Natural World in Eighteenth-Century Britain'. *Appearance(s): Histoire et culture du paraître* 11 (2022), https://doi.org/10.4000/apparences.3713.

Gernerd, Elisabeth. 'Subverting Time: The Banyan, Temporality, and Graphic Satire'. *Eighteenth-Century Studies* 56, no. 3 (Spring 2023): 395–423.

Glover, Katharine. *Elite Women and Polite Society in Eighteenth-Century Scotland*. Woodbridge: The Boydell Press, 2011.

Goggin, Maureen Daly. 'Introduction: Threading Women'. In *Women and the Material Culture of Needlework and Textiles, 1750–1950*, edited by Maureen Daly Goggin and Beth Fowkes Tobin, 1–12. Farnham: Ashgate, 2009.

Goggin, Maureen Daly and Beth Fowkes Tobin (eds.) *Women and the Material Culture of Needlework and Textiles, 1750–1950*. Farnham: Ashgate, 2009.

Gowrley, Freya. 'Taste à-la-Mode: Consuming Foreignness, Picturing Gender'. In *Materializing Gender in Eighteenth-Century Europe*, edited by J. G. Germann and H. A. Strobel, 73–80. Abingdon: Routledge, 2016.

Gowrley, Freya. *Domestic Space in Britain, 1750–1840: Materiality, Sociability and Emotion*. London: Bloomsbury Visual Arts, 2022.

Greig, Hannah. 'Leading the Fashion: The Material Culture of London's *Beau Monde*'. In *Gender, Taste, and Material Culture in Britain and North America, 1700–1830*, edited by John Styles and Amanda Vickery, 293–314. London: Yale Centre for British Art, 2006.

Greig, Hannah. *The Beau Monde: Fashionable Society in Georgian London*. Oxford: Oxford University Press, 2013.

Guest, Harriet. *Small Change: Women, Learning, Patriotism, 1750–1810*. London: The University of Chicago Press, Ltd, 2000.

Habermas, Jürgen. *The Structural Transformation of the Public Sphere: An Inquiry into a Category of Bourgeois Society*. London: Polity Press, 1989.

Haggerty, George E. 'Strawberry Hill: Friendship and Taste'. In *Horace Walpole's Strawberry Hill*, edited by Michael Snodin and Cynthia Roman, 75–9. New Haven: Yale University Press, 2009.

Hartman, Saidiya. 'Venus in Two Acts'. *Small Axe* 12, no. 2 (June 2008): 1–14.

Haskell, Francis and Nicholas Penny. *Taste and the Antique: The Lure of Classical Sculpture 1500–1800*. London: Yale University Press, 1981.

Haslam, Fiona. *From Hogarth to Rowlandson: Medicine in Art in Eighteenth-Century Britain*. Liverpool: Liverpool University Press, 1996.

Haulman, Kate. *The Politics of Fashion in Eighteenth-Century America*. Chapel Hill: The University of North Carolina Press, 2011.

Heal, Felicity. *Hospitality in Early Modern England*. Oxford: Oxford University Press, 1990.

Hellman, Mimi. 'Furniture, Sociability, and the Work of Leisure in Eighteenth Century France'. *Eighteenth-Century Studies* 32, no. 4 (1999): 417–34.

Henderson, Tony. *Disorderly Women in Eighteenth-Century London: Prostitution and Control in the Metropolis 1730–1830*. Harlow: Pearson Educational Ltd, 1999.

Hind, Arthur. *A History of Engraving and Etching from the 15th Century to the Year 1914*. New York: Dover Publications, Inc., 2011.

Hipchen, Emily A. 'Feilding's Tom Jones'. *The Explicator* 53, no. 1 (Fall 1994): 16–18.

Hobson, Janell. *Venus in the Dark: Blackness and Beauty in Popular Culture*. London: Routledge, 2018.

Hollander, Anne. *Seeing through Clothes*. New York: The Viking Press, 1975.

Hope, David. 'Britain and the Fur Trade: Commerce and Consumers in the North-Atlantic World, 1783–1821'. PhD thesis, University of Northumbria, 2016.

Houblon, Lady Alice Archer. *The Houblon Family: Its Story and Times*. London: Constable, 1907.

Hunt, Tamara L. *Defining John Bull: Political Caricature and National Identity in Late Georgian England*. Aldershot: Ashgate Publishing Ltd, 2003.

Inal, Onur. 'Women's Fashions in Transition: Ottoman Borderlands and the Anglo-Ottoman Exchange of Costumes'. *Journal of World History* 22, no. 2 (2011): 243–72.

Inwood, Stephen. *Historic London: An Explorer's Companion*. London: Macmillan, 2008.

Jeffares, Neil. 'Mary Hoare'. *Dictionary of pastellists before 1800*. London: 2006, online edn. http://www.pastellists.com/articles/HOAREM.pdf (accessed 27 June 2022).

Johnson, Maurice. 'The Device of Sophia's Muff in *Tom Jones*'. *Modern Language Notes*, 74, no. 8 (1959): 685–90.

Kidwell, Claudia Bush. 'Are Those Clothes Real? Transforming the Way Eighteenth-Century Portraits Are Studied'. *Dress* 24, no. 1 (1997): 3–15.

Klein, Lawrence E. 'Gender, Conversation and the Public Sphere'. In *Textuality and Sexuality: Reading Theories and Practices*, edited by Judith Still and Michael Worton, 100–15. Manchester: Manchester University Press, 1993.

Kopytoff, Igor. 'The Cultural Biography of Things: Commoditization as Process'. In *The Social Life of Things: Commodities in Cultural Perspective*, edited by Arjun Appadurai, 64–94. Cambridge: Cambridge University Press, 1986.

Kowaleski-Wallace, Elizabeth. *Consuming Subjects: Women, Shopping and Business in the Eighteenth Century*. New York: Columbia University Press, 1997.

Kunzle, David. *Fashion & Fetishism: Corsets, Tight-Lacing & Other Forms of Body-Sculpture*. Stroud: Sutton Publishing, 2006.

Laird, Mark and Alicia Weisberg-Roberts (eds.). *Mrs. Delany and Her Circle*, edited by Mark Laird and Alicia Weisberg-Roberts. London: Yale University Press, 2009.

Lake, Crystal B. 'Needlework Verse'. In *Material Literacy in Eighteenth-Century Britain: A Nation of Makers*, edited by Serena Dyer and Chloe Wigston Smith, 35–50. London: Bloomsbury Visual Arts, 2019.

Lambert, Miles. '"Sent from Town": Commissioning Clothing in Britain during the Long Eighteenth Century'. *Costume* 43 (2009): 66–82.

Lambert, Miles. 'Bespoke versus Ready-Made: The Work of the Tailor in Eighteenth-Century Britain'. *Costume* 44 (2010): 56–65.

Lever, Tresham (ed.). *The Letters of Lady Palmerston: Selected and Edited from the Originals at Broadlands and Elsewhere …* London: John Murray Ltd, 1957.

Llanover, Lady (ed.). *The Autobiography and Correspondence of Mary Granville, Mrs. Delany: With Interesting Reminiscences of King George the Third and Queen Charlotte, Vol. 1*. London: Richard Bentley, 1861.

Llanover, Lady (ed.). *The Autobiography and Correspondence of Mary Granville, Mrs. Delany: With Interesting Reminiscences of King George the Third and Queen Charlotte, Vol. 3*. London: Richard Bentley, 1862.

La Roche, Sophie von. *Sophie in London, 1786; Being the Diary of Sophie v. la Roche; Translated from the German with an Introductory Essay by Clare Williams, with a Forward by G. M. Trevelyan*. London: Jonathan Cape, 1933.

Lemire, Beverly. 'Developing Consumerism and the Ready-Made Clothing Trade in Britain, 1750–1800'. *Textile History* 15 (1984): 21–44.

Lemire, Beverly. 'Consumerism in Preindustrial and Early Industrial England: The Trade in Second hand Clothes'. *Journal of British Studies* 27 (1988): 1–24.

Lemire, Beverly. 'The Theft of Clothes and Popular Consumerism in Early Modern England'. *Journal of Social History* (1990): 255–76.

Lemire, Beverly. 'Peddling Fashion: Salesmen, Pawnbrokers, Taylors, Thieves and the Second-Hand Clothes Trade in England'. *Textile History* 22 (1991): 67–82.

Lemire, Beverly. *Fashion's Favourite: The Cotton Trade and the Consumer in Britain, 1660–1800*. Oxford: Oxford University Press, 1992.

Lemire, Beverly. *Dress, Culture and Commerce: the English Clothing Trade before the Factory, 1660–1800*. New York: St. Martin's Press, 1997.

Lemire, Beverly. *Global Trade and the Transformation of Consumer Cultures: The Material World Remade, c.1500–1820*. Cambridge: Cambridge University Press, 2018.

Mackenzie, Althea. *Hats and Bonnets from Snowhill, One of the World's Leading Collections of Costume and Accessories of the 18th and 19th Centuries*. London: National Trust Enterprises Ltd, 2004.

Mackie, Erin Skye. *Market à la mode: Fashion, Commodity, and Gender in the Tatler and the Spectator*. London: Johns Hopkins University Press, 1997.

MacLean, Gerald, Donna Landry and Joseph P. Ward. 'Introduction: The Country and The City Revisited'. In *The Country and the City Revisited: England and the Politics of Culture, 1550–1850*, edited by Gerald MacLean, Donna Landry and Joseph P. Ward, 1–23. Cambridge: Cambridge University Press, 1999.

Mactaggart, Peter and R. Ann Mactaggart. 'Some Aspects of the Use of Non-Fashionable Stays'. In *Strata of Society Costume Society Conference*, 20–8. London: Costume Society, 1973.

Mactaggart, Peter and R. Ann Mactaggart. 'Ease, Convenience and Stays, 1750–1850'. *Costume* 13 (1979): 41–51.

Marsh, Gail. *18th Century Embroidery Techniques*. Lewes: Guild of Master Craftsman Publications Ltd, 2012.

Marschner, Joanna. 'A Weaving Field of Feathers – Dressing the Head for Presentation at the English Court, 1700–1939'. In *Birds of Paradise: Plumes & Feathers in Fashion*, 141–52. Tielt: Lannoo, 2014.

Marshall, J. P. 'Introduction'. In *The Oxford History of the British Empire: The Eighteenth Century*, edited by J. P. Marshall, 21–7. Oxford: Oxford University Press, 1998.

Martin, Ann Smart. 'Tea Tables Overturned: Rituals of Power and Place in Colonial America'. In *Furnishing the Eighteenth Century: What Furniture Can Tell Us about the European and American Past*, edited by Dena Goodman and Kathryn Norberg, 169–82. London: Routledge, 2007.

Maxwell, The Right Hon. Sir Herbert (ed.). *The Creevey Papers: A Selection from the Correspondence & Diaries of the Late Thomas Creevey, M. P. Born 1768–Died 1838*. New York: E. P. Dutton & Company, 1904.

McClellan, Elisabeth. *Historic Dress in America, 1607–1800: With an Introductory Chapter on Dress in the Spanish and French Settlements in Florida and Louisiana*. Philadelphia: George W. Jacobs & Company, 1904.

McCreery, Cindy. *The Satirical Gaze: Prints of Women in Late Eighteenth-Century England*. Oxford: Clarendon, 2004.

McIntosh, Carey. 'Pamela's Clothes'. *ELH* 35, no. 1 (March 1968): 75–83.

McKeller, Elizabeth. *Landscapes of London: The City, the Country and the Suburbs, 1660–1840*. London: Published for the Paul Mellon Centre for Studies in British Art by Yale University Press, 2013.

McKendrick, Neil, John Brewer and J. H. Plumb. *The Birth of a Consumer Society: The Commercialization of Eighteenth-Century England*. London: Europa Publications Ltd, 1982.

McMillen, Krystal. 'Eating Turtle, Eating the World: Comestible *Things* in the Eighteenth Century'. In *Eighteenth-Century Thing Theory in a Global Context: from Consumerism to Celebrity Culture*, edited by Ileana Baird and Christina Ionescu, 191–208. Farnham: Ashgate Publishing Company, 2013.

McNeil, Peter. '"That Doubtful Gender": Macaroni Dress and Male Sexualities'. *Fashion Theory* 3, no. 4 (1999): 411–47.

McNeil, Peter. 'Macaroni Masculinities'. *Fashion Theory* 4, no. 4 (2000): 373–404.

McNeil, Peter. '"Beauty in Search of Knowledge": Eighteenth-Century Fashion and the World of Print'. In *Fashioning the Early Modern*, edited by Evelyn Welch, 223–54. Oxford: Oxford University Press, 2017.

McNeil, Peter. 'Introduction'. In *A Cultural History of Dress and Fashion in the Age of the Enlightenment*, edited by Peter McNeil, 1–22. London: Bloomsbury Academic, 2017.

McNeil, Peter. *Pretty Gentlemen: Macaroni Men and the Eighteenth-Century Fashion World*. New Haven: Yale University Press, 2018.

McNeil, Peter and Patrik Steorn. 'The Medium of Print and the Rise of Fashion in the West'. *Konsthistorisk Tidskrift/Journal of Art History* 82, no. 3 (2013): 135–56.

Mida, Ingrid and Alexandra Kim. *The Dress Detective: A Practical Guide to Object-Based Research in Fashion*. London: Bloomsbury Academic, 2015.

Mitchell, Robin. *Vénus Noire: Black Woman and Colonial Fantasies in Nineteenth-Century France*. Athens: University of Georgia Press, 2020.

Monteyne, Joseph. 'Enveloping Objects: Allegory and Commodity Fetish in Wenceslaus Hollar's Personifications of the Seasons and Fashion Still Lifes'. *Art History* 29, no. 3 (2006): 414–43.

Monteyne, Joseph. *From Still Life to the Screen: Print Culture, Display, and the Materiality of the Image in Eighteenth-Century London*. New Haven: Yale University Press, 2013.

Moore, Doris Langley. *Fashion through Fashion Plates 1771–1970*. London: Ward Lock Ltd, 1971.

Moore, Lisa Lynne. 'Queer Gardens: Mary Delany's Flowers and Friendships'. *Eighteenth-Century Studies* 39, no. 1 (2005): 49–70.

Morse Earle, Alice. *Two Centuries of Costume in America 1620–1820*. Rutland: VT, Charles E. Tuttle Company, 1971.

Navickas, Katrina. '"That Sash Will Hang You": Political Clothing and Adornment in England, 1780–1840'. *The Journal of British Studies* 49, no. 3 (2010): 542, 564.

Nelson, Charmaine. *The Color of Stone: Sculpting the Black Female Subject in Nineteenth-Century America*. Minneapolis: University of Minnesota Press, 2007.

Nelson, Charmaine. *Representing the Black Female Subject in Western Art*. London: Routledge, 2010.

Nenadic, Stana. 'Middle-Rank Consumers and Domestic Culture in Edinburgh and Glasgow 1720–1840'. *Past & Present* 145 (1994): 122–56.

Newby, Evelyn. *William Hoare of Bath, R. A., 1707–1792*. Bath: Bath Museum Services, 1990.

Newby, Evelyn. 'The Hoares of Bath'. https://historyofbath.org/images/BathHistory/Vol%2001%20-%2004.%20Newby%20-%20The%20Hoares%20of%20Bath.pdf (accessed 28 June 2022).

Nicholson, E. C. 'Consumers and Spectators: The Public of the Political Print in Eighteenth-Century England'. *History* 81, no. 261 (1996): 5–21.

North, Susan. *Sweet and Clean?: Bodies and Clothes in Early Modern England*. Oxford: Oxford University Press, 2020.

Ogborn, Miles. *Spaces of Modernity: London's Geographies, 1680–1780*. London: the Gilford Press, 1998.

Otele, Olivette. *African Europeans: An Untold Story*. London: Hurst & Company, 2020.

Paresys, Isabelle. 'The Body'. In *A Cultural History of Dress and Fashion in the Age of the Enlightenment*, edited by Peter McNeil, 63–86. London: Bloomsbury Academic, 2017.

Park, Julie. *The Self and It: Novel Objects and Mimetic Subjects in Eighteenth Century Society*. Stanford: Stanford University Press, 2010.

Parker, Rozsika. *The Subversive Stitch: Embroidery and the Making of the Feminine*. London: The Women's Press, 1984.

Perry, Gill. 'Women in Disguise: Likeness, the Grand Style and the Conventions of "Feminine" Portraiture in the Work of Sir Joshua Reynolds'. In *Femininity and Masculinity in Eighteenth-Century Art and Culture*, edited by Gillian Perry and Michael Rossington, 18–41. Manchester: Manchester University Press, 1994.

Perry, Gill. *Spectacular Flirtations: Viewing the Actress in British Art and Theatre 1768–1820*. London: Yale University Press, 2007.

Philip, Mark. *Thomas Paine*. Oxford: Oxford University Press, 2007.

Pietsch, Johannes. 'Object in Focus 1: A Robe à l'angaise retroussée'. In *Fashioning the Early Modern*, edited by Evelyn Welch, 83–6. Oxford: Oxford University Press, 2017.

Pinto, Samantha. *Infamous Bodies: Early Black Women's Celebrity and the Afterlives or Rights*. London: Duke University Press, 2020.

Pittock, Murray. 'Treacherous Objects: Towards a Theory of Jacobite Material Culture'. *Journal for Eighteenth-Century Studies* 34, no. 1 (2011): 39–63.

Planché, James Robinson. *A Cyclopaedia of Costume, or Dictionary of Dress. Including Notices of Contemporaneous Fashions on the Continent, and a General Chronological History of the Costume of the Principal Countries of Europe, from the Commencement of the Christian Era to the Accession of George the Third*. London: Chatto and Windus, 1876.

Pointon, Marcia. *Hanging the Head: Portraiture and Social Formation in Eighteenth-Century England*. London: Yale University Press, 1993.

Powell, Margaret K. and Joseph Roach. 'Big Hair'. *Eighteenth-Century Studies* 38, no. 1 (2004): 79–99.

Prince, Michael. *Philosophical Dialogue in the British Enlightenment: Theology, Aesthetics, and the Novel*. Cambridge: Cambridge University Press, 1996.

Prown, Jules. 'Mind in Matter: An Introduction to Material Culture Theory and Method'. *Winterthur Portfolio* 17, no. 1 (Spring 1982): 1–19.

Pristash, Heather, Inez Schaechterle and Sue Carter Wood. 'The Needle as the Pen: Intentionality, Needlework, and the Production of Alternate Discourses of Power'. In *Women and the Material Culture of Needlework and Textiles, 1750–1950*, edited by Maureen Daly Goggin and Beth Fowkes Tobin, 13–29. Farnham: Ashgate, 2009.

Qureshi, Sadiah. *Peoples on Parade: Exhibitions, Empire, and Anthropology in Nineteenth-Century Britain*. Chicago: University of Chicago Press, 2011.

Rasche, Adelheid and Gundula Wolter (eds.). *Ridikül! Mode in Der* Karikatur *1600 bis 1900* (Berlin: SMB, Staatliche Museen zu Berlin, Dumont, 2003.

Rauser, Amelia. *Caricature Unmasked: Irony, Authenticity, and Individualism in Eighteenth-Century English Prints*. Newark: University of Delaware Press, 2008.

Rauser, Amelia. *The Age of Undress: Art, Fashion, and the Classical Ideal in the 1790s*. New Haven: Yale University Press, 2020.

Reboul, Juliette. *French Emigration to Great Britain in Response to the French Revolution*. Cham: Springer International Publishing AG, 2017.

Reinhardt, Leslie. '"The Work of Fancy and Taste": Copley's Invented Dress and the Case of Rebecca Boylston'. *Dress* 29, no. 1 (2002): 4–18.

Ribeiro, Aileen. 'Turquerie: Turkish Dress and English Fashion in the Eighteenth Century'. *Connoisseur* 201, no. 807 (1979): 16–23.

Ribeiro, Aileen. *The Dress Worn at Masquerades in England, 1730 to 1790, and Its Relation to Fancy Dress in Portraiture*. London: Garland Publishing, Inc., 1984.

Ribeiro, Aileen. *Dress and Morality*. London: B. T. Batsford Ltd, 1986.

Ribeiro, Aileen. *Art of Dress: fashion in England and France, 1750 to 1820*. London: Yale University Press, 1995.

Ribeiro, Aileen. 'Re-Fashioning Art: Some Visual Approaches to the Study of the History of Dress,' *Fashion Theory* 2, no. 4 (1998): 315–26.

Ribeiro, Aileen. *Facing Beauty: Painted Women & Cosmetic Art*. London: Yale University Press, 2011.

Riello, Giorgio. *A Foot in the Past: Consumers, Producers and Footwear in the Long Eighteenth Century*. Oxford: Pasold Research Fund/Oxford University Press, 2006.

Riello, Giorgio. *Cotton: The Fabric That Made the Modern World*. Cambridge: Cambridge University Press, 2013.

Riello, Giorgio and Peter McNeil. 'The Art and Science of Walking: Mobility, Gender and Footwear in the Long Eighteenth Century'. *Fashion Theory* 9, no. 2 (2005): 175–204.

Riello, Giorgio and Ulinka Rublack, *The Right to Dress: Sumptuary Laws in a Global Perspective, c. 1200–1800*. Cambridge: Cambridge University Press, 2019.

Roman, Cynthia. 'A Portfolio of Satires from Horace Walpole's Collection'. *Print Quarterly* 25, no. 2 (June 2008): 166–71.

Rosenthal, Angela. 'Angelica Kauffman Ma(s)king Claims'. *Art History* 15, no. 1 (March 1992): 38–59.

Rosenthal, Angela. 'Raising Hair'. *Eighteenth-Century Studies* 38, no. 1 (2004): 1–16.

Rosenthal, Angela. *Angelica Kauffman: Art and Sensibility*. London: Yale University Press, 2006.

Salen, Jill. *Corsets Historic Patterns and Techniques*. London: Bratsford, 2008.

Sandner, Oscar. *Angelika Kauffmann und Rom*. Roma: De Luca, 1998.

Schoeser, Mary. 'A Secret Trade: Plate-Printed Textiles and Dress Accessories, c. 1620–1820'. *Dress* 34, no. 1 (2007): 49–59.

Shaun, Cole and Miles Lambert. *Dandy Style: 250 Years of British Men's Fashion*. New Haven: Yale University Press, 2021.

Shoemaker, Robert. 'Gendered Spaces: Patterns of Mobility and Perceptions of London's Geography, 1660–1750'. In *Imagining Early Modern London: Perceptions and Portrayals of the City from Stow to Strype, 1598–1720*, edited by J. F. Merritt, 144–65. Cambridge: Cambridge University Press, 2001.

Sloman, Susan. *Gainsborough in London*. London: Modern Art Press, 2021.

Solkin, David H. *Painting for Money: the Visual Arts and the Public Sphere in Eighteenth-Century England*. London: Yale University Press, 1993.

Smith, Chloe Wigston. *Women, Work, and Clothes in the Eighteenth-Century Novel*. Cambridge: Cambridge University Press, 2013.

Smith, Chloe Wigston. 'Fast Fashion: Style, Text, and Image in Late Eighteenth-Century Women's Periodicals'. In *Women's Periodicals and Print Culture in Britain, 1690–1820s: The Long Eighteenth Century*, edited by Jennie Batchelor and Manushag N. Powell, 440–57. Edinburgh: University of Edinburgh Press, 2018.

Smith, Chloe Wigston and Jennie Batchelor. 'Patterns and Posterity: Or, What's Not in the *Lady's Magazine*'. In *The Lady's Magazine (1770–1818): Understanding the Emergence of a Genre*. https://blogs.kent.ac.uk/ladys-magazine/2015/04/27/patterns-and-posterity-or-whats-not-in-the-ladys-magazine/ (accessed 19 March 2021).

Smith-Rosenberg, Carroll. 'The Female World of Love and Ritual: Relations between Women in Nineteenth-Century America,' *Signs* 1, no. 1 (Autumn 1975): 1–29.

Sorge, Lynn. 'Eighteenth-Century Stays: Their Origins and Creators'. *Costume* 32 (1998): 18–32.

Sorge-English, Lynn. '"29 Doz and 11 Best Cutt Bone": The Trade in Whalebone and Stays in Eighteenth-Century London'. *Textile History* 36 (2005): 20–45.

Sorge-English, Lynn. *Stays and Body Image in London: the Staymaking Trade, 1680–1800*. London: Pickering & Chatto, 2011.

Spencer, Lizzy. '"None but *Abigails* appeared in white aprons": The Apron as an Elite Garment in Eighteenth-Century England'. *Textile History* 49, no. 2 (December 2018): 164–90.

Spies-Gans, Paris A. *A Revolution on Canvas: The Rise of Women Artists in Britain and France, 1760–1830*. London: Paul Mellon Centre for Studies in British Art, 2022.

Stearns, Bertha Monica. 'Early English Periodicals for Ladies (1700–1760)'. *Modern Language Association* 48, no. 1 (1933): 38–60.

Steele, Valerie. 'A Museum of Fashion Is More Than a Clothes-Bag'. *Fashion Theory* 2, no. 4 (1998): 327–36.

Steele, Valerie. *The Corset*. New Haven: Yale University Press, 2001.

Steorn, Patrik. 'Caricature and Fashion Critique on the Move: Establishing European Print and Fashion Culture in Eighteenth-Century Sweden'. In *Fashioning the Early Modern*, edited by Evelyn Welch, 255–78. Oxford: Oxford University Press, 2017.

Stephenson, Mary A. *Milliners of Williamsburg in the Eighteenth Century: Report*. Colonial Williamsburg Foundation. Early American history research reports, 1951.

Stroomberg, Harriet. *High Heads: Spotprenten over Haarmode in de Achttiende Eeuw/Hair Fashions Depicted in Eighteenth-Century Satirical Prints Published by Matthew and Mary Darly*. Enschede: Rijksmuseum Twenthe, 2000.

Stowell, Lauren, Abby Cox and Cheyney McKnight. *The American Duchess Guide to 18th Century Beauty: 40 Projects for Period-Accurate Hairstyles, Makeup and Accessories*. Salem: Page Street Publishing Co., 2019.

Styles, John. *The Dress of the People: Everyday Fashion in Eighteenth-Century England*. New Haven: Yale University Press, 2007.

Styles, John. 'Fashion and Innovation in Early Modern Europe'. In *Fashioning the Early Modern*, edited by Evelyn Welch, 33–56. Oxford: Oxford University Press, 2017.

Swain, Margaret. *Embroidered Georgian Pictures*. Haverfordwest: Shire Publications Ltd, 1994.

Swift, Jonathan. *The Works of Dr. Jonathan Swift*. Vol. 7. London: Printed for T. Osborne, W. Bowyer, C. Bathurst, W. Strahan, J. Rivington, J. Hinton, L. Davis and C. Reymers, R. Baldwin, J. Dodsley, S. Crowder, and Co. and B. Collins, 1765.

Tague, Ingrid H. *Animal Companions: Pets and Social Change in Eighteenth-Century Britain*. University Park: The Pennsylvania State University Press, 2015.

Tarr, László. *The History of the Carriage*. London: Vision Press Ltd, 1969.

Taylor, Lou. *The Study of Dress History*. Manchester: Manchester University Press, 2002.

Tobin, Beth Fowkes. *Picturing Imperial Power: Colonial Subjects in Eighteenth-Century British Painting*. London: Duke University Press, 1999.

Tobin, Shelley. *Inside Out: A Brief History of Underwear*. London: The National Trust, 2000.

Tobin, Shelley, Sarah Pepper and Margaret Willes. *Marriage à la Mode: Three Centuries of Wedding Dress*. London: National Trust Enterprises Ltd, 2003.

Tozer, Jane and Sarah Levitt. *Fabric of Society: A Century of People and Their Clothes 1770–1870*. Manchester: Laura Ashley Publications, 2010.

van Cleave, Kendra and Brooke Welborn. '"Very Much the Taste and Variety are the Makes" Reconsidering the Late-Eighteenth-Century Robe à la Polonaise'. *Dress* 39, no. 1 (2013): 1–24.

van Horn, Jennifer. *The Power of Objects in Eighteenth-Century British America*. Chapel Hill: University of North Carolina Press, 2017.

Vickery, Amanda. 'Golden Age to Separate Spheres? A Review of the Categories and Chronology of English Women's History'. *The Historical Review* 36, no. 2 (June 1993): 383–414.

Vickery, Amanda. *The Gentleman's Daughter: Women's Lives in Georgian England*. London: Yale University Press, 1998.

Vickery, Amanda. *Behind Closed Doors: At Home in Georgian England*. London: Yale University Press, 2009.

Vickery, Amanda. 'The Theory & Practice of Female Accomplishment'. In *Mrs. Delany and Her Circle*, edited by Mark Laird and Alicia Weisberg-Roberts, 94–109. London: Yale University Press, 2009.

Vigarello, Georges. *The Silhouette: From the 18th Century to the Present Day*. Translated by Augusta Dörr. London: Bloomsbury Academic, 2016.

Vincent, Susan J. *Dressing the Elite: Clothes in Early Modern England*. Oxford: Berg, 2003.

Vincent, Susan J. *Anatomy of Fashion Dressing the Body from the Renaissance to Today*. Oxford: Berg, 2009.

Vincent, Susan J. *Hair: An Illustrated History*. London: Bloomsbury Visual Arts, 2018.

Wahrman, Dror. 'Percy's Prologue: From Gender Play to Gender Panic in Eighteenth-Century England'. *Past and Present* 159, no. 1 (1998): 113–60.

Wahrman, Dror. *The Making of the Modern Self: Identity and Culture in Eighteenth-Century England*. London: Yale University Press, 2004.

Walpole, Horace. *Horace Walpole's Correspondence: The Yale Edition of Horace Walpole's Correspondence*, edited by W. S. Lewis and A. Dayle Wallace. New Haven: Yale University Press, 1965.

Ward, Gerald. *The Grove Encyclopedia of Materials and Techniques in Art*. Oxford: Oxford University Press, 2008.

Warner, Marina. *Monuments and Maidens: The Allegory of the Female Form*. London: Vintage, 1985.

Wassyng Roworth, Wendy. 'Kauffman and the Art of Painting in England'. In *Angelica Kauffman: A Continental Artist in Georgian England*, edited by Wendy Wassyng Roworth, 11–95. London: Reaktion Books, 1992.

Wassyng Roworth, Wendy. 'Anatomy Is Destiny: Angelica Kauffman'. In *Femininity and Masculinity in Eighteenth-Century Art and Culture*, edited by Gillian Perry and Michael Rossington, 41–62. Manchester: Manchester University Press, 1994.

Watts, Carol. *The Cultural Work of Empire: The Seven Years' War and the Imagining of the Shandean State*. Toronto: University of Toronto Press, 2007.

Waugh, Norah. *The Cut of Women's Clothes 1600–1930*. London: Faber and Faber Ltd, 1968.

Waugh, Norah. *Corsets and Crinolines*. London: B. T. Batsford Ltd, 1987.

Wearden, Jenifer. 'Samplers, Stitches & Techniques'. *Victoria and Albert Museum*, 2013. http://www.vam.ac.uk/content/articles/s/samplers-stitches-techniques/ (accessed 19 March 2021).

West, Shearer. *The Image of the Actor: Verbal & Visual Representation in the Age of Garrick & Kemble*. New York: St. Martin's Press, Inc., 1991.

West, Shearer. *Fin De Siecle: Art and Society in an Age of Uncertainty*. London: Bloomsbury Publishing Ltd, 1993.

Whitley, William T. *Artists and Their Friends in England, 1700–1799, Vol. 1*. London: the Medici Society, 1928.

Whyman, Susan E. *Sociability and Power in Late-Stuart England: The Cultural Worlds of the Verneys 1660–1720*. Oxford: Oxford University Press, 1999.

Wilcox, R. Turner. *The Mode in Hats and Headdress, Including Hair Styles, Cosmetics and Jewelry*. London: Charles Scribner's Sons, 1959.

Wilcox, R. Turner. *The Mode in Furs: A Historical Survey with 680 Illustrations*. Mineola: Dover Publications, Inc., 2010.

Williams, Gordon. *A Dictionary of Sexual Language and Imagery in Shakespearean and Stuart Literature, Vol. II*. London: Athlone Press, 2001.

Williams, Laura. '"To Recreate and Refresh Their Dulled Spirites in the Sweet and Wholesome Ayre": Green Space and the Growth of the City'. In *Imagining Early Modern London: Perceptions and Portrayals of the City from Stow to Strype, 1598–1720*, edited by Julia F. Merritt, 185–213. Cambridge: Cambridge University Press, 2001.

Wohlcke, Anne. *The 'Perpetual Fair': Gender, Disorder, and Urban Amusement in Eighteenth-Century London*. Manchester: Manchester University Press, 2014.

Woodforde, John. *The Strange Story of False Hair*. London: Routledge & Kegan Paul, 1971.

Woodyard, Sarah. *Martha's Mob Cap? A Milliner's Hand-Sewn Inquiry into Eighteenth-Century Caps c. 1770–1800*, MA Dissertation, 2017, University of Alberta.

Wrigley, Richard. 'The Formation and Currency of a Vestimentary Stereotype: The *Sans-culotte* in Revolutionary France'. In *Fashioning the Body Politic: Dress, Gender, Citizenship*, edited by Wendy Parkins, 19–48. Oxford: Berg, 2002.

Wrigley, Richard. *The Politics of Appearances: Representations of Dress in Revolutionary France*. Oxford: Berg, 2002.

Wroth, Warwick. *The London Pleasure Gardens of the Eighteenth Century*. London: Macmillan and Co Ltd, 1979.

Yang, Chi-ming. 'Culture in Miniature: Toy Dogs and Object Life'. *Eighteenth-Century Fiction* 25, no. 1 (2012): 139–74.

Yarwood, Doreen. *The Encyclopaedia of World Costume*. London: B. T. Bratsford, 1978.

Yonan, Michael. 'Toward a Fusion of Art History and Material Culture Studies'. *West 86th* 18, no. 2 (Fall-Winter 2011): 232–48.

Zitzlsperger, Philip. *Dürers Pelz und das Recht im Bild: Kleiderkunde als Methode der Kunstgeschichte*. Berlin: Akademie Verlag, 2008.

Index

accessories. *See also* calashes, hats, headwear, muffs
   aprons 17, 50, 59–60, 81, 200 n.43, 208 n.80
   buffont 17–8, 22–3, 26, 189, 193, 195, 200 n.45
   caps 17, 22, 29, 31–2, 36, 44, 47, 99, 212 n.135
   etymology of 10–11
   gloves 47, 50, 132, 171, 189, 193–4
   handkerchief 3, 11, 17, 19, 22–3, 26, 28, 60, 96, 102, 105, 109, 113, 115, 132, 148, 189, 193, 200 n.45, 200 n.49, 221 n.113
   role of 10
   wielding, successfully or otherwise of 48, 56–7, 59, 61
account books, cost of fashion 17, 31, 76, 121, 153
Alexander, David 227 n.104
Alexander, William, *History of Women, from the earliest Antiquity to the Present Time* 64–5
allegory 136–9, 146, 149, 180
Alleyne, Francis 18, 20, 23
Amazons 34, 99, 220 n.88
American Revolution 220 n.96
Austen, Elizabeth Motley 17, 31, 163
Austen, Jane 59
   Persuassion 59

Baartman, Sara 15, 17
Babble, Nicholas, *The Prater* 64
The Back-Side of a Front Row 96–7
baleen, whalebone 7, 11–3, 41, 152–3, 173, 184, 186, 206 n.37, 231 n.19
Banks, Sarah Sophia 32, 93, 198 n.8, 218 n.65
Barker, Hannah 65
Bartolozzi, Francesco 135–6, 140, 228 n.118, 228 nn.111–12
Batchelor, Jennie 124
Baumgarten, Linda 215 n.13, 232 n.28
beau monde, bon ton 3, 26, 36, 56, 70, 82, 123, 179, 193

Bermingham, Ann 230 n.138
Bigg, William Redmore, *A Lady and Children Relieving a Cottager* 9, 61
Birchall, James 142
Body, women's
   alluring 53
   anxieties around women's 85, 179–86
   breasts 1, 3, 6–23, 26, 96, 101, 109, 113, 135–7, 151, 163, 183, 186, 189
   depictions of corpulent 59, 63, 87, 172–3, 179, 184
   depictions of fashionable 50, 168
   depictions of non-white 14–17
   depictions of old 63–4, 87, 172–3
   dressed body *vs.* natural 8, 10–1, 18, 115–8
   mons pubis 14, 115, 118
   unfashionable bodies 172–9
Borsay, Peter 56, 209 n.88, 209 n.90
Boucher, François 195
Bowles, Carington 51–3, 65–9, 124, 168, 170, 194, 208 n.86, 233 n.48
Britannia 14, 180–4, 189, 235 n.73
Brooks, Nicholas 238 n.16
Browne, Claire 224 n.48
The Bumless Beauties 105–6
The Bum Shop 100–1, 105
Burman, Barbara 26, 227 n.99

calash 26–7, 36, 206 n.43, 208 n.83, 211 n.115, 212 n.123, 213 n.147
   advertisements of 47
   'aprons' of calashes 40, 42, 65
   bonnet 39, 47
   The Calash (song/rondo) 44
   collapsible design 26–7, 39–40, 48, 51
   connection with carriage 39, 48, 50, 62, 69–70
   extant examples 39–43

imported 47
made by milliners 47, 70
material construction of 47, 70
as mechanical 48, 50, 53, 70, 207 n.65
Miss Calash 50–5
in motion 48–9
nautical comparison 47–8, 50, 70–1
navigation 39–47
origin story 45
performance of wearing 50, 53
personification of 50
promenade 56–61
Shielded from unwanted glances 46, 56
sociable 62–9
The Triumph of the Calash 45–7, 56
water repellent 56
Campbell, Robert 11, 29, 31, 47
London Tradesman 29, 46–7
Capt. Calipash & Mrs Calipee 58–9
caricature 24, 57, 59, 93, 194, 196, 202 n.76
Carill-Worsley, Thomas and Elizabeth 77, 79
Cavendish, Georgina, Duchess of Devonshire 34, 93, 119
Fashionable cache 36
The Sylph 183
Chalus, Elaine 65
Churchill, Lady Maria 1, 197 nn.4–5
class
elite/polite society 3, 6, 48, 56–7, 59, 61, 64–5, 68–9, 95, 112, 149
middling sort 61, 70
social climbers 54, 57, 59, 62, 107–8, 194
Cleland, John, *Memoirs of a woman of pleasure* 115
coffee house 25, 69, 211 n.113
Collet, John 24, 66–8, 87, 168, 170–1, 180, 183, 193–4, 202 n.79, 234 n.53
Coltman, Viccy 7, 77
consumption 3, 15, 24, 48, 56, 68, 93, 105, 113, 124, 146, 149, 194, 202 n.74, 230 n.138. *See also* shopping
Copley, John Singleton 35, 77
Corfield, Penelope J. 212 n.125
cork
advertisements for 88, 90
in fancy dress 90–1
importation of 87, 90
jackets 87–90, 107, 217 n.47, 217 n.50
Ward, John 87–90, 217 nn.49–50
Wilkinson, John 87–8, 90
cork-cutter 84, 87–8, 90

cork rump and bum 151, 168, 214 n.3, 214 n.5
bum shops, portrayal of 101–3, 105
bums, terminological shift 99–100
composition 73, 77–9, 80, 86, 99
connection with Chloe 50, 80–7, 107
deception 84–5, 99
effect on the dress above 79, 90
erotic appeal of 19, 85, 91
extant examples 23, 27, 77–9, 105, 121
fitting a bum 102
as flotation device 91–2, 95
made by milliners 100–5
material footprint of 27, 77–80, 108
mythical status, lack of non-satirical survival 75–7, 79, 99, 158
obsession with cork 86–92
personification 114, 146, 149
The Cork Rump the Support of Life 91–4
corset. *See* stays
cosmetics 86, 172–3, 184
Coxheath 26, 34

daily routine 64
Damer, Anne (scrapbook) 32, 93, 218 n.66
Darly, Matthew and Mary 24, 30, 58–61, 63–4, 69, 73–4, 77, 82–3, 87–9, 94–8, 101, 168–9, 172, 174, 194–5, 216 n.23, 218 n.65, 218 n.68, 219 n.84
Delany, Mary 130–1, 171–2, 226 n.89, 226 nn.83–4
De La Warr, Lady Mary 17, 163
Delphine (Staël) 189, 194, 237 n.6
Deutsch, Davida Tenenbaum 124
didactic literature 24, 31, 65
Dodsley, Robert 137
Dolefull Dicky Sneer in the Dumps, or the Lady's Revenge 94, 97–8
dolls
doll clothing 23, 36, 48, 90, 96, 130, 164–6, 183
paper dolls 31–9
Donald, Diana 6, 23, 202 n.74, 220 n.97
dress
bridal 84–5, 216 n.30
collections, in museum stores 23, 36, 75–8, 121, 163
as deception 84–5, 99
Turkish 135–6
dressing
getting dressed 184, 189
Gillray 189, 193–4
table 73, 168, 184, 189

The Dress of the Year 1784 146–8
Dyer, Serena 33, 127, 194

effeminacy 61, 103, 237 n. 97
'Elegant Pattern for a Fashionable Muff or Work Bag' 124–5
Emberly, Julia 223 n.21
embroidering muffs 122–32
embroidery
    as female/feminist practice 130, 146, 149
    floral sprigs 79, 122, 126–9
    and the maker's hand 127–30, 149–50
    and satin prints 121–2, 135, 149
    as social conduit 122–3, 130–1
    types of 122–32
embroidery patterns
    acquiring patterns 122–6
    extant patterns 124–6
    out of fashion 130
    professionally drawn 123
    published in books 123–4
    published in magazines 124–5
eyelets
    existence of cork rumps 79, 105, 157, 158, 163
    invention of metal 186
    of stays 155, 157, 171, 179, 186

Farrell, Jeremy 61, 210 n.110, 211 n.114, 211 n.116
fashion
    and change 3, 6, 26, 28–30, 107, 126, 195–6
    definition of 3, 6, 26, 28
    as a goddess 22, 196
    metropolitan nature of 3, 25, 59, 81, 216 n.20
    news and reports 24, 29, 31, 34
    people of 3, 6, 123
    places of fashionable display 3, 6, 8–9, 56–7, 62, 193
    and print 23–6
    reflections on/descriptions of past fashions 6, 23, 64, 68, 151, 153
fashionability 17, 27, 47, 57, 59, 61, 81, 83–4, 87, 98, 107, 109, 112, 119, 123, 146, 164, 167, 171, 186
fashion plates 19, 23–4, 28–9, 31–4, 45, 48, 123–4, 193–4, 238 n.10
    of calashes 45, 48–9
    dress of the year 19–20, 48–9, 146–8
    of hair and headwear 31–9

feathers. *See also* muffs
    ostrich feathers for hair 31, 65, 73, 189, 214 n.1
    peacock 125
Felicity (Kauffman) 136–7, 139, 141
The Female Combatants/Who shall 14, 16
Fennetaux, Ariane 26
Fielding, Henry, *Tom Jones* 114, 223 n.24
Fisher, Kitty 93, 95
fops, macaroni 22–3, 94–7
Fores, Samuel William 18, 100–1, 103–6, 113, 115–19, 173, 175–6, 182, 194, 200 n.54, 220 n.97
Francophobia 61, 183–4
French Revolution 180, 182–3, 186, 195
    French émigrés 182–3
    influence in Britain 180–2, 182
Freneau, Philip, *The Miscellaneous Works of Mr. Philip Freneau Containing His Essays, and Additional Poems* 48
fur. *See* muffs, fur

Gainsborough, Thomas 23, 36, 205 n.29
gender
    attributions to fashion 50–1, 61, 103–5, 113, 153, 179
George, Dorothy 99
gifts 1, 130
Gillray, James 180–4, 189–96, 214 n.2, 235 n.75, 236 n.78, 237 nn.2–3
global trade
    fur trade 112–13, 119–21
    importation into London 25, 119, 195
    importation of clothing from London to colonies 36, 69
    imported from France 159, 182
gowns
    English 73–5, 214 n.3, 216 n.30
    Italian 73–6
    looped-style 74–5, 79, 84, 104, 109, 214 n.3, 216 n.30
    mantua 74, 119
    polonaise 59, 73, 75, 79, 84, 210 n.109, 211 n.114, 214 n.3, 216 n.30
    sacque 74, 95
Grand tour 6
Granville, Anne 130
Greenwich Park 61, 211 n.121
Greig, Hannah 3, 65, 179
Grose, Francis, *A Classical Dictionary of the Vulgar Tongue* 115

hair
  coiffeurs 29, 31–3, 36, 41, 44, 50, 53, 56, 65, 70, 73, 80, 83, 87, 91, 94, 96, 211 n.114, 234 n.59
  cushion 31
  false hair (cignon, curls) 31, 44, 50, 65, 80, 168, 189
  hedgehog 31, 109, 208 n.77
  ornamentation 30, 73, 112, 121, 125
  ostrich feathers for 31, 65, 73, 189, 204 n.12, 215 n.1
  pomatum 31
  powder 31
  wigs 31, 91
hairdressers, frisseurs 31, 73, 168, 189
handkerchief. *See* accessories
Hartman, Saidiya 17
hats
  bergère 34, 36
  brimmed 3, 26–7, 30, 34, 36, 39, 70, 109, 148
  depictions of 64–5
  Devonshire 34, 36, 93, 183, 205 n.28
  military 34–6
  picture 36
  riding 34–6
headwear
  bonnets 31
  caps 22, 29, 31–3, 36, 44, 212 n.135
  poufs 31
  turbans 31, 36, 47, 135, 14
Heath, William 184–5
Heideloff, Nicolaus, *Gallery of Fashion* 193–4, 238 n.10
Hellman, Mimi 48–9, 65
Hoare, Mary 1–3, 7, 15, 26, 197 n.4
Hoare, William 197 n.4
Hogarth, William 6–7, 22, 153–4, 171, 189, 193, 198 n.21
  The Analysis of Beauty 6–7
Holland, William 14
Hopner, John 36
Huddesford, Mary 131–2
  her husband George 131
Humphrey, Hannah 118, 180–1, 189–92, 220 n.97, 221 n.107
Humphrey, William 151–2, 172, 219 n.80, 220 n.97
Hunt, Tamara L. 202 n.79
Hutter, Mark 232 n.28
Hyde Park 1780 211 n.115

Inwood, Stephen 211 n.120
It-narratives 45
  Memoirs and Interesting Adventures of an Embroidered Waistcoat 45

Johnson, Barbara 32
Johnson, Samuel 64
jumps 163. *See also* stays

Kauffman, Angelica 135–42, 146, 149, 197 n.4, 228 n.111, 228 n.115
Kingsbury, Henry 105
Kirgate, Thomas 1, 3, 8, 198 n.8

The LADIES HEAD-DRESS 83–5
A Lady in Waiting (Bowles) 53–5, 208 n.86
La Roche, Sophie von 22–3, 62
Lathom, Francis, *The Dash of the Day* 69
laundry 11, 18, 152
leisure
  pleasure gardens 54, 56, 61, 70, 209 n.90, 209 n.92–209 n.93
  promenade 50, 56–62, 70
  shopping 62, 103, 120, 149
Lemire, Beverly 231 n.6
'Levities of Fashion' 3, 19, 28–29, 100, 193
Lewis, Ann Frankland 146–9, 228 n.109
Liddell, Anne, Countess of upper Ossory 1, 3, 4, 11, 17, 36, 197 n.2
linen 10–11, 17, 36, 77–9, 126, 152–3, 155, 233 n.36
A Little Bigger 173, 176–7
A Little Tighter 173, 175, 178–9
Llanover, Lady 227 n.91
Lockington, J. 73, 75, 77, 94, 218 n.68
London. *See also* leisure, pleasure gardens
  Billingsgate 91, 219 n. 80
  Spitalfields 83
  St. James 47, 118, 189
  The Thames 55, 61, 91–2, 217 n.50
  West End 69, 101, 118–19, 195
Lunardi, Vincenzo 22, 26, 34
  balloon dress 19–22
  balloon hats 22, 34
  balloon mania 22
  hot air balloon 22–3

Macaulay, Catherine 172
Mactaggart, Peter 234 n.52

magazines, periodicals
    growth of 24
    Gallerie des Modes 32, 205 n.28
    The Lady's Magazine, or Entertaining Companion for the Fair Sex 24, 31, 45, 124–6, 128, 1322
    The Spectator 24, 219 n.74
    The Tatler 24, 219 n.74
    The Town and Country Magazine 93, 99, 220 n.88
    Walker's Hibernian Magazine, or, Compendium of Entertaining Knowledge 109–11, 124–5, 133
    The Westminster Magazine 100, 102
Mandeville, Bernard, *The Fable of the Bees* 56–7, 59
A Man Millener 103–4, 113, 115
Mann, Horace 1
mantuamaker 47, 103, 119, 183, 194
Marcuard, Robert Samuel 141
masquerade 24, 95, 194–5
material literacy 24, 127, 159
Matthew and Mary Darly 24, 59–60, 63, 73–4, 77, 82, 87–9, 94–8, 101, 168–9, 174, 194
McCreery, Cindy 64, 172
McKeller, Elizabeth 211 n.120
McMahon, John 184
McNeil, Peter 23, 57, 209 n.95, 238 n.15
mezzotint 24–5, 51–5, 66–8, 80, 84, 134–8, 142, 144–5, 170, 213 n.137
military
    depictions of in satire 59, 108, 118, 132
    influence on women's fashion 34–6, 180
milliners 47
    Dyde, Robert 119–20
    Dyde & Scribe 120–1, 236 n.83
    Harshorn, James 119
    Hunter, Jane 47
    making accessories 11
    man milliners and effeminacy 61, 103–4, 113, 119, 219 n.83
    reputations 46, 50, 103
    shops 103, 207 n.55
A Milliner's Shop 103–5
Miss Calash: Drawn by Miss Calash 1778 50–4
Miss Shuttle-cock 94–5, 97
Mitchell, Robin 15
'A Modern Venus – or – a Lady of the <u>present</u> Fashion in the state of Nature' 1–3, 7–10
A Modern Venus Clothed 3–4, 11, 17
Moore, Doris Langley 23

motifs 27–8, 194
    dress in graphic satire 24
    for embroidery 124–6
    neoclassical 132, 146
    nude *vs* dressed 11, 14
    stays as 153, 167–72, 180, 186
The Muff 113
muffs
    business 119–21
    embroidered silk muffs 121–2, 126–132
    feather, unpatriotic 112–3
    fox fur and politics 121, 180
    fur 109, 112, 114–5, 223 n.29, 228 n.119
    importation and export of 25, 59, 121, 182, 223 n.30
    in portraiture 112, 114, 131–2
    makers 127, 132, 149–50
    metonymic for women's sexuality 113–5, 119
    satirical 113–9
    silk 79, 112, 119, 121–2, 124–38, 142–3, 146, 148–50
    slang 114
muslin 17, 19, 22, 36, 47, 221 n.112, 237 n.5

Nelson, Charmaine 17
The New Rigatta 95–7
newspapers
    Calcutta Gazette 119
    Daily Advertiser 102, 139, 142, 194, 218 n.65, 229 n.124
    editorial attacks on fashion 88–91
    editorial defence of fashion 196
    General Evening Post 91–2, 200 n.45
    London Chronicle 86
    Morning Chronicle and London Advertiser 44, 112, 206 n.44, 228 n.109
    Morning Herald 102, 139, 200 n.51
    Morning Herald and Daily Advertiser 139, 228 n.115
    Morning Post and Daily Advertiser 102, 194, 218 n.65, 229 n.124
    Public Advertiser 84, 200 n.44, 215 n.12
    St. James Chronicle 77, 79
    St. James Chronicle or British Evening Post 103
    Virginia Gazette 195, 203 n.82
    Weekly Miscellany 85
    Whitehall Evening-Post 151

Old Bailey criminal court, London 231 n.6, 231 n. 11
The Old Maids Morning Visit or the Calash Lady's 62–3, 87

Paine, Thomas, *The Rights of Man* 180, 182–4, 189, 235 nn.74–5, 236 n.78
Palmer, William 136, 139–40, 142, 228 n.115
paper dolls 32–33
Parker, Rosika 121
patterns. *See* embroidery patterns
petticoats 11–13, 53, 79, 92, 96, 100, 103–5, 123, 148, 168, 219 n.83, 221 n.107, 232 n.25
Phillips, James 11
Pierres, Philippe-Denis 32–3
A Pig in a Poke 11, 14
Piozzi, Hester Lynch 224 n.41
pleasure gardens 54, 56, 61, 70, 209 n.90, 209 nn.92–3
  Ranelagh 56, 61, 209 n.90, 209 nn.92–3
  Vauxhall 54, 56, 61, 209 n.90, 209 nn.92–3, 210 n.101
pocket books and almanacs 23–4, 29, 31
pockets 11, 23–4, 26, 29, 31, 79, 123, 126, 168, 173, 180, 184, 200 n.45, 231 n.14
Pointon, Marcia 25
polonaise 9, 59, 73, 75, 79, 84, 210 n.109, 211 n.114, 214 n.3, 216 n.30
portraiture
  construction of 29, 105
  fashion in 23, 36, 112, 121, 132, 146
Powell, Margaret K. 219 n.77
The Preposterous Head Dress, or, The Feathered Lady 73–4
print culture 3, 6, 23–4, 27–8, 77, 80, 93, 99, 107, 123, 193–4, 196, 219 n.74, 238 n.15
  assemblage, albums, scrapbooks 32, 93
printed textiles. *See also* satin prints
  development of 132, 167
printshops 25, 93, 101, 118–19, 142, 238 n.16
Progress of the Toilet 189–92, 195
prostitution, sex work
  denoting 153, 171, 208 n.85
  places frequented by 61–2
  portrayal of 115

race 9, 14, 96, 132, 171, 179
The Rake at Rose Tavern 153–4
Rauser, Amelia 238 n.22

Reynolds, Joshua 23, 73, 131, 214 n.2
ribbon 11, 14, 22, 31, 36, 40, 42, 50, 53, 60, 65, 75, 83, 126–9, 133, 135, 155, 157, 159, 180, 194, 208 n.83, 232 nn.26–7, 233 n.36
Richardson, Samuel, *Clarissa* 114
Richardson, William 50
Riello, Giorgio 57
Roach, Joseph 219 n.77
Romney, George 23, 36–7
Rosenthal, Angela 149
Rowlandson, Thomas 173, 175–80, 182, 196, 223 n.25
royal family 103, 116
  George IV, Prince of Wales, Prince Regent 95, 121, 142, 184–6
Rushworth, R. 101, 105, 220 n.98

satin prints 132–3
  applications for 132, 142, 146, 149
  and copperplate printing 132, 142
  extant examples 133–8, 142, 146
  on fire screens 142–3
  their makers/publishers 135–7, 142
  and patronage 149
  as a portable canvas 27, 122, 146–9, 194
  satin print muffs 121–2, 132–46, 149, 194, 229 n.120, 229 n.128
  subjects on 135–6, 139, 141–2, 146
satirical and sartorial dialogues 6, 93–9
satirical prints, graphic satire 23–5, 28, 76–7, 95, 118, 167, 172, 189, 194–5, 197 n.7, 200 n.42, 220 n.96. *See also* printshops
  anthropomorphic, fashion as its material composition 87, 95
  cats and kittens (animals) 14, 63–4
  compositional adaptation 66, 93–4, 180
  cost of 24, 228 n.113
  criticism of as source for dress history 23, 77, 98–9, 195
  display and sale of 25, 118
  dissemination of 24–7, 195
  lions (animals) 142, 182
  pin ups 53, 208 n.85
  relationship to fashion 6, 23–6, 28, 77, 93–9, 118–19, 167, 186, 193–6
  social climbers and depictions of class 54, 107–8, 194
  speed of publication 24, 119, 194–5

toy dogs (animals) 81, 91
typical portrayal of fashionable women 50, 53, 65, 82, 168
use of in dress history 23–4, 77, 195
Sayer, R. & J. Bennett 53–5, 124, 142–4, 208 n.86
Schoeser, Mary 132
servants 60–1, 93, 168, 171, 209 n.93
Sheridan, Richard Brinsley 36, 94–8, 107, 172–3, 183, 194, 219 n.70, 219 n.72, 219 n.80, 234 n.60, 235 n.65
shoes and footwear 56, 84, 87, 100
shopping
    by correspondence 123, 224 n.50
    depictions of 100–1, 103, 120, 132
    new spaces for retail 119–120
The Siege of Cork 87–8
silhouette 3, 8–10, 17, 19, 22, 26–8, 31, 40, 74, 79, 84, 99–103, 105–8, 112–13, 115, 151, 157, 166–7, 189, 193, 195
    pouter pigeon 11, 17, 19, 22, 31, 99, 101, 104–7, 157
    Regency, neoclassical 27, 69, 107, 189, 196
    Southey, Robert 200 n.42
Sincerity 136–7, 140–1
Smith, Chloe Wigston 124, 127
sociability 50, 65, 68–9
spangles 126, 134–5, 137, 142
Sparrow, Frances Mabel 122–3, 125, 128, 130–1, 171–2, 224 n.46, 224 n.51
    her cousin, Henrietta Whitmore 122–3, 224 n.51
    her relationship with Delany 130–1, 171–2
Spencer, Lady Anne, Countess of Sunderland 152–3
A Stage Box Scene; Mrs Bruin, Miss Chienne, Miss Renard 113–14
Stanley, Charlotte 31
staymakers 79, 153, 159, 163, 173, 179–80, 182–3, 194, 235 n.74
    Burchett, John 159
stays. *See also* tight lacing
    busk 155, 189, 231 n.14, 233 n.36
    change in construction 27, 153, 155–67, 183, 186–7
    and class 152–3
    corset 152, 159, 163, 182–3
    effects on the body 151–2, 155–6, 166–7, 183
    extant examples 155–66
    French stays 182–4
    hooks 75, 157, 159, 232 n.27
    linen stays 156–7, 233 n.36
    men wearing 184
    reins of power 179–86
    riding stays 159, 163, 232 n.28, 236 n.81
    material composition of 153, 155, 171
    silk satin stays 158, 160
    strap design 155, 159
    tape straps 159, 163–7, 233 n.36
    terminology 151–2, 182
    and women's morality 167–8
    wool damask stays 155–7, 159
Steele, Valerie 167, 172, 219 n.74, 234 n.49, 234 n.58, 235 n.66
Steorn, Patrik 238 n.15
Stewart, James *Plocacosmos* 31
Stillingfleet, Benjamin, *An Essay on Conversation* 137–8
stipple 24, 80, 104, 106, 115, 132, 136, 138–42, 146, 190–2, 228 nn.112–13, 233 n.40
stockings 10
Styles, John 3, 152
Swift, Jonathan, *Strephon and Chloe* 84

tailor 23, 47, 173
tea
    link with sociability 68–9
    ritual of 68
    table 65, 68–9
temporality 3, 9, 33, 48, 148, 184, 189, 193–6
tête-a-têtes 32
theatre, fashion at the 6, 9, 22, 29, 34, 64, 96, 113, 193
theft, 102 153, 231 n. 11 (*See also* Old Bailey)
The Three Graces 172–3
tight lacing 151–4. *See also* stays
    as fashionable extreme, feminine vanity 168
    as gendered metaphor 171, 183–4, 186
    iconography of 167–72, 186
    introduction of steel eyelets 79, 105, 155–67, 171
    legacy 186
    medical diatribes against 167, 172, 186
    method of lacing 171, 179
    myths of 45–6
    as political metaphor 168, 179–80, 183–4, 186
    straight lacing 167
    use of bodkin 168, 172
Tight Lacing, or Fashion before Ease 168–170
Titus Shapes Figure Frames 151–2
Tobin, Beth Fowkes 9, 199 n.27
The Toilet of Flora 31

The Ton at Greenwich 59–61
toy dogs 64, 82, 83, 91, 94, 102, 109, 216 n. 19
transportation
    carriages 39, 48, 50, 62, 69–70
    gigs 39
    sedan chair 69
    walking 56–7, 59, 62, 69, 71
turtle 59

umbrella 48, 61, 211 nn.113–15
underwear 10, 26, 28, 193–4
    etymology 10
    hoops/panniers 10–13, 27, 74
    shift, linen 10 (*See also* linen)
    structural 3, 6, 10, 105–6 (*See also* stays, cork rumps and bums)
The Utility of Cork Rumps 1777 73, 75

Venus
    as an archetype 6–7, 28, 109
    Hottentot Venus 15–17
    Venus de' Medici 6–7, 10–11, 234 n.59
Vickery, Amanda 65
The Victim 171
The Virgin Unmasked 115–18
Visiting
    cards 64–5, 70
    portrayal of 62–4, 68–9
    social network 62, 64–5, 69
    transportation 62, 70
visual culture 23, 194

Wahrman, Dror 235 n.68
Walker, John 141–2, 228 n.114
Walpole, Horace 1, 3, 7–8, 93, 95, 197 n.7, 211 n.113, 218 n.66
wars
    American War of Independence 99, 195
    Napoleonic Wars 186
    Seven Years War 3, 113
Watson, John F. 39, 205 n.35
Wheatley, Margot 18, 20, 23
Wheatley, William 18
Whiteness 17–18, 137
Whyman, Susan E. 213 n.144
Wicksteed, J. 113–4, 219 n.83
Williamsburg 47, 203 n.82
Woffington, Margaret 93, 95
Woodyard, Sarah 206 n.42, 231 n.19
Worsley, Lady Seymour 73

Yonan, Michael 26